Issues in Ethics and Applied Ethics Series

Vol. 1 Ethics in Business, Applied and Environment
Vol. 2 Ethics in Feminism
Vol. 3 Socio-political Ethics

Forthcoming volumes

Vol. 4 Biomedied Ethics (Part I)
Biomedical Ethics (Part II)
Vol. 5 Metaethics (Part I)
Normative Ethics and Virtue Ethics (Part II)
Vol. 6 Practical Economics, Corporate and Educational Ethics
Vol. 7 Ethics in Charvaka/Lokayata, Morality and Secularism (Part I)
Philosophy and Ethics of the Jainas (Part II)
Philosophy and Ethics of Buddhas (Part III)

About the Editors

Shiva Nath Prasad, after completing his studies, served Bihar Government in several capacities. After retirement he became a full timer in the pursuit of philosophy. He edited a bilingual journal *Abhranta* later edited two journals separately one in English namely Journal of Bihar Philosophical Research and *Darshan Digdarshan* in Hindi. He authored one book *Charvaka/Lokayata Analytical and Hermeneutics Study,* a very unique book, which is a "singular attempt to reconstruct this almost a vanished system of India." He also published an Anthology namely Phenomenology: Methodological Introduction with Prof. V.T. Sebastian of Punjab University. His Multi-Volume Anthology on Ethics and Applied Ethics (more than fifteen volumes) are being published by Concept Publishing Company Pvt. Ltd. New Delhi and some are being processed. His latest book just published is "Reflections on Charvaka/Lokayata, the Gita and Rajneesh."

Avinash Kumar Srivastava, born, December 1955 (at Village Singthu, Nalanda District, Bihar) completed Master's degree (Philosophy) from Patna University, Ph.D. on the topic "A Comparative Study of the Samadhi (Yoga) in Early Buddhism and *Bhagavad Gita*" from Magadha University, Bodh Gaya. Presently he is Professor & Head, P.G. Deptt. of Philosophy, Magadha University, P.G. Centre Darshnik Traimasik (Patna), Nalanda College Biharsharif. He is a prolific writer. He has authored two books *(Living Buddhism and Bharatiya Darshan Ki Mool Samasyayen)* and edited three Anthologies. His about fifty research papers have been published in India and abroad. He is a widely known scholar of India. He was *Joint Secretary and Secretary* of *Akhil Bharatiya Darshan Parishad and General Secretary, Bihar Darshan Parishad, Vice President of Indian Society for Buddhist Studies.* And member of editorial board of *Buddha Prajna Sindhu,* and *Ocean of Buddhist Wisdom (Delhi), Journal of Bihar Philosophical Research, Darshan Digdarshan (Patna).*

Issues in Ethics and Applied Ethics Series

Volume- II

Ethics in Feminism

Edited by
Shiva Nath Prasad
Avinash Kumar Srivastava

CONCEPT PUBLISHING COMPANY PVT. LTD.
NEW DELHI-110059

ISBN-13: 978-81-8069-976-4 (Series)
ISBN-13: 978-81-8069-978-8 (Volume-II)

First Published 2016

Published and Printed by

Concept Since 1974

Concept Publishing Company Pvt. Ltd.
A/15-16, Commercial Block, Mohan Garden
New Delhi-110059 (India)
T : 25351460, 25351794, *F* : 091-11-25357109
E: publishing@conceptpub.com, W: www.conceptpub.com
Editorial Office: H-13, Bali Nagar, New Delhi-110 015, India.

Cataloging in Publication Data—*Courtesy:* D.K. Agencies (P) Ltd. <docinfo@dkagencies.com>

Ethics in feminism / edited by Shiva Nath Prasad, Avinash Kumar Srivastava.
pages cm. -- (Issues in ethics and applied ethics series ; volume - II)
Contributed articles.
Includes bibliographical references and index.
ISBN 9788180699764 (Series)
ISBN 9788180699788 (Volume II)

1. Feminist ethics. I. Prasad, Shiva Nath, editor. II. Śrīvāstava, Avināśa 1955-, editor. III. Series: Issues in ethics and applied ethics series ; volume - II.

DDC 170.82 23

Foreword

Contemporary philosophical temper has been occasionally circumscribed by some major practical concerns which emanate from human condition.

The historical perspective makes it almost true by definition that morality is essentially related to action or conduct. In contrast with predominantly conceptual analysis, present day thinkers have shown greater interest in "praxieal" and pragmatic significance of problems and issues we confront within our lived experience. Philosophical interpretations and examinations have been tied to some specific needs and purposes. Moral discourse does not any more comprise abstract questions and hypothetical answers concerning meanings and definitions of concepts like "good", "bad", "right", "wrong", etc. Areas located within applied ethics were treated as subaltern discourses within the meta-discourse of grand narrative of philosophical ethics. However, it is notable that there are problems which are commensurate with social and political debates. Hence, practical ethics assimilated and deliberated upon large number of issues like suicide, abortion, euthanasia democracy, justice environmental and biogenetic issues, etc.

What is urgently needed, as some thinkers believe, is the return to the Greek spirit from purely intellectual and rational approach.

The essential feature of Aristotelian thinking is employment of practical wisdom (phronesis) which has been highlighted by moral philosophers like G.E.M. Anscombe, Bernard Williams, John Rawls and many post-modernists. The advocates of applied ethics, following Aristotle, justify the acceptance of good life as the ultimate ideal within the bounds of deontology and consequentialism.

The present volume (Feminist Ethics) edited by Shiva Nath Prasad, is an interesting and valuable collection of several chapters written with proper understanding of the subject. The areas of study of the Series include culture, environmental ethics, feminist study, religious understanding, ecosophy, business ethics and various professional and scientific/technological areas where moral issues emerge with significant relevance. It is indeed a praiseworthy attempt on the part of Prasad to collect so many chapters which is a painful, though commendable, project. It will be of great help to scholars working in the area of applied ethics.

S.A. Shaida

Retd. Prof. I.I.T., Kanpur

Preface

The present volume of the series, "Issues in Ethics and Applied Ethics", is devoted to Feminist Ethics. It contains studies of some aspects of gender issues, feminism, its ethics and philosophy as expressed in the views of the thinkers of the East and West down the ages. It focuses on the social attitude towards women, their plight and prosperity as well as philosophy, religion, ethics, science, politics, and the behaviour of social organization relating to the gender treatment in social context. Being an attempt to understand the unequal treatment faced by female population in their everyday life, efforts have been made by the authors of the different chapters to earmark women's problems, their cause, conditions, reason and remedy as thought and observed in modern and postmodern society. Herein an endeavour has also been made to record the history of feminist movement of the West , in brief, as reflected in the writings of the most creative, sensitive and reflective thinkers. It is basically an ethical, philosophical and humanistic approach to the feminist issues wherein some of our authors have tried to view the issues through the lance of women and feminist movement.

It is felt that the traditional man-centric ethics has undervalued and underappreciated the women's moral experiences (the cry of women) and focused the man's perspective predominantly. It has resulted in gender unequal human behaviour and placed women as a second grade citizen. On behavioural part rape, female feticide, maltreatment, eve teasing, oppression and misbehaviour against women in office, common place and even inside the house by her boss, colleague, male friends and family members has become common. This necessitated an urge to recast, reframe the old patriarchal ethics and add new concepts and precepts resonate to the feminist issues. It may contribute to understand issues relating to the women plight and will help us overcome the basic ethical problems of half of human population. Taking into consideration these thoughts and facts our contributors specialized in feminist issues and ethics, have amply reflected on the women plight and problems. This may help create a new framework of feminist ethics, evolve new ethical concepts, precepts and practice and pave path of gender equal society.

From what has been said above, what transpires to us and what the feminists around the world feel is that the human civilization has yet to change its whole mental haze and come up with open human set -up of mind and ponder and pause, how best the human population may be inseparably linked to make a full whole, humanity + unity, one humanity.

Shiva Nath Prasad
Avinash Kumar Srivastava

Acknowledgements

We wish to record our deep sense of gratitude to all the authors of this first volume, under the Series "Issues in Ethics and Applied Ethics ", out of our multi-volume series, for contributing their very scholarly essays. In fact, we have been involved in this work for a longer period and confess that we received numerous enquiries from many of our contributors regarding the fate of their Papers because of inordinate delay in publication. We are extremely sorry and beg their pardon for the delay. We feel remorsement for those contributors who are no more in this world, rather we find ourselves guilty for it.

We express our thankfulness to all the contributors for their perpetual support, confidence and patience shown by them.

We are grateful to all those who have directly or indirectly helped us in our hard and strenuous academic endeavour.

We are thankful to our family members who have cheerfully endured the trial of our work and shared the stress of editing such an anthology.

We express our thankfulness to Shri A.K. Mittal, Proprietor, Concept Publishing Company Pvt. Ltd., New Delhi, for taking personal interest in the publication of this volume and the series.

Bhavatu Sabba Mangalam

Shiva Nath Prasad

Avinash Kumar Srivastava

Contents

List of Contributors

1. **Kumar, Praveen,** Assistant Professor, Department of Buddhist Studies, NISWASS, At & PO. Bhubaneswar, Odisha. Pin-751023
2. **Kumar, Sanjay,** (Asstt. Prof., S.B. College, Chandil, Jharkhand) Residence D-19, Vatika Green City, Dimna Road, Mango, Jamshedpur, Jharkhand. Mob. 08578912345/ 9006775440.
3. **Kumari, Madhubala,** Head of Philosophy Deptt., Z.A. Islamia College, At & PO. Siwan, Bihar.
4. **Mukherjee, Asha,** Department of Philosophy, Vishwabharati University, Shanti Niketan, West Bengal.
5. **Nair, S.M.,** Deptt., of Philosophy, Sree Sankaracharya University of Sanskrit, Kalady, District Ernakulam, Kerala-683574. E-mail–Sree–Kala–nair@yahoo.com.
6. **Prasad, Seema,** Department of English, A.N. College, Patna, Bihar. Pin-800013.
7. **Prasad, Shiva Nath,** Chief Editor of the Series *viz*., "Issues in Ethics and Applied Ethics." Road No. 20, Plot No. 39, S.K. Nagar, Patna, Bihar-800001, Mob. 09905292070.
8. **Sahay, Yamini,** Asstt. Prof. of Philosophy, K.B.W. College, At & PO. Hazaribagh, Vinoba Bhave University, Hazaribagh, (Jharkhand), Pin-825302.
9. **Satya Narayana, Y.V.,** Retd. Professor of Philosophy, Andhra University, (A.P.) Residence-Door No. 8-45-16, Vidya Nagar, Visakhapatnam, Andhra Pradesh.
10. **Shaida, S.A.,** (Retd.) Prof., I.I.T, Kanpur. 34, Kazmi Street, Rani Mandi, At & PO, Allahabad, U.P. Pin-211003.
11. **Sharma, Sunita,** Department of History, B.D. College, Mithapur, Near Gaudiya Math, Patna.

12. **Shrivastava, Umesh Kumar,** C/o. Rajesh Kumar Singh, Deptt. of Philosophy, B.N. College, Ashok Raj Path, Patna, Bihar. Pin-800004.

13. **Singh, Abha,** Head of Philosophy Department of A.N. College, Patna, Bihar, Pin-800013.

14. **Singh, Damodar,** 203, Jayakunj Appartment, Kidway Puri, Near Income Tax round about Patna, Bihar, Pin-800001.

15. **Singh, Deepali,** H.O.D. of Political Science, Department, ARNI University, Kangra, Himachal Pradesh. Residence-14/29, A Deepa Nagar, Purana Hathras Adola, Near Rajdhani Complex, Aligarh, Pin-202001.

16. **Singh, Nibha,** Prof., Department of English, (P.G.) Gaya College, Gaya, Bihar.

17. **Singh, Rajesh Kumar,** Department of Philosophy, B.N. College, Ashok Rajpath, Patna. Pin-800004.

18. **Singh, Shiva Bhanu,** H.O.D. Philosophy, Ewing Christan College, At & PO. Allahabad, (U.P). Residence– 46/23D/1, Ganesh Nagar, Muirabad, Allahabad, U.P. Pin-211002.

19. **Srivastava, Avinash Kumar,** Prof. & Head, P.G. Deptt. of Magadh University P.G. Centre, Philosophy, Nalanda College, Biharsharif, Nalanda, Bihar Editor of the Series. Pin-803101.

Introduction

Feminist ethics is a branch of applied ethics. It is built on the belief that traditional ethical theories are man-centric. Its theorizing has undervalued and under-appreciated the moral experiences of women. Feminist philosophers are of the opinion that traditional ethics pre-eminently focus on man's perspective. Here women's view point is considered very little. Women's virtues, like family responsibilities, caring the husband and children and other moral issues are regarded here as trivial matters. Not only this, in traditional ethics women are portrayed as ethically immature and shallow in comparison to men. For them, the masculine cultural traits, like independence, autonomy, intellect, will hierarchy, domination, culture, transcendence, asceticism, war and death, etc., have been prized by the traditional ethics. On the contrary, culturally, feminine traits like interdependence, community, connection, sharing emotions, trust, and absence of hierarchy, nature, immanence, process, joy, peace and life have been given less weight. The male oriented traditional ethics, views the moral reasoning through a framework of rules, rights, universality and impartiality. While female approaches of moral reasoning gives emphasis on relationship, responsibilities, particularity and partiality. Thus the masculine sense of self worth in our culture has become so entrenched in our habits of scientific thought that it is very hard for men to argue persuasively without recourse to the terms like these for their validation. Women, on the other hand, have socialized them in such a way, as if they are for a multiplicity of contingent tasks and practical labour functions in the home and outside. They do not experience the inhibiting constraints of status validation to the same extent.

The history of feminist ethics goes back to the oblivion of the antiquity, of the Indian religio-philosophical tradition, wherein it has categorically said that "where women are respected God resides there" (*Yatra naryastu pujyante ramante tatra devata*). At another place it is said that "the house is peaceful which is run under women's care. Where women lead a happy life, prosperity comes there." On the contrary, a warning has also been given "that where women are unhappy or subordinated, the house becomes full of misery". This is the reason, that female is presented in Hindu religion and culture as women-power. Goddesses are supposed to be the mightiest force, i.e. Goddess Durga. But in the long run, this concept faded away due to some different reasons. The book *Manusmriti* was wrongly interpreted in such a way, that today it is treated as a source book for women oppression, subjugation and subordination. A detail discussion in this regard is found in the chapter of Avinash Kumar Srivastava and Smt. Sarita Kumari entitled "*Revisiting Dharmashastras in Connection with Gender Equality*" published in S.P. Dube Falicitation Volume (2012), New Bhartiya Book Corporation, New Delhi.

However, in the West, Feminist ethics found it first genuine expression in Mary Wollstonecraft's work *Vindication of the Right of Women*. It was published in 1792. In 1969, John Stuart Mill's essay entitled *The Subjection of Women* was published, that drew the attention of the West towards the unfair treatment against the second sex. The journey of women centric thought that started from Mary Wollstonecraft's work influenced the British and European ideas and social movements. Coming to Mill in 1869, it took a very strong shape, which led to the emergence of feminism in the West as a strong dominant force. With the new ideas from the Enlightenment, individual feminism became able to travel faster than ever before. It generated more opportunities for the exchange of ideas and advancement of women's right. The feminist approaches to ethics were developed around nineteenth to twentieth century A.D., by some powerful feminist thinkers like Catherine Beecher, Charlotte Perkins Gilman, Lucrita Mott, Elizabeth Cady Stanton and many others, who gave specific emphasis on gendered nature morality, which is strongly related to women morality through their powerful feminist writings. C. P. Gilman, an American sociologist advocated economic equality for women. In her book *Women and Economics* (Harper & Row, New York,1966), she opined that so long as women are dependent on men for economic support, they will continue to be known for their servility and men for their arrogance. She sought for the need of women's equality in the economic field in order to develop in them a true human virtue. She gave a call to the women world to work in this direction as this is the only way that will lead the women towards prefect blend of pride and humility, as well as self-respect in the society. In another book *Her land* (Pantheon Books, New York, 1979) and *In a Different Voice: Psychological Theory and Women's Development*' (Harvard University Press, 1982) along with other writings generated much of strength to the Feminist ethics. In *Herland*, she has imagined a male free-society, where women give birth to their daughters, through parthenogenesis and live a superior morality. For Gilman, in this female-centric society, there will be no space for individualistic competition, as it will value both industriousness and motherhood at par. In the concept of her feminine virtue, the masculine virtue is co-extensive. Hence, there will be no competition but co-operation; there will be no domination but equality. She along with Nel Noddings has drawn the attention towards the ethics of feminine care. In late 1984, N. Noddings in her book *Caring: A Feminine Approach to Ethics and Moral Education* (Berkeley University of California Press, 1984) criticized the traditional ethics for their disregard, trivializing and attacking the women's cultural values and virtues. She sought to develop a variety of care, focused on feminist approaches to ethics, as here; the impacts of gender issue are fully appreciated. This is how they advocated very strongly in favour of feminine care ethics.

The continuous and perpetual thinking on this line by different thinkers for a long span of time gave birth to a feminine movement that aims at ending the sexist oppression, elimination of all the factors of traditional ethics that contribute to the continued and systematic domination or subordination of women. In the West, three phases of feminist movement is observed, that grew in a systematic way or steps by steps. This is also called Three Waves of Feminism (The F-World, Row Finkbeiner, Kristine, Emery Ville,

Seal Press). The first wave fought for and gained the right to vote. In the second wave feminist activists struggled for ending the legal sex discrimination and right to work as well as equal opportunity for women to workforce. And the third wave's central issue was social class, sexuality and race as well as to develop an ethics that may promote feminist virtues and values. Its aim was to enable the women to seek for legal and moral rights for equality and equal treatment at par with men. And thus the necessity of framing a women-centric ethics was felt seriously, wherein the women's voice, which was ignored in the traditional ethics, may receive prominence. This is how the Feminine Ethics emerged in a bold way in a global perspective.

The forerunners of the feminist ethics had to perform two-fold commitments, the first, to criticise the male bias in ethics, wherever it occurs and second, to develop women-centric ethics that are not male-biased. These involve articulation of feminist values, such as, value of care, appropriate trust, kinship, friendship, etc., that were lost or underplayed in the main stream of traditional ethics. In doing so, often they were involved in theory-building, by pioneering it in new direction or revamping the old theories in gender sensitive ways. Thus the feminist ethics, on the one hand, rejects the attempts to conceive the ethical theories in terms of trans-historical, universal and absolute abstraction of feminist ethics. Though some attempts have been made to formulate necessary and sufficient conditions for a feminist ethics, but they went astray. However, there are some salient features or postulate of feminist ethics, without which any ethics cannot be termed as feminist ethics. They clarify some of the minimal conditions of feminist ethics. These are as follows:

(a) Since feminist ethic aims at elimination of sexism and sex bias, nothing can be a part of feminist ethics that promotes sexism, racism, classism or any other type of 'ism' of social domination.

(b) Feminist ethics is *contextual ethics*. Its ethical discourses and practices emerge from the voice of the people of different historical circumstances. When a contextual ethics is feminist, it gives central place to the voice of women. Thus feminist ethics can be viewed as a college or mosaic, a tapestry of voices that emerges out of the felt-experiences of women located in different circumstances.

(c) Since feminist ethics gives central significance to the diversity of women's voice, it is structurally pluralistic rather than unitary or reductionist.

(d) For feminist ethics, ethical theories are not objective and final; rather they are theory in process which is subject to change with the change of time, circumstances and context. These are reconsidered ethical theories. It is a fact, that like other theories, feminist ethics too is based on some generalisations. But these generalisations themselves are the pattern of voices within which different voices emerge out of concrete and alternative descriptions of meaningful ethical situation.

(e) Since feminist ethics is contextualised, structurally pluralistic and are always in process, one will have to evaluate its claim in terms of inclusiveness. These terms are less partial, less biased and are felt-experience of the oppressed persons, particularly women. These diverse voices of women (oppressed persons) provide legitimacy in theory building.

(f) There is no objective point of feminist ethics, as it is centralizing of the voices of the oppressed persons. Since it is more inclusive, it is less partial than those who exclude these voices.

(g) The value of care, love, friendship and appropriate trust, that remained typically unnoticed, uninterrupted and misrepresented in traditional ethics, received a central place in feminist ethics.

(h) Feminist ethics rejects meaningless, currently untenable, gender-free gender-neutral descriptions of human ethics and ethical decision making. In other words, it rejects abstract individualism. For it, humans and human's conduct

> should be properly understood in terms of network or webs of historical relationship. It, therefore, tries reconceptualize what is human and it is for humans to engage in ethical decision making.

In short, we can say that feminist ethics is a critique of male bias wherever it occurs in ethics. It aims at providing an ethics which is not male biased. It does so in a way that it establishes a basic characteristic of feminist ethics. It believes that there is an obligation for women's differing points of view to be heard and then to give a form of a inclusive conscious view for them. The goal of the feminist ethics is to transform the society and situations, wherein women are harmed and their potentialities are hampered through violence, subordination and exclusion's. To achieve this end and to push its ethics of gender equality, feminist ethicists are at work.

Another related concept that seems to stem out of feminism is "Ecofeminism". Basically, it is a protest against twin domination of nature and women. Very shortly it drew the attention of a good number of scholars, ethicists and philosophers. They viewed it as an alternative to feminism and environmentalism. Generally, it is believed that this term and the concept was introduced by a French writer, Francois d'Eaubonne in 1974 in her book *Le Feminisme ou la Mort*. The sole purpose of this book was to bring the attention of the people towards women potential for bringing about ecological revolution. Since the text was never translated into English, we think that it could have little impact on the articles and books that were published in the English speaking belt including Asian countries before 1989. However, it is also believed that the concept and the term, *Ecofeminism* is said to have originated at the Institute of Social Ecology in Vermont, North America. It was a dynamic attempt to broaden and transform a political theory to include both feminism and ecology. But after the perusal of the history of this movement, it appears that the concept of Ecofeminism arose out of a real, but internationally observed phenomenon. We can trace its roots, like any other progressive socio-ethical movement and social change movements of 1960-1970. The cumulative effect of the writings of different feminist and environmentalist authors like Richard Carson's book *Silent Spring* (1962), Rosemary Radford Ruther's *Women / New Earth* (1975), Mary Daly's *Gyn/Ecology* (1978), Susan Griffin's '*Women and Nature: The Roaring Inside Her*' (1978), Elizabeth Dodson Gray's *Green Paradise Lost* (1979), Carolyn Merchant's *The Death of Nature* provided a solid foundation to the feminist approach to ecology and environment. Besides these, the first conference, addressing the concept of twin domination of women and nature was conducted at California University, Berkeley in 1974. Its theme was "Women and Environment". It was followed by a number of other seminars, symposium and conferences on the theme of Ecofeminism. These helped popularise the subject and established it as a separate field of *Ethics and Women Studies* and a typical oppressive patriarchal conceptual framework emerged that led to a logic of twin domination of nature and women (*Vide* A.K. Srivastava, *Gender Equality and Buddhism*, Living Buddhism, Impression Publication, Patna, 2011). Hence, it can rightly be said that like other social movements, *Ecofeminism* too has its roots in movement of social change of 1960-1970. These days Vandana Shiva, Bina Agrawal, Greta Gaard, Lori Gruen, Val Plumwood, Karen J. Warren and many others are promoting and patronising the movement of Ecofeminism very strongly.

In the brief historical background of Ecofeminism, it can be said that it is relatively a new concept. It has taken a form of movement which aims at protesting any sort of domination, oppression, subjugation and subordination of women and nature. Etymologically the term ecofeminism is composed of two words, 'ecology' and 'feminism'. It indicates a necessary connection between women and nature. The ecofeminists are of the opinion that there is an essential and important connection—historical, symbolical, logical, and theoretical—between women and the nature. In fact, women's monthly fertility cycle, the tiring symbiosis of pregnancy, the wrench of child birth and pleasure of suckling an infant grounds women's consciousness in the knowledge of being coterminous with nature (*Environmental Ethics*, Vol. VI, 1984). Because of this conceptual connection and identity of women and nature led to an oppressive patriarchal conceptual framework, the nomenclature of that is the '*Logic of Domination*'. This is the reason that ecofeminists are developing a multi-system approach to understand the inter-connected forces that operate to oppress women and the natural world. It is evident from the current global inequality, interpersonal and international violence and environmental degradation contribute to women's subordination. The reason is simple. Even the toxic waste, air pollution, contaminated ground water, increasing militarisation and the like, for ecofeminists, are basically women issues. It is women and children who suffer most in these cases because of their consequences. Through a plethora of examples they have tried to demonstrate the connection between environmentalism and feminism. At the same time Ecofeminists point out a number of ways to demonstrate in which environmental degradation cause a decrease in quality of life for women and children.

After analysing the basic nature and the cause of the twin domination, ecofeminists provide a framework for a distinctively feminist and environmental ethics. It emerges out of the felt connections between domination of women and domination of nature. Since, it is contextual ethics, it spots light on what nature might mean for humans in moral context. It focuses on the relational attitude of men towards women and the nature. It also tries to streamline the grounds of human responsibilities to the non-human environment. While constructing an ethics, it takes into consideration, very seriously, the voice of women and nature and the other oppressed persons. Before we conclude, it seems proper to enumerate its basic characters in brief, because of paucity of space and time, it is not possible to index them all. Since feminism and ecofeminism both are contextual, structuralist, pluralist, inclusive in character, lack objectivity and are ethics in process, we would never like to repeat them as they have been explained earlier, while discussing feminist ethics. However, there are a few more characteristics of ecofeminism that needs to be discussed here. They are as follows :

(a) Ecofeminism is quintessentially anti-naturalistic, because it rejects the ways of thinking and acting which reflects a logic, values and attitude of domination towards women and non-human nature.

(b) Here the relationship of a moral agent becomes of central significance in relationship with the nature. Hence, there is an ethical shift of granting moral consideration from humans to non-humans in a highly contextual account. In moral background, one may clearly observe what a human being is and what non-human world might be for him.

(c) Like feminism, in ecofeminism too, the value of care, love, friendship, trust and appropriate reciprocity are of central importance with the other (nature). This makes us understand who we are.

(d) Ecofeminism denies abstract humanism. It reconceptualises of what it means to be human in historical and social context in relationship of human with non-human nature.

After demonstrating the twin domination ecofeminists show that both are basically feminist concerns, as well as both are vital for environmental ethics. Hence, in order to end the domination of women, feminism must embrace environmental ethics, because conceptually and historically, women's domination is tied with the domination of nature. At the same time an environmental ethics must embrace feminism, because failing in it will lead to a state of mind wherein even the environmentalists will not understand the interconnected domination of nature and women. Today, ecofeminism has to take a holistic analysis of these problems in their human and natural contexts. The reason is simple. These problems stem out from mutually reinforcing oppression of women and natural world. It is impossible to analyse the environmental change without addressing social change. At the same time, it is not possible to discuss the women oppression without explaining degradation of our ecology. Both human and nature are interconnected; it is difficult to address them separately.

The present volume comprises eighteen essays dealing with different aspects of feminist ethics and ecofeminism. The summary of these are mentioned below. The present anthology is given to discuss only a few problems out of so many problems of 'Feminism' and it is our humble attempt to look deeply, sincerely and humanely in the multiple maladies of which women are made prey to. Through a series of chapters in this volume as well. The future volumes to come on Feminism, our aim is to make people aware, how the same human beings 'women' have been neglected and marginalized by human beings themselves and no other, and that the status artificially and contemptuously given to women needs to revised for the greater good of the humanity. Since 'women' represent half of humanity and a healthy and happy humanity, so to say, cannot service at the cost of another half of humanity being living in pain and in pangs of suffuring. Let the feminists also not adopt militant role to gain mileage, political footage at the cost of the other half, but in perfect tune with each other. Since neither can all men be made women or *vice-versa.* Women and men care like the two wings of a birth and no bird can fly with one wing. Women and men are two, they have to play two different roles, indeed, as nature has made them to be two, but the meaning of humanity does not provide for fights, but peace with one and all. If the two separate halves of humanity can develop good will peace and harmony, humanity can be divinized beyond human imgination.

Sri Shivanath Prasad in his chapter on, *Ecofeminism : The Moral Dimension* has extended a supporting hand to the eco-feminist arguments, which is critique of twin domination, nature and women. He is of the opinion that ancient religions, particularly sementic religions have painted women and nature in derogatory colours and placed the status of the both below men. For Christianity God has empowered and instructed men to rule over nature (*Genesis*, 1: 26-28). It is also said that though women and men both are created in God's image, but at the same time Eve (the woman) is held responsible for Adam's fall from the heaven. It is also said that woman was created from Adam's rib and placed below man. (Islam and Christianity both). Judaism's instruction is that women should be subjected to men (*Corinthian*, 11. 3-16). *Qur'an* has equated women with earth (Wives are your farms). In Indian religion women are placed very high in religio-social set-up. The Goddess Durga (The emblem of women power) is the mightiest in the creation, had extended protecting hand to gods even. But with the interval of time, this conception drastically changed. People started worshipping sky gods and nature was seen as his creation. The *Samkhya* concept of *Prakriti* and *Purusa* equated women with nature and placed her below man, as *Prakriti* is *Bhogya* (an object to be enjoyed) and the *Purusa* is the ultimate enjoyer. And thus patriarchal conceptual framework emerged and resulted in the logic of domination. Ecofeminist argument may run as follows : (1) There is an important connection between women's oppression and domination and nature's exploitation and domination; (2) Women are identified closer with nature and men with culture; and (3) Since nature is seen inferior to culture, in the same way women are considered inferior to men. This led to twin domination of nature and woman. The queer situation is found in India. On the one hand, women have been active agent in environmental protection movement and regeneration, (for example *Chipko Movement*), on the other hand, they are victim of environmental degradation in a quite gender-specific way. Ecofeminists try to correct the hierarchal dualism of patriarchy. They raise their voice against the twin domination and criticise the conceptual framework that places women and nature below men in hierarchy and argue for an alternative transformative approach for their development. Sri Shivanath Prasad also speak for demystification of the myth of women and nature equation and asks to paint their real picture wherein instead of considering them as inferior to and competitor of men they should be treated as friendly and cooperative. This will help both attain perfection and enjoy their natural qualities in their own way.

Dr. S.M. Nair in her learned chapter on *An Epistemological*

Approach to Feminist Philosophy of Religion seeks a transformation of women's field from marginalized to their inclusion in the centre of religion. In fact, earlier women's voice was not considered important in religious affair. In the field of epistemology, women have been excluded from being credible witness or informant. They were considered ethically and politically inferior because of their so called irrationality, abjection, deception, dependency, passivity and other womanly values. Now time has come to revaluate these values in religious background and women voice has to be considered as reliable as of men. There is also a need of reflective critical openness, care knowing, strong objectivity and principled autonomy of women's voice. This will motivate feminine pursuit of practice, relationship, thought and principle related to divine. This feminine pursuit will not stop till the achievement of their practical wisdom.

Dr. Rajesh Kumar Singh in his learned article on *Feminist Philosophy : Why and What?* has tried to enquire into the cause of women subordination, oppression and gender imbalance and comes to the conclusion that women's empowerment is the only remedy for its redressal. Like Simone de Beauvoir, he is of the opinion that though biologically both have different inherent roles, but the gender role is the product of culture and society. Hence, there is a need of feminine metaphysics and ethics, wherein women's voice, experience and emotions be given proper representation in order to create an alternative but effective and balanced worldview that will help them improve their socio-religious position.

Avinash Kumar Srivastava in his chapter on *Revisiting the Gender Equality* has tried to explore the reason of the deplorable condition of women in the society. He explores out that it is the conceptual framework in women's perspective which is the cause of women subjugation, subordination and oppression. Since in most of the religio-philosophical world view, woman is compared with the earth, farm or is said to be born out of the bone of Adam, the male, she is considered to be inferior to man. And thus man accrues right to subjugate, dominate and oppress women in order to mould her according to his specification, as per the so called logic of domination. Dr. Srivastava is of the opinion that with the rise of a balanced worldview based on equality of all human beings, the perpetual oppression against women will come to a halt. Such conceptual framework is available in the *Upanishads, Gita* and other sacred scriptures of the East. *Upanishads* say that the *atman* is neither male nor female, nor of neuter gender. For Buddhism all human beings are made up of *pancha skandha*, there is no difference among them. If these conceptual frameworks are upheld by the members of the society there will be no women subordination or oppression and gender equality will never be a utopia.

Dr. Shiva Bhanu Singh in his learned chapter on *Gender Inequality : An Existential Analysis* points out at the very outset, in the tune of Will Durant, that twentieth century should be known as change for women status, not for great wars or Russian revolution. He is of the opinion that earlier women were treated as human chattels, a sexual tool or social ornament. This status was rendered to them by male dominated society, who defined women relative to men as they were not treated as autonomous human beings. From the very beginning girls are taught to be obedient, dependent, weak and different from the male child. For Simone de Beauvoir the essential feminine qualities of sacrifice and narcissism, promoted by these myths, proved to be detrimental to women's identity and were converted into other sex. It is unfortunate that women have accepted this position as they did not resist or revolt against this. The time has come to achieve their lost identity and enjoy autonomous and independent status, as they are giving their valuable contribution in all walks of life. This is how they are proving the so called gender inequality as unscientific and irrational. This has been achieved by dint of women's self endeavour not by the mercy of man.

Prof. Y.V. Satyanarayana in his learned chapter on *Disproportionate Representation of Women in Indian Legislative Bodies* has tried to analyse its root cause and the remedial measures. He is of the opinion that conditioning, restraints on social mobility, lack of encouragement and support of the family members, character assassination and criminalisation of politics, financial problems, lack of education and seclusion or *purdah* system are the main restraints and constraints in the way. If these hurdles are pulled out, their representation may increase. He opines that there is an urgent need of encouragement and cooperation to the women folk from the government, political parties, society and the family members for an effective and meaningful participation of women in the political sphere.

Dr. Asha Mukherjee in her chapter on *Feminist Ethics and its Concern* says that "when feminist regard ending sexual oppression and injustice as a moral imperative at the level of thought and practice", it is called feminist ethics. It no longer realises in the concealment of power relation, but works actively to expose them. In order to transform an ethics into a feminine ethics a priority of the premises of male superiority has to be rejected on the ground of the account of women's experience and their adequate representation. Since gender is a reality, women's subjectivity and specificity of experience is equally important. She opines that normally reason and emotion are associated with man and women respectively. It is unjust. In fact these play a dominant role in nurturing the children and cultivating social relations. These are of great moral importance. These have to be included in framing out feminist moral theories against self-presupposed and self-centred male dominated theory.

Dr. Sanjay Kumar in his analysis of the feminine movement actually makes a survey of the different lines of thoughts that have grown around this issue. He shows a very keen historical sense accompanied with critical insight with utmost objectivity. The discussion he takes up, is all encompassing. His main focus is how these issues have been perceived by different scholars. He also warns against the excesses that are likely to be committed by its advocates and beneficiaries.

The chapter *Women Empowerment and Science*, jointly authored by Umesh Kumar Srivastava and Rajesh Kumar Singh, start with a concern for marginalization of women and domination of masculine values even in value neutral field of science. Pondering over the reason and remedy of this predicament they arrive at the solution that through woman empowerment the androcentric science can be based on feminist value. This can be made possible if in any scientific enquiry, experiment, formation of hypothesis or empirical data collection, the feminist value, emotions, be utilized along with the masculine value, reason.

Dr. Deepali Singh in her chapter tried to spotlight that through 73rd Constitutional Amendment women participation from the very grassroot could become possible. Their 33 per cent reservation in Panchayati Raj to Local Self Government has empowered them enormously and positively. Their journeys from pastoral society to post-modern world of globalization have changed their role from housewife to head of the institution including the policy making agency, the Parliament. This rapidly increasing forceful participation of women in every walk of life streamlines their rapid stride and growing power, which is a good healthy sign for a nation. The credit of this women uplift goes to 73rd Constitution Amendments, which provide 33 per cent reservation for women.

Dr. Yamini Sahaya is of the opinion that feminists are of the view that traditional ethics depreciates and devalues women's moral experience. The moral discourse here are tilted in favour of masculine gender or even written from their point of view. In particular, hence, there is a need to quash them giving place to new conceptions unbiased and unprejudiced. For that there is a need to revise, reformulate and rethink the traditional ethics. The feminist Alison Jaggar has found five ways in which the traditional ethics has devalued women and let them down and has neglected them. However, feminists have developed a wide variety of gender centred approaches to ethics. Some feminist ethicists emphasize issues related to women's traits and behaviours, particularly their care giving ones. In contrast, other feminist ethicists emphasize the political, legal, economic, or ideological causes and effects of women's second sex status. But be these emphases as they may, all feminists ethicists share the same goal; the creation of a gendered ethics that aims to eliminate or at least ameliorate the oppression of any group of people, but most particularly women.

As feminist approaches to ethics is gender sensitive, wherein care focused and status focused approaches to ethics have got their manifestation, what traditional ethicists should have done in the first place. Thus, the feminist rightly suggests that it is not enough for traditional ethics to incorporate women's interests and issues and to recognize women moral agents who must be taken seriously. On the other hand she urges traditional ethics to rethink the onto logical and epistemological assumptions upon which their thinking is based; and to consider the possibility, that far from being sources of human liberation, as their principle, rules, regulations, norms and criteria actually serve to suppose patterns on domination and subordination that demoralizes everyone.

Dr. Madhubala Kumari in the largest part of her chapter, *Gender Discrimination*, spots light on the women's plight in the society all over the world. For this she accuses the masculine worldview, prevalent in the society. Since women are the pivot of any family, society and nation, it is our imperative to dissolve our age old prejudices and create an atmosphere of gender equality that will pave path for women empowerment. This is the only *mantra* all-round development of any society and nation.

In her learned chapter entitled *Buddhist Nun— Past and Present* Dr. Abha Singh narrates the genesis of origin of *Bhikkhuni Samgha* wherein women attained freedom from shacles of male domination and achieved the equal status in the society as well as emancipation from worldly bondage, earlier they were deprived of reading the Vedas, participating in religious rituals on her credit and attaining the *summum bonum* of life. This upward radical change in women status attained its zenith after formation of *Bhikkhuni Samgha* parallel to the *Bhikkhu Samgha.* Primarily unequal treatment was given to it by introducing stringent *Garudhamma* for *Bhikkhuni Samgha* which was humiliating and demoralizing, but latter on the stiffness of the rules was relaxed and equality was maintained during Buddha's time. After the *Mahaparinibbana* of the Buddha, situation changed. Though *Bhikkhuni Samghas* continues to flourish independently in several foreign lands like Sri Lanka, Mynmar, Vietnam,Thailand etc. adopting the traits of the land but in its home land India its status started dwindling down, after fifteenth century. Buddhist model of social equality of sex received a severe jolt under the existing masculine social realities. To change our social outlook, reinstate gender equality and revive the *Bhikkhuni Samgha* as an autonomous unit is the need of the time.

It is commonly believed that women are treated as second grade citizen in Islam. They are the belonging of their husband and they have no role in socio-political affair of the state and its decision making. Contrary to this notion Dr. Sunita Sharma in her chapter *Maham Anaga and Mughal Court Politics* tries to spotlight on the generous ethical principles of Mughal king Akabar whose royal patronage had elevated the political position of a lady to the extent that she became a close confident of the king.From the feminist point of view it was a great leap in the path of women emancipation from a male dominated society wherein women folk have to live behind the curtains. Her importance lies in the fact her untiring efforts caused flux with success in establishing the female voice in mediaeval period dominated by masculine thought of Mughals.

At the very outset of the chapter entitled *Women in Islam and Hinduism. An Analysis in Indian Context*, Dr. Damodar Singh expresses concern on the popular belief that the position of women in both the religions is shrouded in the gist of controversy and confusion regarding the status and position that kept oscillating in the patriarchal society. In order to unveil the curtain from this mistry he revisits both the religion in context of gender equality and feminine presence in Indian society. He is of the opinion that primary in Aryan society the position of women was very high. She was *pujya (Yatra naryastu pujyante ramante tatra devata).* In *Tantra* philosophy she occupies an important position of protecting mother and *Guru.* Her feet is considered here as an object of worship. With the interval of time she became *Sahadharminian* equal partner in religion spiritual life of a man. She is *Bharya,* a real helpmate, here and here after. She is endowed with intelligence, grace and poise. Besides her domestic character of a housewife she had a public character of her own. Slowly but stealthy society changes into a patriarchal one where in her status was maligned and often she is considered as *Bhogya,* an object of enjoyment. Contrary to it Islam has not used such sophistry. Its moral history starts with pre-Islamic Arabia wherein women subjugation, subordination and sexual abuse were rampant. Female, the humanchattels were treated *asan* instrument of pleasure and recreation. With the advent of Islam refinement is marked in their weltanschauung that sublimated women's status up to some extent. Coming to India the social status of women changed drastically. They became equal partners as the explicit consent of the female is a must in marriage. She also acquires share in parent's property, besides a handsome amount of dowry is assured by her husband at the time of marriage that can be used after separation from her husband. These not only secures her future prospect but also help her lead an independent life in the present social set-up. However, the sanction of four marriages, divorce through three *Talaq* and *Halala Nikah* (Marriage) by Islamic Shariat law, for him appears as stigma.

Dr. Nibha Singh, in her learned chapter *Indianness in the Poetry of Sarojini Naidu* hinges on the fact that there is a blend of ethics, philosophy and religion in the poems of Naidu. However, she is not immune of sensuous love and feminist feeling that women had to share in a patriarchal society. Male oriented ethics echoes in some of her poems wherein she tells that women fallen in love is always ready to sacrifice everything for her beloved including her beauty. However, in her poems like *Purdahnashin,* and Suttee her feminist voice becomes loud and she speaks of women emancipation. In Suttee she speaks loudly against the age old *Sati Pratha*. Expressing the feelings of the widow she tells that the lamp of my life (husband) has been extinguished for ever, for that she has to pay heavily by scarifying along with her dead husband. In fact it is the feminist feeling that has manifested through her poem.

Dr. Seema Prasad through her learned chapter entitled *Tagore's Portrayal of Female Consciousness in Home and the World* tries to focus on the fact that when the feminist voice had started emerging the Western world India had started its movement for gender equality and women emancipation and empowerment through the writngs of political thinkers, philosophers, religious leaders, social reformers, poets and novelists. R.N. Tagore raised his voice against these social evils particularly against women plight. The time he came on the stage was not congenial. The country was slave. Indian society was sleeping in dogmatic slumber. A number of super-stitions like *Sati Pratha, Purdah* system and many others were crippling the women autonomy and relegated them to the status of second grade citizen. They were living the life of segregation. Early marriage was common and women's world was governed by mail restriction. Raja Ram Mohun Roy and other social reformers were raising their voice against it. Tagore through his writings was trying to create awareness of gender equality, women empowerment, women emancipation and against subjugation of women in society. He was trying to wake up the Indian society from their dogmatic slumber through his poems, short stories and novels. In his famous novel "Home and the World" throughVimala, who is the pivot of the story, Tagore tries to say that women emancipation and empowerment can be achieved through their education and freedom. For him these two will help women think and act in their own way. It will result in creating their social, political and cultural identity. Thus a bold feminine consciousness emerges through his novel.The uniqueness of her thought lies in this fact that the Western feminine movement speaks of women education for their economic independence while Tagore was creating awareness among the women folk for their all-round development, social, political, religious and spiritual.

Dr. Praveen Kumar in his learned chapter *Status of Women in Buddhism* tries to bring to our knowledge the controversy of *Garudhammas,* which are endocentric in character and had been instrumental for subjugation and subordination of the *Bhikkhuni Samgha* Buddha's social movement was directed against social evils of the then Brahmanic society wherein religion was the prime source of women's exploitation. It was the Buddha who for the first time advocated for gender equality and sublimation of female socio-economic and religious condition. It was his revolutionary decision to open the gate of Buddhist order for women. *Bhikkhuni Samgha* was established, earlier women were debarred from reading Vedas and attaining *summum bonum* of life as it was meant for the men only. However, introduction of eight *Garudhammas* by Buddha himself was astonishing, as these rules are humiliating for *Bhikkhunis.* According to these *Dhammas* a *Bhikkhuni,* whether senior or junior, will have to bow before even a junior *Bhikkhu* and seek permissions for the any activity of *Bhikkhuni Samgha.* The crux of the problem is whether Buddha had introduced it or not. If He has introduced it, what are the reasons behind it? Praveen Kumar apprises us about two types of view of the Scholars. For I.B. Horner the eight *Garudhammas* are the latter interpolations, they are not the Buddha *Vacana*. But others are of the opinion that these are the protecting measures for the safeguard of *Bhikkhunies*. But it is act that women folk attained their freedom and sublimated their life under Buddhist threshold. Unfortunately after Buddha's *Mahaparinibbana* even the *Bhikkuni Samgha* could maintain its independent status, itwas directed by endocentric powers.

Avinash Kumar Srivastava

Chapter – 1

Ecofeminism : The Moral Dimensions

Shiva Nath Prasad

Epithets from most high-sounding to most degrading go to designate the women-kind in the various literatures of the world. Beginning from Indian tradition, women are taken as emblematic of goddess, like Durga, Parvati, Gauri, Sita, Radha, etc., and even as they are designated as goddesses, in the pair of names of gods and goddesses, the name of goddesses find primacy over gods since the names of goddesses occur prior to the names of gods. For example, in the pairs like Radha-Krishna, Parvati-Shiva, Sita-Ram, Lakshmi-Visnu, etc., the names of goddesses are placed prior to the god. This is to symbolise the higher status of goddesses in the Indian traditions. Sita is the power or *shakti* of Sri Ram, Radha is the *ahladini* (*anand*) *shakti* of Sri Krishna, and about Parvati which is the *shakti* or power of Shiva, it is said that Shiva without his *shakti* is only a dead body, i.e. Shiva without his *shakti* is only *sava* or dead body. In the Manusmṛti it has been said that "where the women are worshipped, there gods remain"—*"Yatra naryastu pujyante ramante tatra devatah"*. Further, women are compared to "mother" or cow or Earth which is also called "mother". In the Vedic literature the earth is called mother and sky as father and man is called child of immortality *(mata prithivya* and *pita antarikshah, amṛtasya putra). Pṛthvi* and women are called '*mata*' or mother, in so far as both have super endurance power to bear all onslaughts for the upkeep of child, as also they are compassion, kindness-incarnate. There is still further epithet, that they are *'ardhangini'*, in so far as husband-wife relation, which means that women are half part of man, and thus degradation is far removed to downward scale, but even that due, i.e. the half importance the woman does not get. Another epithet of women is *'bhogya'*, i.e., an article of enjoyment; *dharati* or *vasundhara* is also called '*bhogya*'. We find in the *Ramcharit Manas* of Tulsidas that '*dhol*, *ganwar*, *shudra*, *pashu* and *nari'* are all worth-beating up. Still in the other context, woman is called 'fair sex', 'better half', but it is quite questionable if women are given such fair deal, how woman is called '*gamya*', in the sense of sex-tool meant for enjoyment only. They are said to be most unreliable, because of their excessive sex-urge and they can never be believed in, so far sex. In the *Gita*, there is mention of three things as gates of hell, and one such is woman. Women are devoid of the right to the study of the Sacred *Vedas*, though this right to the study of the *Vedas* has been allowed to women in the *Bhagavad Gita*. It is said that women can not be liberated. It is said that the *Vedas* are not composed by any human being, it is called *'apaurusaya'*, i.e. God's words, though there are also some scholars who say that several of the *Vedic Richas* are composed by some woman of high intellectual excellence. Because of woman's susceptibility to bow down or become prey to passions as it is alleged, they are not allowed to remain free, while she is a child, her father is the guardian, while she is wife, her husband is the guardian, when she is widowed or old, the sons are the guardians. Man is always suspicious of women, while he does not want any control on him from any side. Women are also called 'weaker sex', weaker in the sense of muscle power, and so she is always in need of some stronger power of muscle man to protect, to control. It is a proverb that wealth, property, land and woman all require forceful control and if forceful control is loosened, they go scot-free. Even in *Qur'an*, woman is compared to 'cultivation', *kheti*. Having said all these, what a confused picture we find of woman. In common parlance, what we find is that male is always controlling, oppressing, subduing woman to suit his own interests while keeping the interests of woman to the minimum. Man is subduing nature in the same way, as he is subduing women. Such sort of domination, '*Patriarchal*' subjugation has reacted into ecofeminist movement.

In the present time, ecofeminism is the catchphrase. We may begin with a definition of the word 'ecofeminism' given by Greta Gaard, "Drawing on the insight of ecology, feminism, and socialism, ecofeminism's basic premise is that the ideology which authorises oppressions, such as those based on race, class, gender, sexuality, and physical abilities, is the same ideology which sanctions the oppressions of nature."

Another definition as given by Boyce Nelson runs, "Ecofeminism bridges the gap between ecology and feminism. Analysis of Strands which has existed side by side over the past decades without necessarily intertwining. By making explicit the connection between a misogynist society and a society which has exploited 'mother earth' is the point of environmental crisis, ecofeminism has helped to highlight the deep splits in the patriarchal paradigm."

Thus, "ecofeminism calls for an end to all oppressions arguing that no attempt to liberate women (or any other oppressed group) will be successful without an equal attempt to liberate nature."

The above definitions mean that so long as man's oppression of nature goes unabated, no attempt to liberate woman from man's domination is possible. Nature's liberation and woman's liberation should go side by side, not selectively, separately, since the will to domination works psychologically so deeply in man, that he cannot rest content till his ego sense is fully satisfied. Woman feels affinity with nature, she feels to identify herself with nature, but the patriarchy's myth ties her destiny with her husband, who works as a coloniser, so she has to subdue her inherent nature of nurse, nurture, to aesthetics, to gardens, to flower, to sweet and tender feelings, but to speak not independently but as collaborator, to speak only her husband's voice, work at his dictates willy-nilly, dance to the tune of husband, and in this process of oppression and suppression, her husband's pride find fulfilment, because "he has to pressure his existence, so he must conquer nature" and in each fresh attempt to conquest of some kind, "he tends to increase his vigour and intelligence, until he becomes a new man".

George Meredith in the book *The Ordeal of Richard Feveral*, writes, "I expect women will be the last thing to be civilized by man", which stated most simply means that it is man and man alone who makes woman civilized, otherwise given to woman herself, she will never become civilized. What does this show, other than "man's proprietary arrogance and the 'objectification' or 'think-making' of woman for the purpose of anthropocentric idea of 'civilization'. This is about man's pride and privilege. But Ursula Leguin writes in the book *Healing the Wounds: The Promise of Ecofeminism.*[1] which is about woman's side, "Where I live as a woman is to men a wilderness. But to me it is home". In this utterance, woman identifies herself with nature, but what woman takes nature's ways as her usual, natural life, for man it is tantamount to wilderness, uncivility, unculturedness. This speaks of man's artificiality, snobbery, arrogance frustrating to his self-sense, pride and vainglory and far more, his sophistication worth no price. Are women born fools and end life as fools? And man ever wise, born with wisdom, as wisdom incarnate? Does it not sound like the pride of swollen river of the rainy season? Does it not remind of the story of the *Genesis* which establishes a "dominion" over nature. Is it not "objectification" of woman instead of taking woman as a soul, a spirit, a subject, a living reality like the rest living beings in blood and vein and artery.

The classical Judaeo-Christian thought places man above nature and considers him to be independent of nature, and it offers no apology for holding this view. But having received a superior status, nature is led to be ruled or in other way man finds right to rule over nature. The psalm 8:37 runs thus :

"When I consider your heavens
the work of your fingers
the moon and the stars
which you have set in place
What is man that you are mindful of him,
the son of man that you care for him ?
you made him a little lower than the heavenly beings
and crowned him with glory and honour.
You made him *ruler* over the works of your hands,
you put everything under his feet :
all flocks and herds,
and the beasts of the field,
the birds of the air,
and the fish of the sea.
All that swim the paths of the seas."

The above theme indicates that man is the only creature who has the privilege to "reflect the divine qualities", though he is distinct from the divine, and he is also earthly but he has the potential to have conscious communion and personal and spiritual relationship with the divine, of which no other creature animate or inanimate is endowed with (that power) so he is invested with right to exercise *dominion* over all of God's creation. In the book of *Genesis* 1:26-28, it is stated, then God said, "Let us make man in our image, in our likeness and let them rule over the fish of the sea and the birds of the air, over the livestock, over all earth, and over all creatures, that moving along the ground." God created man and woman in his image and blessed them to be fruitful and increase in number, fill the earth subdue it, rule over the fish of the sea, and birds of the air and over every living creatures that moves on the ground. This right to rule, to have dominion over nature, led the seventeenth century scientists and thereafter to hold that conquest of nature is the goal of science as did Bacon visualise. This domineering right not only remained limited to nature alone, but it extended even to the community of human kind. Judaism (*Corinthians,* 11.3-16) taught that man is above woman, and that woman should be subjected to man. And then a further dominionship on woman, right to rule the woman also came in force. Though God created man and woman both, as human kind, but woman did not achieve equal status with man in religious and social life. "Hebrew religion detested the fertility rite nature cults of Canaanite religion, and it considered the female principle in the cosmos as a vehicle of all evil and pain in the world." The story of the Garden of Eden records that Eve fell an easy prey to the tempting of the serpent and then went to force Adam to fall with her. Woman was equated with nature, mother earth and man was responsible for enriching her with power of progeny-seed, for this woman's needs man, and man by providing seed, secured for himself the right to be ruler of woman. Classical Christian thought taking man's right to rule woman, it "contributed to the designing and enforcing the institution of patriarchy as a social and cultural force and the patriarchy culture dominated the global history for thousands of years, which pleaded for this social paradigm "in which man by force, direct pressure, or through ritual, tradition, law and language, customs, etiquette, education and the division of labour determine what part woman shall or shall not play and in which female is everywhere subsumed under the male." This strictly dominating role of man led to the rise of the new movement of ecofeminism, this is one side of the picture.

There is another theory with regard to the relation of man to nature, which is known by the term "*Stewardship theme*". There is only little difference between Stewardship and dominion theory. What is common to both is that both these "motifs" in the final analysis objectify nature for anthropocentric ends. The Stewardship theme and Dominion theme differ in this that in the Stewardship theme, man is placed at the centre, while in Dominion theme, man is placed above nature. The Stewardship motif is more human than the sadistic overtones of the former. The stewardship theme also withdraws the plenipotentiary rights of human kind in nature. No one can talk of nature as his birth right. Man is held accountable to an external ethical or divine force for the use or misuse of the sacred right that has been entrusted to him."

The question which of the two themes mentioned above should be acceptable to Christianity, is point which has led the Christian theologians to put forth another theory for explanation of man-nature relationship, and this is called 'unity theme'. Unlike the domination and Stewardship themes, which survive on the distinction between human beings and nature, the unity theme affirms the consubstantiality of both human kind and the world. The term 'consubstance' means that the two different objects are made of the same substance. This unity theme is an advance over the two above mentioned dominionship theme and stewardship but "contemporary" theologians are discreet about affirming the unity theme, because it goes against the very fundamentals of classical Christian theology, as well as recognising the validity of certain non-Christian religious systems which operate with unity motifs. This unity theme is more acceptable to Eastern religion's philosophy. This unity is quite new and sudden development and is most in consonance with Eastern thought, as well as very apt from ecological point of view. The science of ecology tells us that there is an unbroken continuity between different elements, objects and forces of nature; there is an unbroken wholeness inherent in the cosmic web of relations at a deeper non-manifest level.

There are some contemporary process theologians like John B. Cobb Jr., Ian G. Barbour, Schubert Ogden and others, consider process theology as the harbinger of ecotheology. Cobb calls *Whitehead the father of an 'ecological philosophy'*, which bring God, humanity and the world into the same pole. The *process metaphysics* has multified the categorical distinction between nature and history, and perceives nature as unbroken process of events rather than static objects. Whitehead's philosophy is called *Organic Philosophy* much like the unity theme which affirms the consubstantiality of God, humanity and the world. This view is unlike traditional Christian, which sees man as the sole object of God's concern, love and redemption and excludes nature from it. It is understood that God is at the highest level, nature stands at the lowest level and man is mid-way between the two, commanding right for being divine, as he is made in the image of God, and since nature is at the bottom, he has right to rule, to 'subdue' and in this, he is an heir of the divine kingdom and sovereign of or ruler of nature. Ecofeminism raises its voice against such attitude of man for a timely correction to save the whole human race from destruction.

Ecological crisis has amply demonstrated that the destiny of both human kind and world of nature is co-terminus, which view is quite in consonance with Eastern religious thoughts. But it is painfully amazing that what even Eastern religious thoughts devise, is not put to exact practice, and leave the theory in the books but not to practice and put the devised theory making a mockery and jeopardy of all theories. Woman and nature are always oppressed, as such, the movement of ecofeminism finds its cause worth propagation and to be ventilated by way of an eye-opener.

Classical Christian metaphysics held time/space as linear as against the Eastern view of Cyclical time scheme. The linear space/time concept or linear historicism sees God's primary involvement in this world in relation to man alone, not any other creatures, it accepts only the destiny of man as the only or ultimate goal of all historical process, while denying any history or destiny to nature. Diametrically opposed to the linear concept is cyclical time schemes as per the Eastern religions. The tribal animism and nature religions held that cyclic time is based on the cyclical flow of nature. Nature's cycles of fecundity and decay are necessary for an ongoing creative process to be kept activated. Cycle time acknowledges the continuous relation and actualisation of the divine dynamics in the creative as well as the disintegrating cosmic process. This cyclic view emerged at a time when primitive consciousness (of primitive people) used to find themselves as part of nature, lived with nature as integrated and as participating entities within the rhythmic cycles of nature. Human birth, sexuality, love, joy, pain, death and after life were transposed on the changing moods of nature and the seasons and their unfailing rhythm. There is no doubt that man has a future, a destiny, to redeem, but this does not go against the life in the kin and lap of nature, living natural life in utter harmony with nature, rather be always fighting. dashing, quarrelling with nature. Ecofeminism which takes nature and women to have the same type of life, wants to adopt this type of life as envisaged in cyclical time scheme, in unison with nature and in harmony with nature, according to the drives and directions of nature rather than opt for destiny, unforeseen destiny, the uncertain destiny guided by God or a destiny dominated and carried by man, the husband, the dictator.

Woman's opting to live according to nature, implies many things to her, i.e. living according to feminine nature. Woman has her own biological rhythms, which is alien to man. Woman can bear a child but not man. It is said that it is only woman who knows the pangs of childbirth. Woman keeps her child in the womb for nine months, if a man has to do this, he will hardly survive, though he has the power of muscle and hardy body quite accustomed for hard work. Man is hardy enough, but he cannot sustain the pangs of childbirth. By nature, woman is tender, she loves beauty, she has more endurance power, almost equivalent to the Mother Earth. She is compassionate and kind. If all natural qualities of woman is snatched and divested of her, she will only remain a neuter gender, material something, a machine, but not a woman. Similarly, if a man is divested and deprived of all his manly qualities, he cannot become a woman either Man will remain man, and so woman and to attempt to womanise man or humanise woman as man would not succeed. Rajneesh says that such attempts would be fatal for both men and women. Further Rajneesh says that woman who claims to be half of man is also a wild-wish. Man and woman are two distinct category and let woman be only woman, let woman enjoy her own inborn qualities and divest from attaining man's qualities, also let man keep his own qualities and remain in his natural limits, not hinder or interfere in the area of the opposite sex, in this lies the glory of man as well as woman. In this regard, Rajneesh would be too much in favour of ecofeminism than any other woman pleading for ecofeminism. Love, compassion are divine qualities, let woman keep these divine qualities in her and lead her kindly light. Man has got muscle power, he can go on for the principle of 'survival of the fittest', but let not this claim of the fittest go to torture woman and rid her from her divine and feminine qualities. Rajneesh asks, why is it that man is immediately, automatically and naturally attracted by the sight of woman, but not by any man? The reason is that she has the charm and beauty, the sex-appeal, etc., so let not woman try to become man in man's race, but let only a real woman, retain her feminine qualities and keep on charming man with her glorious qualities. Such view would be most suitable for the ecofeminist.

In the primitive days, it was said that only man has a soul, woman is not endowed with soul. It was also said that the four *purusharthas*, the last one liberation is meant for man, but not for woman. In the *Samkhya* system of India, the word *prakṛti* is used for feminine power, and *purusa* for man. The *Samkhya* text says that *prakṛti* is for the enjoyment of *purusa* as well as for liberation of the *purusas*, here *prakṛti* is said to be *jada* and the *purusa* as conscious potency. The expression "*Purusosti bhoktri bhavat*" is used, which means that *prakṛti is for purusas bhoga* or enjoyment. But then *prakṛti* not only plays the role of enticement or infatuation, but she also labours for the liberation of the *purusa*. Taken in the mundane sense, woman as emblem of *prakṛti* principle is *bhogya*, gives *purusa* the scope for enjoyment, acting playfully and colourfully the role of a dancer or *nartaki* and then after showing her exquisite dance withdraws from the scene and leaves the *purusa* to realise the higher goals. *prakṛti* plays the active role of cooperation and the cooperative role played by *prakṛti* for *purusa* has been compared in *Samkhya karika* as the cooperation of lame man to go out of burning forest by riding on the shoulder of the blind man, the blind man carrying the lame one, who can move fast but cannot find the way out, the lame one showing the path and blind man moving fast. This is the best example of cooperation of a sturdy eyeless person, helping the indigent partner to win in the hours of difficulty. Interpreted in mundane sense and in the context of ecofeminism, the merciful man can help the biologically and constitutionally weak woman to win whenever difficult days come. Woman can play the role of winning man by her sweet qualities, entice him as well as liberate him from dangers and damaging situations. The ecofeminist movement expects the woman kind to play her own roles and leave man to play the role of unity, harmony, cooperation rather than behave cruelly, heartlessly, subduing suppressing always she succumb to his commands, rather than seek her own divine pursuits of kindness, compassion love and tenderness. This is a significant move towards better understanding and help maintaining harmony rather than remain a captive, a prey to man's passions of violence, subjugation, irrational domination, the false sense of man as carver of women's destiny have the boastful dehumanising effect of de-godding creation which makes man become a scar to civilized ways of culture and even then have boastful claim to 'civilize' woman by his own endeavour. How surprising indeed! This is a bubbling pride of man like foam just to wither away in a moment.

The main project of ecofeminism is to correct the patriarchy's "hierarchical dualism" — by which man equals superior civilization, woman equals wild nature — has ripped the web of life. "Body and nature have been patriarchy's "shadow", easily projected on to woman, who through her biological rhythms and her domestic milieu is easily seen to be close to nature. With further connotations of wilderness, non-civilized state, primitivism, informed conditions, woman in made-made society was seen to require the mediation of man to 'civilize' her away from nature and take her close to the realm of God or morality and social ethics as designed by patriarchy. Hence, emerged what ecofeminists call a "hierarchical dualism" (Joyce Nelson). Man and woman are not just "opposites" but female is subordinate and inferior to male. Man's enterprise in subduing female, nature to his will is analogous to his mechanistic and technological domination over the Earth's original environment. That which resists subjugation causes unease, fear and a sense of evil. The exploitative relation between man and woman and man and nature, is equated.[2]

Ecofeminism seeks to correct the "conceptual error" in the culture/nature dichotomy. Elizabeth Dadson Gray in his book *Green Paradise Lost* has traced this of "Conceptual error" which is continuing from 3000 years old creator myth about which mention have been made (in the paper in the beginning) relating to the first-three chapters of Genesis, in which domination over nature has been expressed by the expression "subdue the earth", have domination overall living beings that Woman Eve was created from Men's ribs, the Eve-serpent collusion, and worst of all *Genesis* 3:17, by which angry God curses the earth, because of Adam Eve transgression in the gaining of carnal knowledge, the knowledge of "embodiment". According to the ecofeminism, apart from the above words of the *Genesis*, the Greeks are also greatly responsible for devaluing women. The Greeks on the one hand devalued woman by keeping them away from economic and political organisation and also spoke for "objectification" of nature, which also means drawing a boundary of dualism between human and nature, the dualism of matter and soul as in Descartes, Idea and Form as in Plato or such many other dualisms, drawing a bifurcation or dividing line between two such pairs, which went on and on, but it was left only to Whitehead who voiced against any "bifurcation in nature". According to Karen Birkeneyer, the male supremacy is based on the supposition that man is endowed with mind and all that is rational and woman has of her nature's gift "anatomy is destiny", biological destiny. She has a body and all that is emotional, hence irrational. According to Birkeneyer, man dissociating himself from body and heart, man is unable to feel the damage he is inflicting on women, on earth and man himself included. Working under this very definition, ecofeminists maintain that the path towards a more safe and healthy society, lies in the capability of man to reconnect his/their (man's) mind, body and spirit, since mind body and spirit do not reside elsewhere than the sense-mansion of the body and to dissociate them is to sound a death knell to his own existence. Woman is a human being, also erected in the image of God, she has also a body, though anatomically a different, she has also a mind and a spirit and qualitatively women cannot be a lesser human being, she cannot be a lifeless something like wood or stone or river.

Helena Cixous draws a distinction between "Man's Realm of Proper" and "Women's Realm of Gift". In the language of the ecofeminist, it signifies a "triumph of Mechanism over Vitalism", the word mechanism may refer to man and vitalism which is a gift, points to woman. In order to gain the lost ground, Vitalism must become a conscious political and spiritual agenda. Consequently, the proponents formulate an Earth-centred spirituality with a wide scope. There are three concepts—(i) immanence, (ii) interconnection, Compassion that all parts of living cosmos are linked; and (iii) the ability to see ourselves as answerable and accountable to those who are different from us, to value other lives as we value our own. These concepts provide an imperative towards action in the world, an activism that links the personal, the political and the spiritual.[3]

II

The term ecofeminism as carried by Francoise d'Eaubonne in 1974 means many things. In its inception stage, i.e. in 1970s, it meant to relate woman to having spiritual relationship with the earth, that women who were in the beginning worshipped in the same way as the other aspects of nature, can alone find an alternative culture to save the earth from ecological destruction. As Vandana Asthana has outlined that ecofeminism tries to accomplish two goals : (1) to establish interconnection between feminism and ecology; and (2) to demonstrate the inadequacies of environmental theory for accommodating insulates of women.

In the Rio Earth Summit 1982 and 1985 Nairobi Conference, the link between productivity of woman and environment first drew attention. *(vide Readings in Environmental Ethics,* Ed. D.C. Srivastava).

It may be mentioned that ecofeminism as a movement does not come or arise from the affluent section of woman, who are safe and secure in their richly state and have not to go out of their homes in search of sustenance, or water or wood. It comes from the poorest section of women, who are most deprived lot, they are invisible work-forces, they are farmers, major food producers all round the year but not recognised as farmers, they are given to more hours of work than men but still not recognized as work-force, they are marginalized women living in remote villages, in the midst of forests, in areas where the trees, forests, fruit trees, dirty water of ponds, etc., are the only source of subsistence, they are nature-dependent folks, for whom there is no alternative source of livelihood. They have either to live or die with nature's bounties or suffer nature fury, pollution, degradation or contamination led diseases or very little food or even death due to hunger. They have to live or die on nature. Their approach is more holistic rather than materialistic. A little statistics would reveal further.

Ecofeminism has grown out of Western scientific industrialised urban culture and from the West it has come to South Asia or India. For Western scientific culture (culture in the special sense that ecofeminism is a matter of culture) according to whom environmental degradation is a matter of physical pollution, a matter of degradation of biosphere but for South Asian woman it is a matter of life, subsistence, a matter of socio-economic sphere, a matter of "international inequitable appropriation and distribution" of national resources. Roughly, 75 per cent of the world's population is among the poorest and the woman and the girl child make up the majority of the poor. All the time, they are reeling under highest burden, working 15-18 hours per day, in bringing water, in bringing wood for cooking, work in the fields and farms in sourcing, weeding, etc., which are back-breaking jobs, then cook for the family both day and night, but little recognition of their hard work is given. They are "invisible work-force and unacknowledged backbone of the family. The Five Year Plan book of India opines that although women represent half of the world's population and one-third of the official labour work-force they receive only 10 per cent of the world income and own less than 1 per cent of the world's property". In spite of the best efforts to weigh the quantum of workload thrust on women, uptill now no foolproof method could have been found out in definite terms, how much load is on women's share or shoulder. Women are greater farmers than men in real sense, they are the major producers of food in terms of value, volume, hours of work, etc., but as yet no say in the family, no recognition as a producer, no definition of labour could have as yet been given for women farmer. According to one assessment, in the Himalayas, a pair of bullocks works for 1,064 hours, a man 1,212 hours and woman for 3,485 hours in a year on one hectare farm. For one hectare farm, women's average work 640 hours for intercultural operations like weeding, 384 hours for irrigation, 650 hours for transporting organic manuring and transferring it to the field, 557 hours for seed sowing, 984 hours for harvesting and threshing, i.e. in terms of total farm work of women constitute 61 per cent of total labour. Still they are kept out of productivity sector, with no recognition at all. Women bake food but they can hardly have full meal for themselves, the girl-child included. All these amount to inequality, partiality of man-dominated culture, hence ecofeminism took rise, whereby it has been attempted to get recognition of the women's close relation to nature, the productivity, the conservation, environmental protection, etc. Since, generally, nature is seen as inferior to culture, women are seen as inferior to men. "The feminist movement and the environment movement both stood for egalitarian systems and need to work together to evolve common perspective, theory and practice.... Ecofeminism calls upon women and men to reconceptualise their interrelationship to one another and to the non-human world, in non-hierarchical ways.

South Asian variants of ecofeminism share many of these assumptions." It also calls for women empowerment, adoption of principles of equity, social justice social ethics, women's participation, recognition of women as "heads of household", gender non-discrimination, to integrate women's identity in different sphere in including women in all decision making and in this way, taking into considerations all these, form an eco-friendly state and government far ahead of eco-friendly family. (*vide Environmental Ethics*, D.C. Srivastava, p. 254).

Turning a gaze at the Indian scene, we find a history which far supersedes the role of women in the discovery of primitive agriculture in the Indus-Valley civilization. "The reproductive creativity of women and the productive fertility of mother-earth, through women's intercession, were imposed on each other in societies based on primitive hoe-agriculture through magic-religious fertility cults. It is this substratum which gave rise to the great '*Tantra*' cults and '*Samkhya*' philosophy which regards '*Prakṛti*' (nature), envisaged as '*Annapurna*' (full of cereals) and the practice of Goddess worship as '*Jagdishwari*' (Master of universe) and '*Jagatmata*' (Mother of universe) with taking over the hoe-agriculture by plough bullock agriculture in the Indo-Gangetic plains after the dense forests were cleared, men's role in agriculture increased." (*vide Environmental Ethics*, D.C. Srivastava).

Women's close relationship with nature is found in the Indian concept of woman as '*Van-Debi*' (forest goddess) and sacred groves in Indian cultural traditions. The rearing roles of women for their children is extended to nature, and due to this relationship of nourish and nurture, the women have been taken as great conservationists of forests, trees, and all that are known by the name of nature. Nature is called '*Prakṛti*', and *Prakṛti* is again taken as the Divine power of production, '*Maya*', '*Shakti*', and since *Prakṛti* is in the feminine gender, it is symbolic of women, women's creative power, women's carefulness, women's tenderness, women's sisterly relation with nature's bounties, etc.

Ecofeminism has been recognised (as a movement) quite early as 1787, when Arunita Debi gave her life with 363 women against the king of Jodhpur to save Khejri trees in Rajasthan by hugging and embracing trees. In 1970, Gauri Debi and a group of women hugged trees in Tehri Garhwal to protect the felling of trees. The name of Sharmistha Agrawal, Medha Patkar are important who fought for the rights of the tribal. Vandana Shiva with ner great writings have done great service in this regard. The Chipko Andolan led by Sunderlal Bahuguna who was a Gandhian, was started in the villages of Uttarakhand in 1973. The word '*Chipko*' means 'to hug'. In the British regime, large quantities of trees were cut for preparation of ships, railway girds, etc., but there were no tree plantation. The trees which constituted a wealth as well as source of livelihood were cut which resulted in the loss of survival and subsistence of the forest dwellers, etc., also led to floods, environmental pollution, loss of wild life, decrease in rains, etc., and this Chipko Movement was struggle of the tribal for repairing or reallowing survival source. This movement symbolises looking at the natural product, e.g. trees "not as a commodity' for being sold, but to be taken as something sacred, the "very basis of life". In his campaigns Chandi Prasad Bhatt joined Sunderlal Bahuguna. In 1981, he undertook 5,000 kms *yatra*. Bahuguna has given great weight to this movement by alluding to the texts of the sacred book, *Bhagwad Gita*, whereby knowledge, action and devotion are emphasized, which according to Bhauguna is comparable to the three "H" i.e. Head, Hands and Heart which go to constitute full personality. Bahuguna says that "Modern man has a big head, very feeble hands and no heart", and "our destinies are decided by intellectual prophets, technocrats" scientists, and this had made man's life quite unbalanced, the result is destruction. The reason is that "today, we are seeing problems in pieces, whereas we should have a holistic view of the whole thing. We are just like the traveller going from one country to another and collecting stickers on the baggage—this airline, that airline—and in the end the whole baggage is covered with stickers and the actual thing disappears. Similarly, today, we view problems from different angles and the real problem disappears. We only see the "isms" outside. Sunderlal Bahuguna resorted to fast by way of protest against felling of trees while construction of Tehri dam was being done, since such construction would lead to heavy deforestation, will lead to environmental hazards like submerging of 11,000 acres of Himalayan valley, displacing 80,000 people, and this according to him is a "illusory magnificence after a great deal of destruction. "This is practically cheating the people." A folk singer wrote his song 'The Appeal of a Tree" dedicated to the Chipko Movement, and it is very amusing and thought provoking, and deserves to be quoted—

I have been standing for ages,
I wish to live with you.
Do not chop me, I am yours,
I wish to give you something in the future.
I am milk and water for you.
I am thick shades and showers.
I manufacture soil and manure.
I wish to give you foodgrains.
Some of my kind bear fruits.
They ripen for you.
I wish to ripen with sweetness.
I wish to bow down for you.
I am the pleasant season.
I am spring, I am the rains.
I am with Earth and life,
I feel pain, so my name is tree.
Rolling of logs will create land slides
Remember, I stand on slopes and below is the village.
Where we were destroyed,
Dust is flying there.

The hilltops have become barren.
All the water sources have dried up.
Don't cut us, decorate the Earth.
What is ours is yours.
Leave something for posterity.
Such is Chipko Movement,

One of the Chipko folk song provides a dialogue with a forest officer who persuades the village force to stop their movement.

The forester asks—

What does the forest bear?
Resin, timber and foreign exchange.

The village woman says—

What does the forest bear ?
Soil, water and pure air.
Soil, water and pure air.
Are the basis of our life.

Air, water, soil are life of plants as well as human being, so why should there be any discrimination between man and nature. The message of Hindu culture is to be one with nature, one with environment, oneness of life in all creation, trees, birds, animals, insects are all one—Hindu culture provides a worshipful attitude to all life, trees are no more timber, wood but endowed with life. In India, there are *sadhus* and *sannyasis* who have to live in forests, for peace and tranquillity, more so, for the sake of oneness with all creatures, trees and forest. A *sadhu* is called one, who lives alone devoted to religion with few possessions; the *sannyasi* is one who has given up his family in order to teach and accept disciples, the *brahmin* teacher who lives on charity. The hermits who have nothing to give is respected in India only because their needs are for less and they take less from nature also. Lord Krishna is the greatest God, and he lived in Vrindaban, the forest of Vrinda. The problem of pollution was the main concern of the Lord, who killed Kaliya Nag for making the water of the river Yamuna clean and fit for drinking. War, pollution and hunger linked together are the three enemies of mankind, all these require to be tackled simultaneously and they can be tackled in the light of the teachings of the *Gita*, where *jnana*, *bhakti* and *karma* are to work in unison. Devotion or *bhakti* is the easiest path. When mind is adopting an arguing bent, the two hands are engaged in fighting, only devotion can help, it will allow us to accept everything. Asked from Bahuguna, if he is hopeful of environment protection, he said, "There are three types of people. Firstly, the humanitarian scientist who are able enough to mitigate the miseries of human beings and Mother Earth; secondly, there are social activists, who are impatient to bring a change through non-violence means; thirdly, the compassionate artists, musicians, journalists and literary man and women." All these three should come together and they can help make a combination of *Satyam*, *Shivam* and *Sundaram*. Though such persons are a small portion of their number are few, but only such small minority can change the course of society, they swim against the tide, but ultimately, they only come out with solutions of humanity's problems, they change everything.

III

Some of the books by Judhith Plant, Ursula Le Gunis papers, Greta Guard's papers, Janat Bichl, Lorraine Anderson, Karen Birkenevy, Irene Diamond and Gloria Feman Orenstein's, Judith Plaskow and Carol P. Christ, Andree Collard and Joyce Construcce, and Van Dane Shiva[5] are written to elaborate the ecofeminist approach towards holism. Ecofeminism is based on a new paradigm of 'social and ecological justice for all beings on this planet' for the reason that due to the mad rush of patriarchy towards Apocalypse the ecosystem is currently being dismantled at the rate of 400 species group extinct per day or 1,50,000 species per year. This is a worry not only of the ecofeminist but the concern of whole existence, a multi-disciplinary multi-dimensional concern. According to Petra Kelly "Just Repairing the Existing System, whether capitalist or state socialist, cannot be answer for us. Our aim is radical, non-violent change outside and inside of us."

REFERENCES

1. *Judith Plant* (ed.) Philadelphia: New Society, 1989.
2. *Sisters of Earth* : ed Larraine Audeson – New York, Vintage Books, 1991.
3. Joyce Nelson, see also *The Reweaving the World: The Emergence of Ecofeminism* (Sans Francisco, Sierra Club Books, (1990) and "*Weaving the Visions: New Patterns in Feminist Spirituality*", (Ed.). Judith Plaskow and Canol P. Christ, New York, Harper 1989.
4. Thomas Weber; *Hugging the Trees,* Penguin, Delhi, 1989.
5. Some of books by Judith Plant, *Healing the Wounds: The Promise of Ecofeminism* (Philadelphia: New Society 1989), Ursula Le Gunis Papers, Greta Guard's papers, *Mary Daly's Gyn/Ecology: The Meta-ethics of Radical Feminism* (Boston: Beacon 1978); Janat Bichl's (ed.) *Finding Our Way: Rethinking Ecofeminist Politics* (Montreal. Black Rose Books 1991). Lorraine Anderson's (ed.) *Sister of the Earth : Women's Prose and Poetry About Nature*, Karen Birkeneyv's Writings, Irene Diamond and Gloria Feman Orensteinse (ed.) *Reweaving the World : The Emergence of Ecofeminism,* San Francisco : Sierra Club Books (1990) Judith Plaskow and Carol P. Christ's (ed.) *Feminist Spirituality* New York : Horpa (1989), Andree Collard and Joyce Contrucci's Bloomington, Indian University Press, 1988, book *Rape of the Wild : Man's Violence Against Animals and Earth*, Vandane Shiva's, *Staying Alive: Women, Ecology and Development* London, Zed Books, 1988.

Chapter – 2

An Epistemological Approach to Feminist Philosophy of Religion

S.M. Nair

In certain fields of study, for instance in social and political fields, feminism is thought to be a thing of the past: discrimination against women is no longer a live issue, at least theoretically nothing stands to be discerned. However, on feminist philosophy of religion, it is undeniable that the course of theorizing has barely begun. The field continues to exclude women in thought and practice. In fact the problem with defining the field "philosophy of Religion" itself is indicative of this situation. It is virtually impossible to give a definition without reinforcing the devaluation of terms associated with the female. Anglo American tradition of philosophy of religion for instance seems to have adopted one method consisting logical proofs/rational demonstration and one model, namely tradition theism, excluding any association with the body. If someone enthusiastic to put forth a revised definition of the field, we will be told "Well, that is not really Phi of religion but go ahead if you want to. Further, the lively debates currently taking place in the field concerning God's existence/attributes, justification of theistic beliefs, etc., cannot be related to feminist concerns about love and truth, reason and emotion. Thus in order to make oneself comfortable, we tend to segregate feminist theology, a totally separate field from those who are real philosophers of religion. Such alternatives. I resist at the start itself. This chapter seeks a transformation of the field by the inclusion of women and marginalized others and of methods, thought to be impossible for women. One way to realize how far we are from achieving feminist goals is to consider the number of authors of philosophy of religion text books. "Needless to say that men constitute the majority, women simply lack the social and material markers which would give them any epistemic authority in the field." We still find new books coming out on or about philosophy of religion in which there are no female contributors, no mention of feminism, no discussion of emotion, sexual or romantic love, care or justice. beauty or birth. Presumably the response to pointing out such omissions would be, what do such topics have to do with "religion?" Alright, then what is religion. and incidentally who defines "religion"? As feminist philosophy of religion, we are to grapple with critical appraisals of definition of "religion" philosophy and even our definition of "feminist". Questions like "why have our emotions and feelings been excluded from debates in philosophy of religion, why are philosophy of religion white male, mainly Protestant— virtually always Christian — Western and largely Anglo-American?" etc., though are relevant to the theme are consciously kept away from the discussion for the sake of brevity.

A. Philosophy of Religion in Different Voices

In this section, I shall make certain feminist inroads into philosophical debates about religion. My purpose here is to consider the ways in which philosophy of religion is currently being written in different, voices and to offer a critique of the dominant direction of the discipline. By critique I mean the practice of showing the limits of a mode of thinking by forging an awareness of alternative, more liberating ideas, symbols and discourses.[1]

Ranging from the scalding critique of Stanton to the reconstructive reflections of Irigary, feminist philosophy of religion has been marked by a complex set of relations to religion as well as to philosophy in general. Whether offering critique or reconstruction, women are rewriting philosophy of religion today according to a variety of strategies. Although I believe that gender as an analytic category and gender studies as a body of knowledge cannot only challenge, but also enrich and inform the methodological and substantive assumptions of philosophers of religion. I do not mean to suggest that gender hierarchy comprises a simple/exclusive category of analysis. Given the interflowing streams of class, race, ethnicity, age, sexual orientation, etc., it is unlikely that all women speak in a single voice or describe themselves as sharing uniform experience. Nevertheless, gender constitutes perhaps the most fundamental factor creating human difference, and it remains among the most ignored philosophically. Like the cultural phenomenon of religion itself, philosophy of religion originated in a male tradition of production and transmission, with a history of excluding and devaluating women. It has also been defined by many concepts and symbols marked as 'masculine'. which stand in oppositional relation to those marked as 'feminine'. Unlike the cultural phenomenon of religion which is embedded in multiple cultural contexts, philosophy of religions has been largely Eurocentric and Anglo-American in its orientation. In addition to gender bias, its ethnocentrism constitutes the second major weakness of the field. However, undaunted by these two severe deficiencies, gender bias and ethnocentrism — the dominant Anglo-American analytic school of philosophy of religion has proved surprisingly healthy. After long decades of dormancy when logical positivism seemed to yield only negative conclusions in the philosophy of religion, a resurgence of interest in traditional theism is occurring in "mainstream philosophy of religion". Thanks to the work of a variety of analytic philosophers, we now know, for example, that modal logic can be used to formulate a more perspicuous version of the ontological arguments, that Bayesian models of probability can breathe a new life into inductive justification of religious belief; and that language game analysis can offer a *prima facie* justification of religions language. Such developments, imported from other areas of philosophy, have prompted Richard Yale to suggest that (phi of religions is to the core areas of phi, as Israel is to the pentagon. The former are a proving ground for the weapons forged in the latter.[2] None of the new and sophisticated military hardware, however, engages the questions posed by feminist inquiry or aims at disarmament of the sexist elements of the traditional theistic mode. Instead, in the works of philosophers such as Richard Swinburne, Alvin Plantinga, William Alstan, D.Z. Phillips, philosophy of religion has been deployed in defence of the cogency of a standard form of monotheism, in the service of a conception of 'God' that is patriarchal, and in the vested interest of staunchly traditional forms of Christianity. Philosophy of religions needs to shed both its gender bias and its ethnocentrism, if it is to open out in new directions adequate to the twenty first century.[3]

B. Epistemological Approach to Feminist Philosophy of Religion

When it comes to women in relation to epistemology, they have been excluded from being credible witnesses/informants, from seeing reality objectively and from acting autonomously as equally rational agents. Yet, my proposal is that these exclusions can be avoided with the free cultivation of four intellectual virtues, reflexive critical openness, care-knowing, strong-objectivity and principled autonomy[4]. These virtues are meant to unite ethical and epistemological components in a form of virtue epistemology. That is, our perspectives and practices would be shaped by the development of certain virtues with capacities for cognition guided by reflexive, imaginative and interactive capacities for decreasing truth, a feminist philosophy of religion would aim for practical wisdom.

To grasp the significance of their approach we should recall certain reasons why women have been excluded from epistemology. Basically the associations of women with their bodies and bodily functions, with irrationality, passivity lack, slim, abjection, deception and dependency rendered female persons ethically and politically inferior. These associations, then rendered 'Female philosophers' an oxymoran. Those feminist philosophers of religions following Luce Irigaray's psycho-analytic, theological and political writings, aimed to revalue. These female associations, they sought to raise up the repressed values of female becoming. However, this attempt at revaluations was disliked by a group of feminist philosophy of religion. They maintain that feminist theories are better if they do not mainly reject the biased value hierarchy. So passion or female interior should not simply subvert reason. Therefore, what is proposed here is a transformation of the philosophical domain and care concepts of philosophy of religion, not reversal of values.

What is it to call something an intellectual virtue? Intellectual virtues get defined as those forms of motivation to have cognitive contact with reality. It is more than saying that people desire truth and hence involves no truism whatsoever. There are types of intellectual virtues, some aiding us to acquire justified true knowledge, some others enhancing the quality of knowledge and yet others, a few stellar virtues, render motivation to advance knowledge for the human race itself. The virtues that I have referred above, needless to say, falls under the last category.[5]

First of all this feminist epistemological approach to philosophy of religion needs to address quires about knowledge and power. For each claim to knowledge, we are compelled to ask whose knowledge is it? In each use who and what are excluded as subjects and objects of (divine) knowledge, respectively? More generally, who is a good informant? These queries find a response in Miranda Fricker's account of 'reflective' critical openness.[6] As an intellectual virtue, reflective critical openness ensures against our unjustly giving either too much/too little credibility to certain people. It is characterized by a sensitivity to reasons for believing/not believing what we told. preventing us from being indiscriminate in whom we believe. As a cognitive disposition, it is associated with testimonial sensibility which develops according to upbringing and education. If despite clear evidence for the truth of her testimony, a witness is not believed because of certain social markers, whether there are sexual or racial features, ethnic manners or ever a particular accent our testimonial sensibility would seem to be unfairly biased. Reflective critical openness would then function to expose the ungrounded prejudice created by unfair stereotypes, especially those which make women untrustworthy witness and unreliable informants. As such this intellectual virtue should have a pivotal role in any future philosophy of religion. In particular for philosophers of religion should learn from feminist critiques to develop less biased testimonial sensibilities, since testimony itself remains a significant source of religious knowledge and a model for our 'epistemic practices'.[7] Incorporation of reflective critical openness into philosophy of religion means thinking more effectively by shaping our epistemic practices with the help of the philosophical capacities for reflective imaginative and interactive understanding. We seek to listen to the testimonies of those who are not early trusted became of certain largely exclusive social markess of rational authority but because the informant generally acquires and offer a true account of the matter. The specific questions guiding the development of this virtue is: are we motivated to bring about reflective critical openness towards the testimonies of women and those persons who lack the power necessary for rational authority due to their social location. Consider the information of Fricker :

> "If you want the full story you had probably better listen especially closely to the accounts of experience that are given by people who are among the least powerful in society. There hermeneutical disadvantage can become a positive epistemic resource, so long as one can listen."[8]

Thus the definition of thinking reflectively can be extended to listening to female informants of a conflict of points of view. Her Christian philosophers of religious may think of the woman is in the *New Testament* Gospel story who saw and witnessed Christ after he rose from the dead on the third day, but none of the (male) disciples believed the female testimony.[9] Yet the problem is not mainly one of a particular (sort of) women being thought to be worthy of interest. It is also the more wide ranging problem of the history of philosophy silencing by mistrusting all women.

If gender is to be taken seriously is religious epistemology, it is necessary to assess the content (what?), acquisition (how?), content (when?) and possess or (who?) of knowledge. Once cognitive power includes the ability of the human knower to reflect critically upon what is known, how it is known, and who possesses it, then the reliable acquisition of knowledge by both men and women of particular thing taking place at particular times is a particular location can become a gender inclusive virtue, aiming at wisdom. Such a capacity for knowledge gained by critical reflection represents a greater sort of truth and power than divine omniscient conceived as knowledge in timeless propositional form.[10]

Yet the problem is women's ideas have not been recognized as reliable sorts of information let alone knowledge. Think of the derogatory connotations attributed to 'women's institutions'. And Yet pity the male philosopher who knows all true prepositions but fails to "know that he should avoid a particular life threatening situation about which he could have learnt from the insight of a woman. Think of the king of message of his own daughter, Cassendra, foretelling of the disaster awaiting him, if he went to war. Hence, Troy fell in, true the story assumes that Cassendra in infallibly informed by the god Apollo; yet the point is to trust the integrity of the Knower.

Eve herself leads Adam to acquire knowledge of the difference between good and evil and so to develop virtue through reflection, imagination and interaction. Such wisdom thus becomes the superior sort of knowledge while divine knowledge becomes a regulative idea guiding open and critical reflection upon the trust worthiness of particular ideas and the particular knowers. To recognize that the motivation to know is first represented by Eve and in whom we have personified a misplaced mistrust of all women we need to imagine her social identity differently and then we need to develop a reflective critical openness to the testimonies of those who, like Eve symbolically and literally, have lacked rational authority.

1. Care Knowing

Dalmiya demonstrates the cognitive value of caring by linking the interactive dimension of what have been traditionally women's practices (in the West) and to the wider concerns of epistemologists globally[11]. She identifies care knowing as relibilist virtue which exhibits a distinctive sort of 'knowing how'. Reliable means here that the success of care receiving is dependent as much on the one caring as it is on the cared for. This virtue involves critical self-reflection on the interactive practice of caring. And this means an ability to listen to and register what the other says or, simply, needs. In externalist beliefs about one's own and others care practices produced in a reliable way are likely to be true. Note that it is necessary to embrace carrying as a form of cognition. Like reflective critical wisdom care knowing is developed as a disposition for practical wisdom.

The crucial question is, are we motivated to bring about the know-how of caring as a distinctive epistemic virtue? For this first we need to register and recognize the interactive practices of women and others, who can equally important is the proper understanding of the terminology "care". Then ideal of the career can have negative associations in the all too clear stereotype of a woman bound up with an oppressive construction of feminity, whose "care" allows her to be clear exploited by other. Neverthless self-critical reflection or what Dalmiya calls caring about caring should ensure our critical assessment of the relationship governing, the lives of both the carer and the cared for.

As a cognitive disposition care-knowing requires for its development a process of self-revaluation and self-making,

Dalmiya explains caring as a five-faceted disposition establishing the possibility of an interactive cognitive practice between the one caring and the cared for. The five faces include caring about caring for taking care a care reception and caring about caring.

2. Strong Objectivity

Sandra Harding explaining her notion of strong objectivity in feminist philosophy of religion, exposes the weak objectivity of the male neutral ideal of Enlightenment Philosophy. This ideal is assumed by man to be neutral but, in fact, exhibits male qualities exclusive to the men who assume neutrality. Today along with warning Hartsock and Harding we can find an alternative to the modem ideal agent theory in what is called feminist stand point epistemology.

The development of strong objectivity involves the cognitive social abilities implied in the virtue of reflective critical openness. The challenge is to develop the capacities of reflexively and imaginatively listening, not just for ourselves, but for the other. In thinking from another's point of view about our own social location we (i) recognize the injustice both of our epistemic practices and in our drive to become intellectually virtuous, (ii) eliminate this injustice; and in this way, and (iii) change how we see ourselves the problem with this challenge is potentially a self-contradiction be just and gain knowledge of the other for the cultivation of oneself. P. S. Anderson truly suggests that a feminist standpoint is the result of an epistemological struggle; it is not a spontaneous perspective which a woman possesses by virtue of being a woman, strong objectivity becomes the goal of this struggle demanding less partial knowledge and more justice in our interactive practices. However, neither feminist nor epistemological proper find it easy to work out this sort of "objectivity" can be coherent. Here a distinction between two different sorts of objectivity helps: absolute objectivity and objectivity as a process. Thomas Naval seeks, for example, absolute objectivity as a view from now here. The second kind, incorporates subjectivity rather than trying to eliminate it, objectivity is thus achieved by understanding our and more about one's own subjectivity and especially the limits of other perspective. The feminist standpoint theorists strong objectivity is closer to this second conception.

In Fricker's terms social facts reflect the epistemic pluralism which results from convergence on the truth of the matter. Instead there is bounds to more than one rational point of view in any social or religious fact of matter. The critical point for developing strong objectivity is to preserve possibility of the full story. As P.S. Anderson points out, "By listening closely to the accounts of religious experience that are given by people who are among the least powerful in society, we find that far from advocating a view from now here or the vantage of an ideal observer we seek to incorporate the ever greater understanding of our subjectivities in the pursuit of practical wisdom.[11]

3. Principled Autonomy

O'Neill in his rethinking of Kant's ethics rejects the popular idea of individual autonomy, and instead promoted a principled autonomy expressed in action whose maxims or laws could be adopted by all others. Here a revised conception of principled autonomy can serve as an intellectual virtue for Feminist philosophy of Religion. This virtue is associated with this model idea of seeking to recognize and to know how to apply principles that all could follow. Similar to strong objectivity, principled autonomy is a virtue which would make redundant any notion of an ideal agent/observer in ethical and epistemological theories. And yet this does not eliminate the functioning of certain limiting ideals or guiding principles. The mission is to achieve "self-legislation" that puts the stress on legislation not self-legislation means a reflective act which is free not oppressive in enabling each self-reflexive agent to follow general principles legislative or law-like means according to principles that all could adopt.

This would include principles such as supporting and assisting others. In other words, we would not advocate individual autonomy as represented by the male ideal of the detached agent who acts gratuitously. It would also include trust, which is the general principles behind what is its opposites, i.e. suspicion/ deception. We could not will that deception becomes a universal law because it is only possible to deceive against a background of persons who trust.

This virtue can be posed as an alternative to the ideal observer theory which treats god as the unmatchable ideal of cognition and morality. The ideal observer theory would be decisively challenged by the reflexive, imaginative and interactive levels of principled autonomy. This traditional theory is so impoverished philosophically that it seems to render the ideal agent someone who values only his own supposedly omniscient individual self. Since he is unable to reflect upon his own locatedness, to imagine the points of view of others or to interact thought struggle and dialogue with each other.

Reflective critical openness, care-knowing strong-objectivity and principled autonomy together motivate the feminists as pursuit of practices, relationship thoughts and principles related to the divine. This grounding would link the rational authority and autonomy of every woman and man with the accompanying virtue. This pursuit will not end until it achieves the practical wisdom which is the very essence of philosopher, i.e. the love of wisdom.

REFERENCES

1. Indicative of this resurgence is the volume *Contemporary Perspectives on Religious Epistemology* edited by R. Douglas Geivett and Brendan Sweetman (New York: Oxford University Press, 1992).
2. Richard Gale on the *Nature and Existence of God* (Cambridge: Cambridge University Press, 1991), p. 23.
3. Nancy Frankenberry, "Feminist Approaches" in *Feminist Philosophy of Religion,* Pamela Sue Anderson and Beverley Clack. ed. (London and New York: Routledge, 2004).

4. Pamela Sue Anderson, "An Epistemological Ethical Approach to Philosophy of Religion: Learning to Listen" in *Feminist Philosophy of Religion,* Pamela Sue Anderson. Beverley Clacked. (London & New York: Rautledge 2004).
5. P.S. Anderson. "Feminist Theology as Philosophy of Religion" in Cambridge *Campanion to Feminist Theology*, S. Parsons, ed. (Cambridge: Cambridge University Press, 2002), pp. 51-55.
6. Mtiranda Fricker; "Epistemic Justice and a Role for Virtue in the Politics of Knowing" in *Meta Philosophy* 34, V. 2 (Jan 2003), pp. 154-173.
7. S. Harding "Rethinking Standpoint Epistemology" in *Feminist Epistemologies,* L. Alcafvf & E. Patter. Ed. (London, Routledge,1993) pp. 49-8L.
8. Miranda Fricker; "Power, Knowledge and Injustice" in *New British Philosophy: The Interviews*. J. Eaggini and J Stangram; ed. (London, Routledge, 2002), p.190.
9. See Lucke 24:1-12:cf. John 24:1-18 .
10. G. Such as presented in P. S Anderson.
11. V. Dalmiya "Dogged Loyalties A Classical Indian Intervention in Care Ethics" in *Ethics in the World,* Relip-ion Vol. III. J. Runzo and N. Martin, ed. (Oxford, One world, 2001), pp.293-308.

Chapter – 3

Feminist Philosophy : Why and What ?

Rajesh Kr. Singh

The condition of women and the question how to bring about the empowerment of women is a global anxiety. The year 2001 has been recognized by the Government of India as the "Women Empowerment Year". My purpose in this chapter is not to cover the vast area of the topic, but to acquaint the readers with how this commonly unknown but emerging branch of philosophy tried to attempt the problem in a novel and interesting manner.

(1) What Women Empowerment Is ?

The Original Sin in the Garden of Eden was women's. She tasted the forbidden fruit, tempted Adam and has been paying for it ever since. In *Genesis* the Lord said, "I will greatly multiply thy sorrow and thy conception, in sorrow thou shall bring forth children and thy desire shall be to thy husband, and he shall rule over thee."

Gender difference is an innocent natural biological phenomenon. All animals are males or females. But in human beings this gender difference has resulted into so many unjust developments like : Gender Imbalance (inequalities), Gender Roles, Gender Subordination, Gender Oppression, Gender Torture (like dowry deaths), etc. Masculinity or femininity does not entail these things in other biological species. Then why in human beings alone should socio-cultural development produce such inhuman constructions? With the rise of education more and more women are becoming aware of their demoralizing status and a global feminist movement against this is building up. The movement of Women Empowerment takes up the problem not as a destiny of women, but as a challenge and it takes up two tasks: (i) rational enquiry and understanding of the roots of the problem; and (ii) social action to uproot it and thus make women equal to men. Feminist Philosophy is concerned with the first one.

(2) The Philosophy of Feminism

The feminist scholars have come to realize that the problem is philosophical in nature, because it does not consist in some social or political customs or practices, but is rooted deep into the basic identity formation (the search of self as men or women) and its expressions. Peeping into the identity formation would mean to take into account their basic outlook (i.e. male epistemology *vs.* female epistemology), their metaphysical reality (as males or females), different value systems, goals of life, ways of fulfilment, traditional religious identities, expressions of femininity and masculinity in work, behaviour, language, art and drama.

(3) The Function of Feminist Philosophy

Feminist Philosophers raise a basic question regarding the nature, purpose and method of philosophy, sciences and social sciences. They say that these subjects claim general, universal and objective knowledge, hence they are applicable to all. But the basic question is : who is the subject (or author) of these disciplines, whose purpose do they serve and whom do they empower? For example, when we say that "The Englishmen have such and such concept of society or give the women such and such rights and duties", it seems that the subject "Englishmen" is a gender neutral or bisexual entity covering all persons of England. But if we analyse properly we find that the real subject is male, white bourgeois man of England. So, if we reform the language by saying "The white bourgeois males of England give the women such and such rights and duties", the oppressive nature becomes evident. This is why the knowledge and system developed by such authority (subject) confirms gender, class and race oppression. The females, the blacks and the poor are only the objects of study and the study is done from white male and bourgeois point of view.

Thus feminist philosophers argue that androcentric scholarship is not only partial (i.e. half of the story), but also untrue and deceptive.

Thus the function of feminist philosophy is to demonstrate the androcentric, gender oppressive character of scholarship and replace it by an androgynous one and construct a parallel world-story more true and complete, in which feminine experiences, values and work can find fullest expression and place.

(4) The Feminist Philosophy of History

The discovery of the nature of male and female identity and expression needs a philosophical interpretation into history and changing modes of cultures.

According to the majority of feminist scholars the reason for the inequality between men and women is the difference between male and female roles, i.e. the sexually based division of labour. There are men's jobs and women's jobs from the primitive hunting and gathering bands to the most complex societies. Women do subordinate jobs under male authority like producing children, caring and serving as mothers and wives, cooking, washing; all these largely excluded from high status occupations and positions of power. This has been highly debated between the feminists and therefrom two main positions have emerged:

1. The Gender Roles are determined by biologically or genetically based psychological dispositions between male and female.

2. The above view is opposed by those who argue that the gender roles are culturally determined and socially constructed :

   (i) (a) *Lional Tiger and Robin Fox : The Human Biogrammar Theory* : Biogrammar is a genetically based programme which predisposes mankind (men and women) to behave in a certain way. In comparison to women, men are more competitive, aggressive, dominant, risk-taking, adventurous, rational, etc., whereas women are more emotional, loving, caring, subservient, peace-loving, protection-seeking, cowardly, etc. All these characteristics are genetically based and hormone-governed psychological predispositions. Thus men and women are wired to do male and female jobs, which we see from the primitive hunting societies to the House of Commons and House of Lords. From this it follows that attempts to abolish gender roles and replace them by unisex roles, however, desirable this may be, will go against nature.

   (b) *George Peter Murdock : Biology and Practicality* — Murdock does not agree that biology-based predispositions direct men and women to adopt their particular roles. In a cross-cultural survey of 224 societies, he found that it is out of sheer preference and practicality that men and women found to adopt particular types of roles. Otherwise what is man's job in one culture, place or period of time is female's job in another culture, place or period of time (as hunting, cooking, ploughing, etc.). But in each culture, place or time sexual division of labour based on male or female propensities does exist.

   (c) *Talcott Parsons* : Biology and "Expressive Female" : Parson says that the biological dispositions of women and men find their expression and satisfaction in their respective gender roles. Men do not find pleasure and satisfaction in women's jobs and women in men's.

(ii) *Gender Roles : Product of Culture and Society :* According to this view norms, values and roles are culturally determined and socially transmitted. It is not the product of biology.

Ann Oakley argues that Murdock's data from 224 cultures are itself a proof that no job is exclusively man's or woman's. Today women are armymen, pilots and cosmonauts and men are cooks, domestic servants, and in child caring jobs. Bruno Battelheim, Ernestime Friedle, Sherry B. Ortner, etc., come heavily against biological theory. They say that there are enough materials in male dominated culture, education, family and social structure, labour market and politics which make it impossible for women to compete with men and thus are compelled to feel comfortable in their own homes. I do not want to go into details of these things. They are frequently and amply highlighted in the newspapers and periodicals.

(iii) *Women and Social Stratification :* Many attempts in history have been made to free women from mother housewife role and bring them into equality with men. Some most prominent ones are these :

The Marxian Perspective : Marx and Engels saw female subordination as a result of the emergence of private property. To transfer the property to one's own offsprings, men needed control over women to ensure the indisputed paternity of their offsprings and heirs. They believed that true equality between the sexes could be achieved only in a socialist society in which the forces of production are communally owned. Thus the wife would not be merely property for the production of heirs. Private housekeeping is transformed into a social industry. The care and education of children becomes a public matter.

(iv) *Evaluation :* The case of USSR–Studies have shown that :

(a) The status of women in family does not depend upon outside job.

(b) Most of the Soviet women do their house work themselves.

(c) 30 per cent of Soviet women (in a sample survey) thought it better for the wife to devote herself exclusively to the home and children.

(d) In 1975, after a long communist regime, a total 51 per cent of labour force in USSR were women, but most of them concentrated in areas like communication, housing, domestic service, health, education, culture etc. Only 6 per cent of them were highly placed as factory directors, etc.

(e) In politics women made up 47 per cent of the membership of local Soviets, but only 1 per cent of the Council of Ministers of USSR. In Czechoslovakia also the trend was very much the same.

All these developments were great jerk to the socio-cultural theorists and in favour of bio-psychological theory of Tiger and Fox.

(5) Feminist Metaphysics

Thus the problem is that whenever we try to remake society or culture the metaphysical reality of men and women (men as rational, aggressive, competitive, etc., and women as emotional, non-competitive and subservient) will again and again make the social system male-dominating. Again man cannot be held responsible for this bio-psychological function of nature. The question of ought can be attached only to voluntary actions.

Feminist Philosophers like Ann Fergouson say that there is little objectivity in the reality. Anything like chair, cow, rape, marriage, etc., is understood from man's point of view (i.e. value, culture, use, etc.). Likewise the reality of man and woman is also a socio-cultural product. There are three levels of self-formation :

(i) At the first level of primary process (of Freud) men and women struggle for their material survival from hunger, thirst, cold, dangers, etc. This level is free from gender or race norms and social meanings attached to it.

(ii) The second level of identity formation of the self-process is called *status quo* level. Since human beings are social animals we need social acceptance. Thus we have an interest in accepting meanings socially important, others put upon our body types and we need to act accordingly. At this level our gendered psychical body image is formed. Now the society being male-dominating, women internatise the body image and norms as desired by men. For example, women are charged to be more emotional and, therefore, irrational. But we can see that in contemporary societies emotionally more expressive women are desired, whereas same type of men are looked down upon as homosexual. In another example we can find an answer to the question many persons ask against the possibility of women empowerment. "Why women often desire things which are against their interest?" As women desire empowered (i.e. dominant and possessive) man, rather than women empowerment. Feminist philosophers would say that such desires are socially constructed by male dominant society.

(iii) The third level of the process of self-formation is the level of self-understanding or the reconstituting level. Here we start to think what we are (at *status quo* level), what we ought to be and what action should we follow for it, it is at this level that the moral question of responsibilities arises both for the dominant class and the subordinate class for continuation of the unjust system. The dominants can change the habits and the subordinates can resist the system.

(6) Feminist Epistemology : Knowledge, Reason and Emotion

It is argued that men dominating in reason and knowledge are empowered to dominate emotional women. In traditional epistemology reason is considered as the basis of knowledge (logical and scientific) and the power to control nature. Women being nearer to emotions (subversive to knowledge) instinct and nature (*prakṛti*) need to be controlled by rational men (*purusa*).

Feminist scholars argue that emotions are helpful rather than hostile to construction of knowledge and social behaviour.

(i) Though emotions are continuous with the instinctive response of our pre-human ancestors, mature emotions are learnt, suppressed or reformed. A child is taught appropriate emotional responses to certain situations like to fear strangers, enjoy food, swim or respect teachers, etc.

(ii) Truth and reality are not objective, but depend upon our value judgements, upon what we mean by truth and what type of truth we want.

(iii) Again, values are nothing but certain types of emotional responses of approval or disapproval.

(iv) So far as knowledge is concerned, Plato says that it requires a higher level of love.

(v) Knowledge starts from perception which is a selective (valuational) process.

(vi) Knowledge is the evaluation of perception (data) which is based upon values and we have seen that values are nothing but emotional attitudes towards the world.

Thus the question is not whether reason or emotion should be the basis of knowledge, but whether masculine or feminine emotions be given priority. The feminists argue that knowledge based upon feminine emotions and experiences can construct an alternative world theory where women can find themselves more fit and successful. They are engaged in constructing a new social moral, political and religious philosophy.

Chapter – 4

Revisiting the Gender Equality

Avinash Kumar Srivastava

Gender equality has been a much-hyped topic both in the Print and Electronic media. Even more than that tons of ink have dried upon the blank sheet of paper producing essay, criticism, analysis, searching history, geography, philosophy and social studies. On the face, it appears that inequality does exist in society all over the world in respect of women's position, prestige, status and respect. In contemporary social scenario women have received the status of a second grade citizen. Despite the development in science and technology, global economy, standard of living and evolution of some novel and brilliant thoughts in the field of social, political, religious and philosophical, at the root, man's vision for women have not entirely changed as she is subjugated, oppressed and exploited whenever and wherever opportunity is found. Rape, foeticide, dowry-death, sex-oppression, and exploitation are taking place everyday. With the rise of market economy women's body is being utilized in different ways for promoting consumerism. In fact the Western patriarchy's economic vision is based on exploitation, exclusion and degradation of women. This is why throughout the Third World, women are struggling for the liberation from the clutches of patriarchy's domination as we were struggling for our liberation from the British rule. This has resulted in the rise of feminist movement, movement for women liberation, etc. This macro-analysis, however, needs a revisit.

To make this point crystal clear, let us analyze the social framework in which we live. There are numerous societies in the world,[1] but in each of them exists microcosm that is, societies within society. These can be divided into three strata, namely social album of the elite, social album of the middle class, and the social album of lower class. In elite society, there has been little or no differentiation on the ground of 'Gender'. In its fold we find rich and affluent people with sprinkle of knowledge and information who, at best, believe life is to be lived and enjoyed. The desire to enjoyment neglects all steps between man and woman's interaction. They share together the fruits of life and make their presence felt in the society, they do at times fight and show dissensions but not with the idea of domination and subjugation. These are only mundane tantrums.

Lower strata of the society have at no stretch of civilizational history either tasted the fruits of knowledge or dreams of affluence. So they have been devoid of both, aspiration and affluence. They work together [manually], bite poor bread together and sleep together. In simple phrase, they live hand to mouth. Although much is talked and written about their plight, they have remained immune to praise and abuse. In this frame of mind, there never was or is any issue of 'Gender Equality' among them.

Quite different is the story of the middle class people. Broadly speaking, this consists of intelligentsia who are teachers, philosophers, clerks, bureaucrats, farmers etc. They have 'Inspirations' as their sole acquisitions with a very little back-up from affluence. Their attempt is to seek the level of elite but their poor or inadequate economic condition keeps the strings downward. So they keep hanging between aspirations and semi-poverty [achievements]. This peculiar existential dilemma forces them to make adjustments, curtailments and shelving things off to uncertain future. In the process inhibitions, taboos, oppression and subjugations are imposed. Because till recent past the bread earning segment was man, woman was the target of all these.

Gender equation was and to some extent is the problem for middle class. This chapter aims at revisiting, evaluating and exploring the cause and solution to the problem. For the purpose of clarity, this chapter is divided into three parts apart from introduction. They are : (i) the historical background, (ii) the reason behind the gender inequality, and (iii) the solution to the problem.

The Historical Background

Cultures preceding the rise of state and society was matricentric and this social set-up is found in some parts of our country even today. It is reflected through this popular saying, "where woman is worshipped there reside the gods."[2] Even religious supreme powers were created in the feminine colour. The creator of this universe and even some of the gods [*Brahma, Vishnu* and *Mahesh*] were created by the *Adi Shakti*, the woman power, the female one. Not only this, the concept of God is not supposed to be complete without Goddess. Even gods received their strength from feminine power, as she was the embodiment of strength, power, virility and source of energy. It is evident from the Hindu religious scriptures that whenever gods, saints and even mighty kings became helpless, powerless and were on the brink of being vanquished by the evil forces, women appeared as the mightiest one and helped them, protected them and even defeated or destroyed their enemy [the evil forces or demons] too. This is the reason we worship *Goddess Durga, Laksmi, Saraswati, Parwati,* etc. and pray them for strength, wealth and knowledge. Their names are written before the names of gods, viz. *Sita-Ram, Radha-Krishna, Laksmi-Narayan,* etc. It is remarkable to note here that in matriarchal social set-up, there is no ideology of domination because women are filled with sympathy and care. It appears that this social set-up continued to be in vogue for a longer period. Later on it was felt that women are physically weak in relation to men. Though they are superior to men in tolerance, working capacity and often in managerial skill, they are inferior in physical strength. Their fertility cycle, pregnancy period, etc., are hurdle in ways of their working hours and capacity. Slowly and stealthily, situation changed. Both became equals and all the decisions began to be taken together. In other words, there was full participation in decision making, income producing as well as equal status in the family and society. But this situation could not continue for a longer period. Patriarchy replaced the matriarchal system of society. Man's domination over woman started. This inferior status is reflected in the scriptures of different religions.

Buddhism and *Jainism* arose and developed in a patriarchal socio-religious milieu. Both the religions could not remain immune to the ethos and air of the time. Hence, they too maintained distinction between men and women throughout their history. Perusal of their sacred texts reveals the fact that both advocate or assume women's subordination in both religious and secular realm. The *Vinaya Rules* for *bhikkhunis* insist on their formal subordination to *bhikkhus* in all matters of monastic life.[3] Women, in general have been looked down in Buddhist fold. They never received equal status. In *Anguttar Nikaya,* it is said, "Monks women folk end their life unstated and unrepeated in two things, sexual intercourse and child birth".[4]

Jainism is milder to *Buddhism* in this respect, though its texts also reflect patriarchal assumptions about inherent nature and appropriately subordinate role in society and religious community. Later on *Jainism* got split into two folds, *Shwetambar* and *Digambar*. The former accepts the women's capacity to attain *moksa* [*kaivalya*], while the latter did not accept their capacity.[5]

Women's subordination attained its zenith in *Manusmriti* and other *Puranas* wherein women's autonomy at anytime in her life is explicitly condemned, as she should do nothing independently, even in her own house.[6] It is said, "In childhood, subject to her father, in youth to her husband, and when her husband is dead to her sons, she should never enjoy independence.[7] It is further said, "though [her husband] be uncouth and prone to sensual pleasure, though no good points at all, the virtuous-wife should ever worship him as god."[8] At one place, it is said that for women marriage ceremony should be considered as *Vedic* rites, husband her *guru* and serving him is equal to the service of her *guru.* Husband's house is her *gurukul* and her domestic work is the ritual of worship [*agnihotra*]. She is not entitled to observe fast, *vrata*, and *yajna* for anyone except her husband as she can attain *summum bonum* of life through unwavering devotion and service to her husband.[9] These verses convey the message that women are not entitled to take their own decision and exercise their own prudence. And thus definition of a wife starts with her husband and ends in her husband. She does not have her own independent existence. This conceptual framework spoke very heavily on women, which culminated in oppression, exploitation and degradation of women to the extent that they are being treated as second grade citizens even now in certain societies.

During colonial rule women impoverishment increased. The Western rulers who spent centuries subjugating and crippling their own women into deskilled, deintellectualized appendage also disfavoured the women of colonies on the matter of access to the land, technology and employment.[10] Their political and economic process were also based on Western patriarchal mind-set, that impoverished women in a large number. The privatization of land for revenue generation displaced women critically. This eroded their traditional land-use rights. With the expansion of the cash crop, the food production was undermined and women were left with meagre resources to feed and care for their children, the aged and the infirm, while men were made to migrate or were conspired into forced labour by colonizer.[11] With a few exceptions, women's relative access to economic resources, income and employment worsened. Their burden of work increased and their relative and even absolute health, nutrition and educational status declined.[12] By expansion of developmental project, women's productivity was destroyed, as it was rooted largely in the manner that women be displaced from their productive activity. The reasons are three fold. They are mentioned below :

(a) There is pre-existing gender division of labour. In tribal and poor peasant house, it is women who do much of gathering and fetching from the forest, village common river and wells. Due to environmental degradation such as deforestation, etc., women have to go far from their houses for subsistence and survival. In addition women of such households are burdened with a significant responsibility for family subsistence and they are often primarily, and in many female headed houses, the sole economic providers.[13]

(b) Secondly, it is from the survey that there is systematic gender difference in the distribution of subsistence, resources (including food and health care) within rural houses. This has resulted in higher rate of female morbidity. Hospital admission data and sex ratio has decreased (93 females per 100 males in all over India).[14] These differences especially in health care are widespread in India and in South Asia.

(c) Thirdly, there is significant inequalities in women's and man's access to the most critical productive resources in rural economics, agricultural land and associated productive technology. Women have systematically disadvantageous position in labour market as thy have fewer employment opportunity, less occupational mobility, lower level of training and lower payment for same and similar work.

The Reason

Now in this analytic backdrop of "Gender Equality", we need to examine the reasons behind this subjugation, subordination and patriarchal system, the oldest tool of women oppression that has gone sharper with the development. We all agree that sex oppression and gender inequality exist, it is wrong and it must be abolished, while some may disagree about the nature, reason and solution of the subordination. In order to understand this problem one has to understand the conceptual framework that contributes to women degradation. Feminist philosophers also claim that the issues are conceptual one. They concern how one conceptualizes main-stay conceptual notions as reason and rationality, ethics and what is said to be human. We all know that conceptual framework is a set of basic beliefs, values, attitudes and assumptions that shape and reflect how one views oneself and one's world. It is a socially constructed lens through which we perceive ourselves and others. It is affected by such factors as gender, race, class, age, effectual orientation, nationality and religious background. Some conceptual frameworks are oppressive. It explains, justifies and maintains the relationship of domination and subordination. When an oppressive conceptual framework is patriarchal, it explains, justifies and maintains the subordination of women by men.[15]

When we cast a glance over the Indian culture and philosophy, we find such a conceptual framework is present here. There is a popular saying that "the mother earth and women have to bear a lot [*dharani aur dhatri ko bahut kuch sahana parata hai*], has adversely affected women. It, on the one hand, pampered the emotions of women by equating her with mother earth, on the other hand, she is asked rather advised to tolerate the male dominance, subjugation and oppression. Women's monthly fertility cycle, the tiring symbiosis of pregnancy, the wrench of child's birth and suckling of an infant grounds women's consciousness in the knowledge of being similar to nature. On the other hand, this tacit or conscious identity has prepared her to tolerate man's subjugation oppression and domination, willingly or unwillingly. The *Samkhya* concept of *Prakṛti* and *Purusa* have helped man's chauvinism grow as here *Prakṛti* is the object of enjoyment [*Bhogya*] and *Purusa* is the ultimate enjoyer [*Bhokta*].[16] In this conceptual framework nature and women are turned into passive objects to be used and exploited for the uncontrolled and uncontrollable desire of alienated man. From being creator, and sustainer of life, nature and women are reduced to being 'resources'. This identification has bruised the women's status to a derogatory patriarchal attitude towards motherhood. And thus oppressive conceptual framework came into existence.

A feminist writer Karen J. Warren[17] is of opinion that there are three significant features of oppressive conceptual framework. The first is value hierarchal thinking, which places higher value, status or prestige on what is 'up' rather than what is 'down'. Second, are the value dualism (i.e.) disjunctive pairs in which disjuncts are seen as oppositional (rather than complementary) and exclusive (rather than inclusive) and which places higher value (status, prestige) on one disjunct rather than the other, e.g. the dualism which gives higher value or status to that which has historically been identified as 'mind', 'reason' and than to that which has historically been identified as 'body', 'emotion' and 'female'. And the third, is Logic of domination, i.e. a structure of argumentation, which leads to a justification of subordination.

The third feature is the most significant here, as it is not just a logical structure rather it involves substantive value system. It needs an ethical premise to permit or sanction the subordination of that which is subordinate, justified. This justification is given on the grounds of some alleged characteristics (i.e. rationality, etc.) which the dominant (e.g. Men) have and the subordinate (e.g. women) lack. This logic runs as follows in argument [A] :

[A1] Humans do, and plants and rocks do not, have the capacity to consciously and radically change the community in which they live.

[A2] Whatever has the capacity to consciously and radically change the community in which it lives is normally superior to whatever lacks the capacity.

[A3] Thus humans are morally superior to plants and rocks [the nature].

[A4] For any '*X*' and '*Y*', if '*X*' is morally superior to '*Y*', then '*X*' morally superior to '*Y*', then '*X*' is morally justified in subordinating '*Y*' .

[A5] Thus humans are morally justified in subordinating plants and rocks (the nature).[18]

In above argument, the two assumptions that humans are morally superior to [at least some] [A2], and that superiority justifies subordination [A4] entails human domination over nature. Now on this basis, the patriarchal society has woven a net of logic of domination against women, which springs out of the oppressive conceptual framework, which sanctions twin domination of nature and women, i.e. "*dharini aur dhatri ko bahut kuch sahana padata hai*". This logic runs in the following argument 'B'—

[B1] Women are identified with nature (*prakṛti*) and the realm of physical; men are identified with human [*purusa*] and the realm of mental.

[B2] Whatever is identified with nature and the realm of physical is inferior to [below] whatever is identified with the human and the realm of the mental; or conversely the latter is superior to [above] the former.

[B3] The women are inferior [below] to men; or conversely men are superior to women.

[B4] F or any '*X*' and '*Y*' , if '*X*' is superior to '*Y*' then '*X*' is justified in subordinating '*Y*'.

[B5] Thus men are justified in subordinating women.[19]

The above argument '*B*' establishes patriarchy and the conclusion given at [B5] that the systematic domination of women by men is justified. Thus the logic of domination results in women's inequality, subordination, subjugation and even oppression. The echo of which is heard in *Ramcharit Manas* wherein Tulsidas has said that "*dhol, ganwar, shudra, pashu aur nari, sakal tadana ke adhikari*". It means "drum, idiots [fools] lower castes, animals and women are liable to thrashing.

Now let us evaluate the logic of domination, whether it is tenable or not. As we know that it is a general rule of deductive logic that any conclusion of deductive logic is true if and only if its premises are true. Now let us examine each and every premise of the above mentioned argument from which conclusion [B5] is derived. On the minute observation, it is found that [B5] is justified by three features of oppressive conceptual framework. They are value hierarchal thinking at [B2], value dualism, and the assumed dualism of physical and mental, *prakṛti* and *purusa*, at [B1] and the assumed inferiority of physical *vis-à-vis* the mental at [B2] and logic of domination at [B4]. Hence, in so far as an oppressive conceptual patriarchal conceptual framework has functioned historically, within Indian and Western cultures, to sanction twin domination of women and nature [argument B] needs to be rejected. But in order to reject the logic of domination premise [B4], on which argument 'B' rests has to be opposed whatever truth value status of [B1] and [B2] outside the patriarchal context,. Again in order to oppose the logic of domination one has to be the critique of three assumptions B1, B2 and B4 on which the logic of twin domination, i.e. nature and women, rests. The critique of above mentioned three assumptions amounts to a critique of patriarchal conceptual framework where man is put up and woman down.

Let us evaluate the first premise of logic of domination B1. It says that women are identical with nature and the realm of physical; men are identified with human and the realm of mental. The critical analysis of it may reveal the fact that the premise B1 is itself a fallacious, erroneous and wrong due to the below mentioned reasons :

1. The woman nature metaphor is, in fact, a definition imposed by *Patri* centric culture to further the subordination. But this is not the true picture of the woman. To equate them with nature would not only situate them outside culture and history altogether, but would deprive them from the humanity itself, that will never be just on their part. In fact, women too are the pare of culture as men are. This is the thing that clearly distinguishes human beings from animals. Truly speaking, women are not any closer to nature than men, as both have consciousness, intelligence and mortality.

2. The argument 'B' is linked with, rather based on argument 'A'. It is the very first premise 'A1' does not support 'B1', wherein it is said," Humans do, and plants and rocks (nature) do not have the capacity to consciously and radically change the community in which they live. Now under connotation of 'humans' women are also included as they do consciously and radically change the community in which they live. If we take into account the biological fact of genetic parenthood or women's reproduction, it is apparent that women have greater role in human development and shaping the society. Right from the birth of a baby and development from infant to child and child to adult, man is dependent on women. All have to undergo a long period of dependency and learning from mother, as she is the primary school for children. All have a great need for, among other things, unconditional love and affection in order to develop a sense of individual self. It is women who fulfil, up to a great extent, these needs. In such a situation to equate women with rock and plants (i.e.) nature, is unjustified and wrong and hence, it is untenable.
3. In premise 'B1' women are considered in the realm of physical, on the contrary, men are considered in the realm of mental. It too is untenable and irrational, as it is false erroneous and wrong. The reason is simple. The survey of women population reveal the fact that in field of mental excellence women are competing men in all walks of life. In ancient India, we find the reference of two great scholars named Maitrei and Gargi, who were not inferior to many male scholars of their time. The great Shankaracharya was defeated by the wife of Madan Mishra of Mithila. Today very many scientists, astronauts, historians, politicians, players, film directors, physicians, surgeons and even head of the states are women. They are in no way inferior to men in their mental capability. In such a situation, to consider them inferior to men in

> the realm of physical is not only improper and unjust but also amount to deny the basic fact of life.

It is apparent from the above discussion, that in patricentric world-view, women are identified with physical and considered closer to nature; and men are identified with mental and are considered closer to culture. Secondly, nature is seen inferior to culture and women are seen inferior to men. In the logic of domination 'B4' looks to be wrong *prima facie*. It wrongly presupposes, "For any '*X*' and '*Y*' if '*X*' is superior then '*X*' is justified in subordinating '*Y*'." Here a question arises, who gives the right to dominate, subordinate and oppress the inferiors. On the contrary, the ethics of care advices the senior's superiors and elders to help, protect and extend love and affection to juniors, inferiors and the people of weaker section. This idea is reflected in our everyday life. Parent take care, love and groom their children who are physically weaker and mentally inferior to them. The teacher teaches their students and guides them properly. If this is forgotten and seniors and superiors start behaving adversely, as is stated in '*B*' the human development will start going in reverse gear. The entire human development is based on the ethics of care where in juniors, subordinates, inferior's students children younger brothers and sisters are taken care of by their seniors, elders, parent, elder brothers and sisters. Thus 'B4' is again proved to be wrong on the practical parameters.

Now let us evaluate the third premise of logic of domination 'B3' which expresses value hierarchy and places men up and women down as it says, "Thus, women are inferior to [below] men; or conversely men are superior to [up] women." The perusal of 'B3' reveals that it is based on 'B2', a false premise, which says, "Whatever is identified with nature and the realm of physical is inferior to [below] whatever is identified with human and the realm of mental. When we carefully go through the arguments 'A' and 'B', it is found that 'B2' and 'B3', are linked with or based on 'A2' which categorically says that "whatever has the capacity to consciously and radically change the community in which they live is superior to whatever lacks this capacity". On the basis of this, 'B2' holds that women are inferior to nature and 'B3' declares that women are inferior to men, which is thoroughly false. It has already been argued that women too like men have the capacity to change the community consciously and radically. Hence, nature-women identification is unjust. They in no case be equated with nature and considered to be in the realm of physical. In fact, they too are in the realm of mental. Now the question of considering women inferior to men, 'B3', does not arise as technically nature and women are qualitatively different to each other. When B1, B2, B3 and B4 are declared to be false, incorrect and wrong, the conclusion 'B5', 'Men are justified in subordinating women" which is based on B1, B2, B3 and B4, the wrong premises becomes wrong, unjust, false and untenable.

The Reason

After the collapse of the logic of domination, two points need to be discussed, one, how this wrong and erroneous logic continued to be operative for such a long period? Second, how this erroneous conceptual framework, that supported the logic of domination, came into existence? The last question needs to be answered first. In order to answer it properly, we need to address few more questions relating to it. They are how there came a paradigm shift from matricentric thinking to patricentric in human society? How value hierarchy and value dualism between man woman arose? And what necessitated to construct the logic of domination that led to actual domination of women? A brief discussion on these questions will spotlight the reason behind the gender inequality.

In Indian context woman-nature identification had never been negative in its import. It was never derogatory for women. Right from *Rig Vedic* age, nature worship is in practice. Even today people worship natural entities such as Sun, Moon, banyan, *peepal* trees, *tulsi* plant, snake, etc., and they are considered to be sacred. The nature and natural entities were considered to be divine and greater than humans. According to the *Hindu cosmological* view of [animate and inanimate] nature as *prakṛti*, as "an active and diversity" as an expression of *"Shakti"*, was the feminine creative power of the cosmos [*Adishakti*]. In such context to equate women with nature was never the reflection of negative vision of man, nor was it a derogatory one. It was positive in that context as this equation placed women superior to men. As nature gives birth, protects and helps life to grow, women were considered to be the embodiment of these qualities. Like nature woman too was considered to be a nurturing mother, full of sympathy and care.

A radical conceptual shift occurred with the introduction of male divine concept, *Shiva.* Now, it presupposes *Shiva* for creation. With the conjunction of this masculine principle, *Shiva* and *Shakti*, the feminine principle, could create this world. With the advent of *Samkhya* philosophy, the masculine principle gained power, as here the entire creation is said to be completed with the union of *Purusa* and *Prakṛti*. Later on, *Purusa* was defined as male and the *Prakṛti* as feminine, female or women. *Prakṛti* is incapable to create this universe alone, for this, it has to take the help of *Purusa*. And *pralaya*, the total destruction, is a state in which the two principles are separated with each other. *Samkhya* has used a number of epithets for *Prakṛti*, they are *cancala, bhogya* etc., that is, feminine in character. On the contrary it has used different words for *Purusa*, they are *drasta*, and *bhokta* etc., that denotes masculine character. These gave a radical shift in a conceptual framework or the worldview of that time. In this shift, the living nurturing relationship between man and earth as mother earth was replaced by the notion of man as a separate entity, dominating over inert and passive nature or women embedded in nature. This, for Bina Agrawal, was aggressive and violent".[20] Slowly and stealthily this led to a patricentric society.

However, it seems proper to mention here that in ancient India, there were several ideological strands regarding nature-women relation operating simultaneously. This gave India an ethnic and religious diversity. This is the uniqueness of the Hindu religion itself that is pluralistic, fluid and contains several coexisting discourses with varying gender implications. It is not clear that in which historical period the concept of feminine principle, affected in practice, the gender relation. It is really very difficult to indicate that when and by what concrete process and institutions the ideological constructions of women nature identity have changed.

In Western civilization, the rise of patriarchy and women's domination have different stories. Mirja Gimbutas,[21] Monica Sjoo,[22] Merlin Stone,[23] and Riane Eisler[24] are of opinion that the history of the rise of man's oppressive nature towards women goes back to 4500 B.C., well before scientific revolution. This was the time when we mark the beginning of the shift from goddess worship culture to male deity. In goddess religion there was no gender hierarchy. Earth and women's fertility was seen as sacred, and divinity was seen immanent. With the advent of patriarchal religion, there came a paradigm shift in people worshipping. Instead of earth and goddess the sky god worship started and earth was seen as his creation. The role of male in reproduction was elevated above the role of female. Women started to be compared with field (earth) and later on with nature, which gestate and bear the male seed. The time taken in this change, from goddess centred culture to male deity, was very long. Coming to the age of Jews and Greeks this change became rapid. In Judaeo-Christian tradition, a great leap of change is marked wherein God was established on the top. He appointed Adam to be in charge of entire creation. It is evident from that woman was created from the rib of Adam and placed under him and below the divinity appointed animals and rest of the nature to serve the man. Thus the patriarchal domination over women and nature was justified in the Western culture by divine command.

On the contrary, Elizabeth Fisher,[25] Donna Harway,[26] Andree Collard and Joyce Contrucci[27] are of opinion that patriarchal domination is the result of human evolutionary development. This evolutionary shift from matricentric society to patricentric, occurred as a result of hunting behaviour of male hominids.

Hunter's destructive, competitive and violent activity directed towards his prey differentiated men from nature. Woman who was smaller, weaker and reproductive was an obstacle in his way as she could not participate fully in the hunt and thus she was relegated. Her reproductive capacity as well her life bearing activities were taken as contrast to hunting, a death oriented activity, which was underlying the culture. This is how women, like animals and nature, were considered inferior to cultural activity of men. Thus the biological difference and women's nature of love and care became the reason of gender inequality, gender hierarchy and dualism of value came into existence. This gave birth to value hierarchy where things associated with male are valued higher in comparison to other than male. This value dualism is manifested as culture/nature, man/woman, and human/non-human, etc.[28]

Carolyn Merchant holds altogether a different view regarding gender equality and women's subordination. She explains its reason in the context of present reality faced by everyone. In her opinion that with the rise of modern science and modern mechanical civilization, the market oriented culture grew in Europe. It undermined the image of an organic cosmos with the living Mother (female) Earth at its centre. Due to this new way to view the nature a mechanical worldview emerged wherein nature was reconceived as something to be mastered and controlled by humans. Since women were identified with nature for a longer period because of their sublime qualities, as discussed earlier, the twin idea of mechanism and domination over nature supported male domination over nature and women. Merchant says, "The ancient identity of nature as a nurturing mother links women's history with the history of environment and ecological change. . . . Investigating the roots of our current environmental dilemma and its connections to science, technology and the economy, we must re-examine the formation of a worldview and a science that, by reconceptualizing reality as a machine rather than a living organism, sanctioned the domination of both nature and women.[29]

From the above discussion it has become clear that men and women differ each other biologically. With the change in our vision they have been reified as having different essential nature, value and cosmology. The reification of male nature and female nature oddly resemble masculinity and faminity. The masculine sense of self worth has become so entrenched in scientific habits of thought that it is very hard to argue persuasively without recourse to terms like these for validation. Women on the other hand, have socialized themselves in such a way for multiplicity of contingent tasks and practical labour functions in home and out, that they do not experience the inhibiting constraints of status validation to the same extent. In fact the traditional feminine role runs counter to the exploitative technical rationality, which is the requisite masculine norm.

The Solution

The twin domination of women and nature is a social problem. It is rooted in very concrete historical, socio-economic, and in oppressive patriarchal conceptual framework which maintains and sanctions these circumstances. Now there is a need of a new social structure, new conceptual framework, and new values, which are not based on domination of women and nature but on full expression of male and female talents. This involves three fold commitments :

(i) To critique the conceptual framework, which justifies women's domination, as well the ethics, which is implementing the said subjection.

(ii) To develop a new ethics where there is no male bias.

(iii) To construct a conceptual framework that may be the basis of gender equality.

A brief discussion of above mentioned three commitments is desirable here.

I

Any conceptual framework is a social construct, so is the case of the conceptions of 'gender and nature'. It does not require any one to deny that there are actual women, actual trees, actual rivers and actual hills. But how women and nature are conceived identical is a matter of historical and social reality. It is again a fact that these conceptions vary from time to time and culture to culture. Hence, any discussion on women's domination involves the reference of specific form of social domination of women by men in a historical context. Although it is not my intention to repeat the historical facts relating to the roots of this identity and women's subordination, but it cannot be denied that there is a historical connection between the domain of women and of nature. The claims of B1 and B2 of argument 'B' indicate that in a patriarchal society the 'feminization' of nature and 'naturalization' of women are crucial to historically successful subordination of both.[30] When we give a repeated thought over this problem it seems that women, her relation with nature and her subjugation is rooted in a system of ideas and representation, values and belief which place women and nature hierarchically below men. This idea was introduced into contemporary feminist discourse by Sherry Oterner for whom "women are identical with or, if you will, seem to be a symbol of something that every culture devalues, defines as being lower order of existence itself. . . . women are (everywhere) is being symbolically associated with nature as opposed to men who are identified with culture.[31] In this connection it relevant to mention that the formation of nature women identity is rooted, as is the realm mentioned, in the biological process of reproduction. But it is also a fact that like men, women also mediate between nature and culture. In fact women are not only closer to nature than men. Both are closer and different to it as both have consciousness and both are mortals.[32]

Secondly, women are supposed to have some sublime qualities such as care, sympathy, love, affection, etc. For historical or social reasons women, even today, are retaining these characteristics that many men, for sociological reasons, have lost. Hence, women are considered to be the social repositories of ethics of care. They remain a strong hold for the values on which a society depends. They may be called the moral missionaries on whom a moral agenda is imposed to somehow save the society from the damage that some men have historically wrought. In this way they are comparatively superior to men. To consider them inferior or subordinate is not only wrong and unethical but also amount to ignore the women's contribution in creating, sustaining and protecting the society.

II

To Develop a Social Ethics wherein there is no Male Bias

This proposition is advanced by the feminist thinkers who have seen the women oppression through the magnifying glass and have held responsible male only for all sorts of women's plight. They advocate for developing an ethics, which are not male biased, and where women voice is prominent. It involves two fold commitments, (a) critique of male bias in ethics and (b) creation of new social values as well as reinterpretation of old values in the light of changing realities.

(a) Critique of Male Bias in Ethics

Up to some extent I do agree with the feminist thinkers that earlier ethics had a male bias as it was the creation of male vision only where women were considered weak and meek. In order to protect them and save the society from peril the moral agenda was imposed on them. But with the change of time and situation, social condition and social institution also suffered change. The modern technological advancement has caused a major innovation in modern society. The male domination has become irrelevant. Men and women both have the equal status and ability to utilize the tools of higher technology. Not only this we have notable examples before us that have proved the superiority of female mental (often physical) ability than men. This necessarily requires a radical change in our outlook and orientation of ethics. We have to accept certain human qualities, which are certainly not the monopoly of men. Hence, ethics should not be based on male bias.

On the contrary, some feminine thinkers and activists are of opinion that since long man-oriented ethics was in vogue wherein women voice was suppressed. Now with the changing situation, women voice has to be given proper and prominent place. Perhaps this will amount to give "social justice" to the oppressed class. They assume that "whatever bias it has as an ethics centralizing the voices of oppressed persons is a better bias—than those which exclude these voices."[33] To my mind both the views and propositions are partial. If we base our social ethics on female bias, it will amount to beat the same drum from the opposite side. Hence, care should be taken to provide an objective point of view while developing a social ethics. It should not be based either on male or on female bias, in reaction, rather it should be free of any sort of bias.

(b) Creation of New Values as well as Reinterpretation of Old Values in the light of Changing Reality

In order to develop a bias-free objective ethics we must take into account the ethical discourse and practice as emerging from the voice of the people located in different historical circumstances It must be the expression of the felt experiences as it makes a way to raise philosophical germane issues in ethics that is often lost or underplayed in the main stream philosophical ethics. Such a narrative gives voice to a felt sensitivity in which one conceives oneself as fundamental in relation with others. Such expression of the felt experience provides a way to conceive ethics and ethical meanings as emerging out of a particular situation and moral agents find themselves in, rather as being imposed on these situations and the individuals. In this process a multiplicity of cross-cultural voices are centralized and narrative is able to give expression to a range of attitudes, values, beliefs and behaviours which may be overlooked or silenced by imposed ethical meanings and theory.[34] Thus it is like a collage or mosaic wherein ethical propositions and commands emerge out of the different voices of the people located in different circumstances irrespective of their caste, class, gender and race. Hence, it reconceives ethical theory as theory in process which may change in course of time and like all theories it also has to be based on some generalization.[35] However, this generalization is a pattern of voices within which different voices emerging out of concrete and alternative descriptions of ethical situations have meaning. Therefore, it is structurally pluralistic, temperamentally contextual and characteristically inclusive. It ensures that diverse voices of oppressed person (mainly women) be given legitimacy in ethical theory building. It thereby helps to minimize the empirical bias.

The above mentioned discussions logically culminate in developing a new ethics wherein above mentioned instructions may be taken into account. This may lead to articulation of certain rules, such as value of care, love, mutual understanding, mutual trust, appropriate reciprocity, kinship, friendliness, equality etc. that have remained unnoticed, underplayed, lost and misinterpreted in traditional ethics.[36] Endeavour should be made to place these values in the centre of ethics. These are the value of care they presuppose our relationship with nature and women are centre to our understanding.[37] It, thereby gives voice to the sensitivity that one is doing something in relationship with other has to be treated with care and respect. This understanding should grow from within. This feeling emerges from the voice of the oppressed, i.e. women and nature. Since we are immune to listening to the voice of the nature the voice of women has to be heard carefully and patiently. Because it is the women who experience the harmful domination of nature and the way it is tied with the domination of women. This is the reason that in Indian tradition, women have been placed in centre and special instructions have been made it that for the happiness of the society and family women's voice has to be taken into consideration properly, sincerely and sympathetically.[38] A special instruction has also been passed not only to love and care and keep the women happy but also to respect them. A warning has also been given that in a family wherein women are not given due importance, not respected but oppressed, it is destined to be destroyed. Where women live a happy life happiness is bound to spread in the entire family. On the contrary, if women are not happy the entire family members live in an unhappy state.[39]

But this does not mean that certain other values such as right, utility, rule, etc. be excluded as these had been instrumental in women's oppression and exploitation. Our work should be to reinterpret these values in terms of gender equality. Let these values be utilized by women in a positive way. For instance women have the right to be taken care of by their husband. The female child has the right of education and equal share in parent's property. In the same way civil and social rules should be framed in favour of female and these be utilized to protect their interest. Earlier men exercised their rights to subordinate the women as is shown in [B5] of the argument 'B'. Now women have the right to fight or raise their voice against such fictitious and oppressive rights of men. This needs a theory building by pioneering a new direction or by revamping or by reinterpreting the old values and theories in a gender sensitive way for establishing an oppression free gender equal society.

In this background if we cast glance over our ancient scriptures we find that references are available of values as that are helpful in changing man's oppressive vision. They are compassion, happiness, friendliness and equanimity (*karuna, mudita, metta* and *upekkha*).[40] These are the four *Brahmavirahas* propounded by Buddha which can prove to be the foundation stone of a new emerging gender ethics. If one is filled with the virtues one cannot think of oppressing, dominating, subordinating and subjugating the weaker one rather he will extend love and affection to them. The reason is very simple. His unbounded compassion will compel him to help, protect and take care of others in need. The internal wave of his *mudita* (joy/happiness) will spread happiness and joy in all the living creatures that come into his contact. The virtue of friendliness (*maitri*) will help him befriending and winning the heart of others. And the virtue of equanimity (*upekkha*) will develop the vision to treat everyone alike. In the same way the virtue of non-violence and celibacy (*ahimsa* and *brahmacarya*) are widely accepted by every religions of the world. Gandhijee used non-violence as his weapon for acquiring *swaraj*, the independence.

This non-violent vision will never allow anyone to oppress the women and nature. Gandhiji wanted to inculcate the culture of non-violence in Indian mass. Buddha has provided empirical *modus operandi* for generating non-violent thoughts in human mind that may accordingly purify his vision and action. He says, "All tremble punishment, all fear death. . . . all love their own life. Remembering that thou art like unto them do not kill and cause no slaughter."[41] this is his empirical way to cultivate non-violence. When it is cultivated the question of any kind of oppression or domination does not arise as these are the different modes or expression of violence. In this connection it seems relevant to point out that the word *ahimsa* and its practice has been advocated by most of the Indian sacred texts. *Hitopadesa* says, "As life is dear to one self, it is dear to all other living beings, by comparing oneself with others good people bestow pity on other beings."[42] The same thing has been said in Patanjali's *"Yoga Darshan"*.[43]

Celibacy (*brahmacarya*) is another virtue, which needs to be inculcated in developing a social ethics. Self-control is another word that can be used for *brahmacarya* as it has a wider connotation. Many moral thinkers are of opinion that this should be made the basis of our ethical structure as it may control many types of male violence. Rape, as many feminists consider, is a pure male violence. It is the kernel of all sorts domination of women. Behind it misogyny is supposed to be the strong force. They are seriously concerned of it. But let it be known that these are caused not only by misogyny alone but also due to man's oppression in their own right under other system of domination. For understanding the relationship of misogyny and other factors that provoke men to dominate women as well as the analysis of its different reasons is required. But to my mind the basic reason behind this social evil is lack of self-control. Sex impulse is natural, but unregulated sex, either by man or woman, leads to women oppression in terms of rape, molestation, prostitution, etc. Hence celibacy (*brahmacarya*) or self-control should be made the basis of social ethics and this has to be observed by men and women both equally. The provocative dress, showing body in common place, in fashion-shows or in cinema, etc, are the dominant reasons of such oppression. In Indian tradition these are called '*brahmacarya*' and much emphasis has been laid on abstaining from it(*brahmacarya*).[44] It has been further said that one should observe it mentally, orally and in action (*manasa, vaca, karmana*). An emphasis has also been laid here to observe penance (*tapa*) and always keep the mind filled with pious thoughts.

Finally, it can be said that the problem of gender equality and women oppression are, partially, due to the fact that we have permitted our actions to divorce the values, virtues and ideals and allowed them to move in different directions. The set of values, sublime ideas, virtues and ideals act as the cohesive forces and keep the different parts of the society integrated. When these are weakened or lost, society tend to break into conflicting groups and civilization decline. The present problem of gender inequality and women oppression is due to neglect of moral ideas and lack of spiritual insight, not because lack of scientific knowledge, technical education and material equipments. We need mature conception of right and wrong. There is a need to recover the moral insight of our culture and spiritual heritage and bring them into harmony with our modern personal and social relationship.[45] These are the time tasted values that can be used in every age and clime.

While developing a new social ethics these values, virtues and ideals have to be reinterpreted in a scientific, empirical and impartial way in the light of contextual realities.

III

Construction of a Conceptual Framework that may be the basis of Gender Equality

Before constructing any new conceptual framework, it seems proper to re-evaluate the old concepts that was supposed to be the reason behind gender disparity. It is found that the question of "woman and nature identity" is generally held responsible for the present plight of women. But when we give a critical perusal to it we find that "woman-nature" metaphor tells a different story. In fact, the comparison of women with nature might have been used for certain strategic purposes, or in Indian context its designation to subjugate *prakṛti* (the nature) and establish dominance of *purusa* might have been based on certain teleological grounds which are certainly not applicable in the present context. Even if we accept this identity, we must consider the nature in a wider dimension. Nature is a symbol of peace, serenity, cohesion and affection and men are certainly subject to such requirements. And in that perspective superiority of women is a logical conclusion.

Secondly, there is a life affirming connection between nature and women, women, as has been earlier discussed have a greater role not only in giving birth to an infant but also in grooming and making them without being, as nature gives birth, protects, sustains and help the entire animate and inanimate things to grow and get stronger. Hence, the notion of women can be replaced by defining them as cultural beings. This train of thought was influenced by cultural feminism that gained ascendancy not only on the traditional view of gender equality but also on the feminist view of the West. It executed enormous revision in our old notions, feminist concepts and its thinking too.[46] Hence, there is a need to replace the old notion of women having an interior status with the new notion of women as a cultural being. That is why Susan Graffin categorically declares "we know ourselves to be made from this earth, we know this earth is made from our body. For we see ourselves. And we are the nature."[47] Thus, there is nothing derogatory in this women-nature identity, as from nowhere it smirks of interior position of women.

The thought and ideas of cultural feminism, in the West, influenced the Eco-feminist thinkers as they also tend to see women as "closer to nature" than men's. For them modern men must learn from society who were gender equal, non-dominating to nature and women were considered nearer to or identical with nature. They are of opinion that in the interpretation of "nature-women identity concept" there is a possibility of an Ecological society wherein female value can be infused in nature, women-hating culture.[48] Although this treatment falls into atavism, as if no change has taken place since about 3,000 BC. But, it is a fact that after some refinement this conceptual framework can be used for a gender equal society.

There is also a need of building of a theory by pioneering into gender free direction or by revamping the old theories, as is done by cultural feminist and by Eco-feminist, in a gender sensitive way. By analyzing sex-gender and by reflecting on whatever analysis reveals about gender experience and genders social reality, a new conceptual framework may also emerge. In this connection it seems proper to quote an Eco-feminist author who is opinion that we should utilize the old concept in a new way instead of constructing totally a new framework. In her words, "If someone has laid the foundations of a house it would seem sensible to build on these foundations rather than import a pre-fabricated structure with no foundations to put beside it.[49]

However, while reinterpreting, renovating, revamping or redefining the old concepts, we must take into account their negative aspects, their positive and negative impact on our life and society as well as the changing realities of the day. We cannot accept or implement any old conceptual framework in its original forms only because it is old and is of our own cultural heritage. It has to be purged as per the needs of the time, context and situation. For instance, we cannot ignore that the Neolithic culture has hierarchies and were brutal in their own right; it has to be taken into account that the question of individuality was decided according to the rules of custom and tradition and the problems of organizing the culture were sorted out on a biological line of age and gender. And above all we all have to consider the ground realities of the present time that were not in Neolithic culture. The basic thing of the present society is that science and technology have done a lot to change our life style and way of living. It has removed drudgery of women's life up to a great extent. As a result the women participation in every walk of life has become the women's heritage as much as it is of men. In short our Weltanschauung, in the context of gender has entirely changed.

Now in view of the major innovation of modern society with special reference to the advancement of science and technology there is both a need and urge to reconceptualize the older ideologies, thoughts and values of life. It also needs to redefine and reinterpret the older presumptions in consistence with changed situation. We certainly do not mean reversing the older *Weltanschauung* but we are definitely concerned with their new interpretations, which may change the basis of fallacies of premises.

In this background if we peep into our sacred texts we find that balanced conceptual frameworks are very much available there that hinges upon gender equality, mutual understanding as well as essential harmony of men, women and nature. *Vedas*, while explaining the origin of this Wavers says that the *Virat Purusa* was one. He willed to be many एको' हम बहुस्याम[50] and this multiple word came into existence. Thus the one Brahman manifested Himself in and through the things and beings of this world, whether it is plant, rock, animal, man and women. Hence at the root it is the *Brahman* that cannot be bifurcated into man, women and nature. All these differences are unreal and illusory coming to the *Upanisads* we mark the transition from Brahman to *atman*. The Brahman of *Veda*, from subjective point of view, turns into the *atman* of the *upanisad* as for it *Brahman* and *atma* are identical.[51] There is *atman* not only in man but also in all the objects of the universe. . . . and *Brahman* is this *atman*.[52] It is needless to impress upon that *atman* is the central point of *upanisadic* religious and metaphysical beliefs. After going through its contents there remains no doubt that *upanisads* accept rather emphasize that *atma* has no gender bias as it is neither male nor female nor of neutral gender.[53] At another place it is said that *Brahman* or *atman* is male and female both. The verse runs like this "only you are female only you are male, only you are bachelor only you are male."[54] These lines of *upanisads* categorically indicate that in reality there is no gender division. There should not be any difference between male and female as the same atman or *Brahman* is seated in both. The *Bhagavad Gita* explains this fact in a beautiful way. Lord Krishna says, "God is seated in the heart of each and every individual. He through the power of *maya* is moving the entire according to the merit of their *karmas* (deeds)."[55] Now there remains little doubt that in *upanisadic* worldview there is no scope for gender disparity, there is equality among all the creatures of the world, whether it is male or female. This is the reason *Gita* says "The men established in wisdom and morality sees (considers) cow, elephant, dog and downcast people alike."[56] The way man considers the limbs of this body, viz. legs, hands, head, etc., equal in the same way wise men considers men, women and downcast people (*sudra*) alike as he finds the same *atman* in all of them. This is an ideal state wherein there is no room for gender, class, and race. Everyone is equal as everyone is the manifestation of the same *atman*. It is only because of ignorance the cases of gender problem, sex oppression is found in the society. In reality there is no gender difference.

However, we cannot ignore the scientific factor the brute reality that there is a difference between man and woman. We cannot outright reject the animal biology. We should not hesitate to accept the biological difference between the two sexes particularly obvious difference in reproductive capacity, women menstruate, gestate, give birth and lactate, men do not. Women on the whole not as tall or heavy as men of the same ethnic group. Most of the women are physically weaker than men. *Upanisads* do accept this biologism, but it does not allow us to dominate, subjugate or oppress women or make any sort of discrimination on biological line. For *upanisads atman* is the soul or self, is divine but it is clogged by flesh. The different biological structure as well as function of both the sexes give birth to gender problem. Some feminist build biological differences into elaborate theories of "female nature" of the minimize biological differences excessively and regard present difference as wholly a socially construct, and in effect they anathematize biology. But *upanisads* hold a different view altogether. It categorically says that "although *atman* is neither male nor female nor of neutral gender but it is protected by the body it adopts", whether it is of male or female. This biological difference of sex or gender never comes in the way of perfection. *Gita* says, "everyone attains perfection whosoever performs one's own duty honestly."[58] Because in the eyes of God everyone is equal. Krishna further says, "Any individual can achieve the *summum bonum* of life provided one worships the creator of this universe dedicatedly.[59] At another place of *Bhagavad Gita,* Lord Krishna hinges on gender equality as He says "whether one is female, sinner or downcaste if one surrenders unto me with unwavering confidence attains the highest state, the liberation."[60] These verses delineate that there is no place for sex or gender difference in *upanisadic Weltanschauung*. This phenomenon is caused by mind, it is a social construct. if this conceptual framework is adopted in our culture it may change our vision as well of society and an ideal state of gender equality will never remain an utopia. This alternative conceptual framework of the *upanisads*, if engrained in our social behaviour and custom as well as in our scientific habit of thought it will be very easy for men to get rid of this oppressive vision against women and gender equality can easily be established in our society.

REFERENCES

1. Vandana Shiva, Judith Plant (ed) *Healing the wounds: The Promise of Ecofeminism*, Philadelphia: New Society Publishers, 1989, pp. 80-90.

2. *Yatra naryastu pujyante ramante tatra devatah /*
Yatraitastu na pujyante sarvastatraphalah kriyah //
— Manusmriti, III. 56
3. *Bhikkhunis* had to pay homage to all *bhikkhus*, even very junior *bhikkhus*; *bhikkhunis* could not spend their rains independent of *bhikkhus; bhikkhunis* had to ask *bhikkhus* the date of *uposatha* rites; *bhikkhunis* has to confess transgressions before both the orders; *bhikkhunis* must accept discipline from both orders; *bhikkhunis* had to be ordained by both orders; *bhikkhunis* cannot abuse or revile a *bhikkhu* in anyway; and *bhikkhunis* could not admonish a *bhikkhu* for any reason.—*Therigatha*
4. *The Book of Gradual Saying*, vol.III (F.L. Woodward trans.) London:Luzac & Co. Ltd., 1932, pp. 55-57.
5. Padmanabh Jaini, "Gender and Salvation: Jain Debate on the Spiritual Liberation of Women", Berkeley University of California Press. 1991.
6. *Balaya va yuvatya va vriddhaya vapi yoshita /*
Na svatantrayena kartavyam kincitkarye griheshvapi //
—Manusmriti, V. 147
7. *Balye piturvashe tishthetpanigrahasya yauvane /*
Putranam bhartari prete na bhajetstri svatantratam //
—Manusmriti, V. 148 also see
Pita rakshati kaumare bharta rakshati yaunane /
Rakshanti sthavire putra na stri svatantryamarhati// —*Ibid.*, IX, 3
8. *Vishilah kamavritto va gunairva parivajitah /*
Upacaryah striya sadhvya satatam devavatpatih // —
Ibid., V. 154
9. *Nasti strinam prithagyajno na vratam napyuposhanam /*
Patim shushrushate yena tena svarge mahiyate // —*Ibid.*,V. 155
10. Ester Bserup, *Women's Role in Economic Development*, Allen & Unwin, London, 1970.
11. *Ibid.*
12. DAWN, Development Crisis and Alternative Vision: Third World's Women's Perspective Christian Michelsen Institute, Bergsen, 1985 p. 21.
13. Bina Agrawal, "The Gender and Environmental Debate, Lesson from India", *Environmental Philosophy*, Edt. J. Baird Callicott and Clare Palmer, Vol. II, Routledge, London and New York, 2005.
14. This data is based on Radio and T.V. broadcast by Govt. of India; Bina Agrawal, "Women Poverty and Agricultural Growth in India" *Journal of Peasant Studies,* 13 July, 1986, pp. 165-220.

15. Karen J. Warren, *The Power and the Promise of Ecological Feminism, Environmental Ethics*, 12, pp. 125-46.
16. *Samkhyakarika.*
17. Karen J .Warren, *The Power and the Promise of Ecological Feminism, op. cit.*
18. *Ibid.*
19. *Ibid.*
20. Bina Agrawal, *The Gender and Environmental Debate*, *op. cit.*
21. *God and Goddess of Old Europe* 6500—B.C. Berkeley and Los Angeles : University Press, 1982.
22. Monika Sjoo and Barbara Mor, *The Cosmic Mother; Rediscovering the Religion of the Earth*, Harper & Row, San Francisco, 1976.
24. Riane Eisler, *The Phalic and the Blade; Our History, Our Future*, Harper Collins, New York, 1987.
25. Elizabeth Fisher, "Women's Creation, McGraw Hill, New York, 1979.
26. Dona Harway, *Primate Vision*, Routledge, New York 1989.
27. Andree Collard and Joyce Contrucci, *Rape of the Wild: Man's Violence Against Animal and the Earth*, Bloomington: Indiana University Press, 1988.
28. Elizabeth Dodson, *Gray, Green Paradise Lost*, Wellesley, Mass : Roundtable Press, 1981; also see Susan Griffin, *Women and Her Nature: The Roaring Inside Her*, Harper and Row, San Francisco, 1978.
29. Carolyn Merchant, *Tne Death of Nature, Women*, Ecology and Revolution, Harper & Row, San Francisco, 1980. p. 144.
30. Gray Green *Paradise Lost*, Eliizabeth Dodson, *op.cit* ; *Women and Her Nature*, Susan Graffin, *op.cit.*
31. Serry Orterner, "Is Female to Male as Nature is to Culture?" in M.Z. Rosaldo and L. Lamphere, (ed.) *Women, Culture and Society*, Standford University, 1974.
32. *Ibid.*
33. For more information regarding mail bias and impartiality in ethics, see this article by Karen J. Warren, "Critical Thinking and Faminism", *Informal Logic,* 10 no. 1 Winter, 1988, pp. 31-44.
34. Jim Cheney, "Ecofeminism and Deep Ecology" *Environmental Ethics* 9, 1987, p. 14.
35. Kathryn Addelson, "Moral Revolution in Women and Values": *Reading in Recent Feminist Philosophy,* ed. By Marilyn Pearsall, Belmont, Calif Wasworth Publishing Co., 1986, pp. 291-309.

36. *Ibid.*
37. Jim Cheney, "Ecofeminism and Deep Ecology", Published in *Environmental Ethics*, 9, 1987, p. 122.
38. *Manusmriti,* III 55.
39. *Ibid.*, III 56-62.
40. *Ibid.*
41. *Sabbe tasanti dandassa sabbe bhayanti maccuno /*
    Sabbe tasanti dandassa sabbe sam jivitam piyam /
    Attanan upamam katva na haneyya na ghataya //
    —Dhammapada, Danda Vaggo 129 and 130
42. *Prana ythamanto abhishta bhutanam api te tatha /*
    Atmaupamyena bhutesu dayam kurvanti sadhavah //
    —Hitopadesa, I, 2
43. *Mahabharata* XIII 5568; Patanjalyogadarsanam.
44. *Brahmacaryam sada raksestadha laksanam prithaka /*
    Smaranam kirtinam kelih preksanam guhyabhasanam //
    Sankalpo adhyavasayaca kriyanivrittireva ca /
    Ẹtanmaithunmastanga pravadantim manisinah //
    —Daksasmriti, VII, 31,32;
    Brahmacaryam—Guptendriyasyopasthasya sayamam, Vyasya Bhasya , p. 250, ed. Damodar Shastri,Chaukhambha Varanasi,1935;
    Karmendriani samyamya ca aste mansa smaran /
    Brahmacarya tadevoktam grihasthaasram vasinam // Gita, III-6.
    Visuddhi maggo (with Hindi translation) I, pp. 42-47.
45. Harold H. Titus, *Ethics for Today*, Third Edition Euresia Publishing House (Pvt.) Ltd., Delhi, p. 5.
46. For detailed description please see Alice Echals, "The New Feminism of Yin and Yang" in A. Snitow, C. Stanseil and S. Thompson edited, *Power of Desire*, New York, Monthly Review Press, 1983.
    The Taming of the Id: Feminism Sexual Politics, 1968-83 in C.S. Vance edited. *Pleasure and Danger, Exploring Female Sexuality*, Boston Routledge and Kegan Paul, 1984; and Hester Ceisenstein, Contemporary Feminist thought, Boston, G.K. Hall, 1983.
47. *Women and Nature: The Roaring inside Her,* p. 226.
48. Janet Biehl, *What is Social Ecoleminism.*
49. Ariel Key Salleh, "Contributions to the Critique of Political Epistemology", Thesis Eleven 8, 1984. pp. 15-17, also see M. George Foster, *Traditional Society and Technological Change*," Allied Publishers, Delhi, 1973.
50. Ṛg Veda. Puruṣa-Suktā

51. *Tat tvam asi.*
52. S.N. Dasgupta, *A History of Indian Philosophy*, Vol. I, Ist Indian Edition, 1975, Motilal Banarsidass, Varanasi, Delhi, p. 48.
53. *Naiva Stri Naiva Pumamesana caivaya napunsakah, Svetasvataropnisad*, V. 10.
54. *Tvami stri tvam pumanasi tvam kumar utava kumari, Svetasvataropanisad*, IV, 3.
55. *Iswarh Sarrabhitanam hriddesearyun tisthati, Bhramayansavvabhutatni yantrarudhani mayaya, Gita,* XVIII, 61.
56. "*Vidya vinayasampanne brahmane gaxi hastini*", *Suni Ceiva Svapake ca panditah sandarsheh.*
57. *Naiva stri naiva pumamesa na caivaya napunsakah, yadaccharira madatte tena ten samiraksyate, Svetasvataro upanisad*, V.10.
58. *Sve sve karmnyabhiratah sansiddhi labhate narah, Gita,* XVIII, 45.
59. *Gita*, XVIII, 46.
60. *Mam hi parth vyapasritya ye'pi syuh papanyonayah, striyo vaisyastatha sudraste'pi yanti param gatim.*

—*Gita*, IX, 32.

Chapter – 5

Gender Inequality : An Existential Analysis

(With special reference to Simone de Beauvoir)

Shiva Bhanu Singh

In his illuminating book "*The Pleasures of Philosophy*", great contemporary philosopher, writer and historian Will Durant comments that if asked about the outstanding feature of human events in the first quarter of the twentieth century, we shall perceive that it was not the great war, nor the Russian Revolution, but the change in the status of woman. History has seldom seen so startling a transformation in so short a time. The "sacred home" that was the basis of our social order, the marriage system that was our barrier against human passion and instability, the complex moral code that lifted us from brutality to civilization and courtesy, are visibly caught in that turbulent transition which has come upon all our institutions, all our modes of life and thought, since factories outwooed the fields, and cities absorbed the natural and human resources of the countryside.[1]

Earlier in past centuries woman was treated as household slave, a social ornament or a sexual tool. The roots of sexual discrimination and prejudiced outlook towards woman can be traced in ancient theology where Eve is depicted as made from what Bossuet called 'a supernumerary bone of Adam'.[2] Thus humanity is male and man defines woman not in herself but as relative to him; she is not regarded as autonomous being. Male supremacy and prejudices towards woman are not common in ordinary persons rather some great philosophers and theologians also had such kind of evil tendency. For instance, Aristotle said, "The female is a female by virtue of certain lack of qualities. We should regard the female nature as afflicted with a natural defectiveness." The medieval theologian St. Thomas pronounced woman to be an 'imperfect man', an 'incidental being'.[3] In *Pleasures of Philosophy*, Will Durant quotes, 'Gorki and Tchekov were walking in Crimea. They came upon Tolstoi as he sat on the beach, his great head bent in meditation, his beard sweeping the sand. They squatted down beside him and began to talk about women. For a long time Tolstoi listened in silence. Then suddenly he said, "And I will tell the truth about woman only when I have one foot in the grave. I shall tell it, jump into my coffin, pull the lid over me and say, 'Do what you like with me now."[4] Will Durant again cites an example by saying that when Bernard Shaw was invited by Count Keyserling to contribute an essay to *The Book of Marriage*, Shaw refused by saying, "No man dare write the truth about marriage while his wife lives".[5] Even in contemporary age some philosophers and psychologists have observed major psychological and biological differences between females and males. It has been argued that while social conditioning plays some role in determining psychological differences between the sexes, biological factors are also at work. The evidence for this view is particularly strong in respect of aggression. In "*The Psychology of Sex Differences*", Eleanor Emmons Maccoby and Carol Nagy Jacklin give four grounds for their belief that the greater aggressions of males has a biological component.

1. Males are more aggressive than females in all human societies in which the difference has been studied.
2. Similar differences are found in humans and in apes and other closely related animals.

3. The differences are found in very young children, at an age when there is no evidence of any social conditioning in this direction.
4. Aggression has been shown to vary according to the level of sex hormones, and females become more aggressive if they receive male hormones.[6]

Besides above mentioned differences, some moral and mental differences between females and males have also been advocated but latest studies and feminist's analysis have demonstrated that none of the moral and intellectual differences are innate or hereditary rather these are due to social conditioning and environmental influences. H.B. Thompson quotes in '*Mental Traits of Sex* (p. 178), "Boys are encouraged to individuality. They are trained to be independent in thought and action . . . . They are encouraged to experiment and make things for themselves. Girls are taught obedience, dependence and deference. They are made to feel that too much independence of opinion or action is a drawback to them not becoming or womanly. A boy is made to feel that his success in life . . . . will depend upon his ability to accomplish something new . . . . No such social spur is applied to girls."[7] It has been advocated that industrial revolution and feminist's movements have bridged the moral and mental gap between the sexes. It has been argued that given equal opportunity female can rival male in all walks of life. More than half a century after the publication of the *Second sex* in 1949, Simon de Beauoir is still recognised as the first philosophical thinker to have systematically raised the issue of 'sexual difference'. Her work has inspired many subsequent developments in feminist theory as well as shaping the gender critique within the discipline of philosophy itself. While it is true that Beauvoir's position has often been criticized for some of its existentialist assumption, it is equally true that even her most trenchant critics credit her with having the courage and tenacity to systematize a topic ignored by Western philosophy for over two millennia. Simon de Beauvoir is one of the leading exponent of a Philosophy of existence that privileged freedom, transcendence and authenticity. She was of the opinion that the ideal of freedom, as expressed by being for itself could be seriously impeded by the socio-cultural structures and institutions limiting individual development. For de Beauvoir, the oppression of women throughout history represented the paradigm case of this constraint. She maintained that "man" has consistently defined himself as pure being—for itself, leaving only the role of an inessential and objectified other—for 'Woman' to fill. Moreover, this attitude had been internalized by women themselves, thereby reinforcing the invisibility of this oppression. Simone de Beauvoir has attempted to unpack the generalogy of women's peripheral status as well as to suggest how this status could be actively and historically changed.

De Beauvoir vigorously rejected as too simplistic, the commonly accepted biological, psychological and economic explanation for women's marginal condition. While she acknowledged that the reproduction facts of sexual difference did perhaps burden women more than men, she claimed that the context of social values and attitudes counted for more than the physical facts themselves. She did not support Freudian explanation of woman's oppression. In the same manner she remained sceptic of Marxist attitude of explaining women's oppression due to capitalist tendency. However, Beauvoir located the site of women's continuing oppression in patriarchal institutions and myths. The 'essential feminine' qualities of sacrifice and narcissism promoted by these myths were targeted by Beauvoir as particularly detrimental to women's identity. All of women's efforts towards freedom and transcendence would face in surmountable odds as long as they remained passive and accommodating in their social roles. She suggested that women seek their economic independence through work outside the home, while simultaneously challenging themselves intellectually to understand their own history and prospects for the future.

Simone de Beauvior observes that man defines woman not in herself but as relative to him, because she is not regarded as an autonomous being. Michelet writes, "Women, the relative being . . . . " and Benda is most positive in his Rapport : 'Uriel', "The body of man makes sense in it quite apart from that of woman whereas the latter seems wanting in significance by itself . . . . Man can think of himself without woman. She cannot think of herself without man".[8] Beauvoir observes that woman is simply what man decrees, thus she is called "The Sex", by which is meant that she appears essentially to the male as a sexual being. For man woman is sex—absolute sex, no less; she is defined and differentiated with references to man and not he with reference to woman; she is the incidental, the inessential as opposed to the essential. He is the subject, he is the Absolute, she is the other. Men deprived women of their subjectivity, individuality and were treated as "object". Beauvoir observes that it is unfortunate that women have accepted the position given by men. They did not resist against it nor did they revolt. They do not authentically assume a subjective attitude. They have gained only what men have been willing to grant. They have taken nothing, they have only received.

Demonstrating the above prejudiced and biased attitude towards woman, Dorothy Parker writes in *Modern Woman : The Lost Sex,* "I cannot be just to books which treat of woman as woman, my idea is that all of us, men as well as women, should be regarded as human beings."[9] Pointing out the main reasons of woman's marginal condition in human being, Beauvoir observes that woman lack concrete means for organizing themselves into a unit which can stand face to face with the correlative unit. They have no past, no history, no religion of their own and they have no such solidarity of work and interest as that of the other oppressed class like proletariat. They live dispersed among the males, attached through residence, house work, economic condition and social standing to certain men—fathers or husbands, more firmly than they are to other woman. Woman has always been man's dependent if not his slave. These two sexes have never shared the world in equality and even today a woman is heavily handicapped, though her status has changed a lot. She is gaining almost equal legal status but still long standing customs and traditions prevent the full expression of legal rights. In economic sphere too, woman are competing men in getting all kinds of jobs. However, in industry and politics men are still occupying better positions and key posts.

Simon de Beauvoir observes that change in women's condition began in eighteenth century when genuinely democratic man began to view the matter objectively. Diderot for instance strove to show that woman is like man, a human being. Later John stuart Mill came frequently to her defence. But these philosophers displayed unusual impartiality. In the nineteenth century the feminist quarrel became again a quarrel of partisans. One of the consequences of the industrial revolution was the entrance of woman into productive labour and it was just here that the claims of the feminists emerged from the realm of theory and acquired an economic basis, while their opponents became more aggressive. Even within the working class the men endeavoured to restrain woman's liberations because they began to see the woman as dangerous competitors. In proving women's inferiority the anti-feminists then began draw not only upon religion, philosophy and theology as before, but also upon science, biology, experimental psychology, etc. At most they were willing to grant equality in difference to the other sex.

In twenty first century women are achieving their lost identity and are enjoying autonomous and independent status. They are giving their valuable contribution in all walks of life. However, women have still to fight for their complete subjectivity and individual identity. By their ability, merit and competence woman have proved all psychological, moral and mental differences as false and baseless. The existentialist approach towards woman has demonstrated them as free, autonomous and independent human being. Women are successfully fighting for their individuality, subjectivity, freedom and autonomy. She is not an 'object', or 'other sex' rather a conscious human being, an individual like a man. All kinds of sexual discrimination and inequalities have been proved as unscientific, irrational and baseless. Beauvoir emphatically observes that this status will be established only by the efforts of woman, men will not give this status by themselves.

REFERENCES

1. Will Durant : *The Pleasures of Philosophy,* Chapter IX, 'The Modern Woman', page 128. A Touchstone Book published by Simon and Schuster, 1953.
2. Simone de Beauvoir : *The Second Sex* (Introduction), London : Cape, 1953, trans. D Baired. H.M. Parshley, p. 97.
3. *Ibid.,* p. 97.
4. Gorki, *Reminiscences of Tolstoi,* p. 65, quoted from Chapter VIII, 'Men and Women' from Will. Durant's book '*The Pleasures of Philosophy*', p. 115.
5. *Ibid.,* p. 115.
6. Quoted from the book *Practical Ethics* by Peter Singer, p. 34. Cambridge University Press, 1993.
7. Will Durant, '*The Pleasures of Philosophy*', Chapter VII, 'Men and Women,' p. 127.
8. Simone de Beauvoir, *Introduction to the Second Sex,* p. 97.
9. *Ibid.,* p. 96.

Chapter – 6

Disproportionate Representation of Women in Indian Legislative Bodies

Y. V. Satyanarayana

This chapter is intended to analyze reasons for disproportionate representation of women in Indian Politics and to suggest appropriate remedial measures to enhance their representation in the legislative bodies at the State and National level.

The word "discrimination" connotes two different meanings. Discrimination, in general, means "the act of differentiating one person from another or recognition of the difference between one thing and another". In addition to its usual and primary meaning, the word "discrimination" also means "making an unjust distinction of the people on the grounds of caste, colour, creed, race and sex and treating them differently".

In one aspect, the act of discrimination is quite essential to differentiate equals from unequals in the distribution of benefits and burdens, which society distributes competitively. The people, who have a duty to be impartial, must also have a duty to discriminate human beings on the basis of relevant reasons in question. Hence, the exercise of discrimination, at all times and in all contexts, is not wrong. But discrimination of people on the consideration of irrelevant factors in question such as — caste, colour, creed, race and sex and treating them differently is morally wrong. These factors or characteristics are almost irrelevant in the distribution of burdens or benefits in our social life.

Gender discrimination may be defined as "differentiating people as male and female on the basis of gender or gendered based functions and treating them unequally in the matters of social functions or treating them unjustly in the distribution of burdens and benefits in the society."

For centuries together, women in India have been excluded from their rightful role in social, political, economic, educational and cultural spheres of activity; deprived from occupation of society's high and reputed positions; restrained from getting their equal share of wealth and power; prevented from developing their competitive abilities and skills on par with men in the society.

How can a developing country like India progress and prosper without inclusion or active participation of half of its population in social development?

The differences we conceive between a male and a female are just like any other difference between one individual and the other, with reference to their functional aspects such as ability, efficiency, capacity, capability and so on. The unequal treatment between a male and a female in most of the societies is not based on natural inequality existing between them. In fact, they are man-made inequities or socially induced inequalities, which exclude women from their rightful role in social participation. Therefore, to differentiate a male and a female on the basis of gender or gender-based functions and treat them unequally in the matters of their social functions is not morally justifiable. The moral law demands that all man-made social inequalities, which are unnecessary and unjustifiable, ought to be eliminated.

What is Political Participation?

Political participation does not mean merely exercising of political rights like franchise. It also means involvement of women in a wide range of political activities such as — membership in political parties, living contact and communication with political leaders and legislators, propagation of political ideas and programmes of the political parties among the electorate, extension of voluntary services to the people, contesting in elections, involvement in the decision-making bodies of the government and other related activities. These activities are very crucial because they provide an opportunity to the women to acquire the necessary political experience, knowledge, skills, and recognition, which are essential for public life.

FACTORS RESTRICTING PARTICIPATION OF WOMEN IN POLITICS

Traditional Thinking and Social Conditioning

The traditional gender based division of labour in the family mostly limits the activities of women to the generation of children, their care and nurture and household duties. The role of women, as a wife and as a mother, progressively confines her to the home and keeps her away from participation in the wider aspects of socio-political and economic fields. She is not having sufficient leisure time to contemplate on political issues and problems. These constraints are more or less common to all sections of women irrespective of their class or community.

Socialization of Children

Socialization is the process by which society prepares children for adulthood. We see much difference in the socialization process among the pre-adolescent boys and girls. The younger girls and boys, during the formative period of their life, learn societal values and norms as at home. In the socialization process, the older women and mother play an important role in our families. They usually aim to inculcate respect for traditional social norms, into the minds of the young.

Restrictions on Social Mobility

The restrictions imposed on movements of girls and their engagement in domestic work obstructs the girls' exposure to the outside world. In most of our families, the voice of a daughter counts less when compared to the son in matters of decision-making and this creates a sense of ineffectiveness in the minds of girls during their childhood. Even after marriage, she does not have much important role in decision-making in her in-laws' family. In many families, we find, a difference of treatment between sons and daughters in their day-to-day activities. The parents give less importance to the education of their daughters in comparison to their sons for various reasons. This type of biased or differential treatment between sons and daughters in a family, creates a sense of inferiority in the minds of girls and it has a great impact on the personality development.

Age Factor

Age is an important factor for women to participate actively in politics. The attitude of traditional thinking prevents entry of young and unmarried women in politics because they become an object of public attention. Women, in general, prefer to play a "two-role" function—the traditional house-wife-mother functions, and socio-political functions simultaneously. Many women believe that the ideal age for them to enter the political arena is 40, because the women of this age group are relatively free from gender responsibilities; mentally more matured and experienced; possibly less to the pitfalls of scandals and character assassination. The choice of political parties is also in favour of elderly women with less of familial responsibilities. The electorate is also having strong reservations to elect young and unmarried women.

Encouragement and Support of Family Members

Moral support of husband and other family members constitutes a crucial factor for the active participation of women in politics. The husband and other members of the family have to bear the prolonged absence of her at home due to her long hours of political activity and sometimes her preoccupation of legislative business, etc. In such a situation, they have to forego the services generally they expect from her.

Character Assassination and Criminalisation of Politics

Women's entry into politics is severally restrained by the contemporary political atmosphere in the country. Threats of political violence, criminalization of politics and character assassination are preventing women to enter into political arena in large numbers. Under these conditions, many men are reluctant to encourage their women to participate in politics. The unmarried educated girls are also not allowed by their parents to enter into politics or to hold any political post or position.

Financial Status

The financial status of women in the society is another impediment for women's participation in politics. Money plays an important role in politics. Most of the women in our society are neither economically independent nor having sufficient financial resources for active participation in politics. Because of high cost of electioneering, the choice of political parties, at the time of selection of candidates to contest in elections, is always in favour of women with good financial background.

Importance of Education

Illiteracy is another factor for non-participation of women in politics. An uneducated woman generally feels less self-confidence and less control over external environment. An educated woman feels politically more confidence and competent than a less educated women.

Purdah or Seclusion

Keeping woman in *purdah* or seclusion is also a notable factor, which hampers women's public life. It is an evil relic of a barbarous custom which imprisons the body and mind of many women and restricting their free movement in the society. For whatever purpose it might have had introduced in the beginning, it is doing great harm to the women and to the nation[1].

Freedom Struggle and Liberation of Indian Women

The freedom struggle under the leadership of Gandhi, and the legacy of freedom movement has brought a radical change in the status and position of women in India. Gandhi brought a dramatic change in the attitude of Indian women and at his bidding a large number of women came out of their homes to take part in the struggle for India's Independence.

1. The freedom movement provided an opportunity to the women to play an active role which includes—participation in processions and protests, shouting slogans, singing patriotic songs, facing lati-charges and police firing, courting arrest, going to jail, etc.
2. It contributed for the liberation of women by themselves from many inherited customs that enchained her and dragged her down.
3. It helped women to prove their organizational abilities, moral courage and intellectual capacities and potentialities.
4. It created political awareness among Indian women; minimized the inferiority complex developed in them ages together; and raised their dignity and status in the society.
5. The legacy of freedom struggle enabled women to achieve equal rights on par with men and these rights are guaranteed by the Constitution of India. All the political

leaders of freedom movement recognized the organizational abilities and intellectual competencies of the Indian women participated in freedom struggle and consequently many women held high positions like Governors, Chief Ministers, and Ambassadors in Independent India.

Referring to the participation of women in civil disobedience movement in 1930, Jawaharlal Nehru observed—

> "Most of us menflock were in prison. . . . our women came to the front and took charge of the struggle. . . . not only the British Government but by their own menflock by surprise . . . . It was not only that display of courage and daring, but what was even more surprising was the organized power they showed . . . . when news of this reached us, the enormous pride in the women of India that filled us. We could hardly talk about all this among ourselves, for our hearts were full and our eyes were dim with tears."[2]

Measures suggested for Improvement of Women's Participation in Politics

1. Education is an essential factor for an effective and meaningful participation of women in politics. It enables women to assert their rights, to exercise them wisely and to work for their liberation from all social evils and age-old customs. It provides political awareness, political commitment and involvement in political activities. It also makes them to act independently and take autonomous political and administrative decisions. Compulsory education up to high school level and free education to all girls up to degree course may be helpful to them.
2. The political parties can play a crucial role in motivation, training and involvement of women in political process.

They should motivate and attract more number of women into the party and allot a reasonable number of positions in the party organization at all levels. The political parties must evolve a policy, to allot a reasonable number of seats to women to contest in the elections at the State and national level.

3. The media, both print and electronic, can play a very potential role in bringing out the inherent qualities and potentialities of women. Because women are less mobile and less exposed to the contemporary problems and issues, media can act as educative as well as conscious-raising role among women. The media should give wider coverage to various activities of women, highlight their problems, and motivate them for an active participation in politics.
4. Economic independence makes women to feel more secured, more independent and freer. The rights of a wife in husband's property and daughter's right of inheritance along with the sons must be admitted. The government should bear the total electioneering expenses of women, contesting in elections on a party ticket.
5. The local bodies, like Panchayat Raj Institutions and Municipal Corporations, constitute as an important ground for political training to women. The 73rd and 74th constitutional amendments, which reserve one-third of the seats to women in local bodies, provides a good opportunity to women for direct participation in self-rule at the local level. These institutions help women as training grounds for the emergence of leadership.
6. As time is an important factor to woman to play a double role — domestic as well as political— husband and other family members should cooperate and share some of her burden in discharging her duties.
7. The women should be given proper representation in all decision-making bodies of the government. They should

have a rightful place in all important committees, commissions and delegations constituted by the government from time to time.

8. The women should actively participate in protests and demonstrations — against the evils like child marriages, dowry deaths, molestation of women, price-rise and other such related activities, which make them aware of the social problems and help them to develop leadership qualities.
9. The evil customs of child-marriages and *purdah* or seclusion can be curtailed through legislative measures or by the pressure of public opinion. Compulsory registration of marriages may check the evil practice of child-marriage to a considerable extent.

Conclusion

Women constitute more or less half the population of the Indian society. When compared to their population, it is true that the representation of women is quite less in the State Assemblies and Parliament. But the question is — how to enhance their representation?

In recent times, the government, after consulting many political parties, introduced a Bill in the Parliament to amend the Constitution to reserve one-third of the total number of seats to women in the State Assemblies and Parliament. This act of Government evoked a strong reaction among some people and political parties in India. Under these circumstances, we are compelled to contemplate on alternative measures available to enhance women's representation in the legislative bodies.

1. Is reservation of one-third of the seats in the legislative bodies, only alternative available to increase women's representation?
2. Can't we evolve some other method to enhance their number in the legislative bodies?

3. What are the alternative means and methods available and acceptable to the people as well as political parties?

Is women's claim for reservation of one-third of the seats in the legislative bodies through constitutional amendment morally justifiable? Is not reservation of seats to women, a violation of men's right to equality?

An important moral issue is involved in this question and one must respond to the question in a most convincing manner and establish the rightness of one-third reservation of seats to the women in the legislative bodies. The justification or unjustification of a policy depends upon the reasons that strengthen it.

For centuries together, women have been discriminated and as a consequence of past discrimination, they are in a most disadvantaged position to compete equally with men in different spheres of social life. The practice of discrimination against women in the past resulted in under representation of women at the higher levels of political institutions. The doctrine of compensatory justice states that the people belonging to victimized groups should be adequately compensated for the injustices done to them in the past. The principle of equality sought for a balanced distribution of political positions and power among the groups of the social system. Hence, women's claim for equal representation in legislative bodies and compensatory benefits seems to have a moral justification. It is the duty of the government to take necessary measures to rectify the injustices done to the women and ensure equal opportunity or equal access to most desirable positions competitively available from the society.

As an alternative to constitutional amendment to reserve one-third of the total number of seats to women in the legislative bodies, we may suggest other means, to enhance women's representation.

1. The first alternative suggests that — the Election Commission may amend its law and make it mandatory

to all recognized political parties to allot at least one-third of the total number of seats to the women that the parties contest to the State Assemblies and Parliament, considering each State as a unit. This kind of arrangement gives a better choice to the political parties to select suitable, active and efficient women members of their own party, belonging to different sections of the society.

2. The second alternative suggests that—the government may bring a constitutional amendment, as a temporary measure, to nominate women to the State Assemblies by the respective State Governors and to the Lok Sabha by the President of India, considering each State as a unit. After the completion of the election process, the Election Commission may provide data to the State Governors and the President of India concerning — (a) State-wise percentage of votes polled to each political party in the election, (b) the number of women candidates elected from each State, and (c) the number of deficit seats to be filled through nomination, to maintain at least one-third women members in the State Assemblies and Lok Sabha.

The political parties may submit their lists of women members to the State Assemblies to be nominated by the State Governors and to the Lok Sabha to the President of India. On the basis of the percentage of votes polled to each political party in the elections, the State Governors and the President of India proportionally nominate women members belonging to different political parties to the State Assemblies and the Lok Sabha. This kind of arrangement may be acceptable to the people as well as political parties, and also contribute to the enhancement of women's representation in the Legislative bodies.

The Constitution of India guarantees gender equality and a number of laws have been enacted from time to time to implement these guarantees. Many legislative measures have been taken by the government in the matter of inheritance of the property, employment, marriage, maternity benefits, crimes against women and so on. However, the equal rights legislation itself cannot ensure gender equality as long as majority of women do not claim or its entitlement.

We have to bring a change in the attitude of men and women, bring a change in their mindset or in the thinking process, through education or by the pressure of public opinion. Legal rights can never ensure social practice. Legislation by itself fails to offer a complete solution to the problems of women. Unless the women are politically conscious, and actively participate in large numbers in politics, it is neither good to them nor desirable to send them to legislative bodies, because they cannot function in an effective and meaningful way. The Indian women "have to free themselves from the tyranny of man-made customs and laws; they have to carry on this struggle by themselves."[3]

The government, the political parties, the public in general, and the family members in particular, should encourage and cooperate for an effective and meaningful participation of women in the political sphere.

REFERENCES

1. *Cf.* M.K. Gandhi, *Women and Social Injustice*, Ahmedabad, Navajivan Publishing House, 1942, p. 96.
2. Jawaharlal Nehru, *The Discovery of India*, Bombay, Asia Publishing House, 1974, pp. 41-42.
3. S. Gopal (Ed.), *Jawaharlal Nehru: An Anthology*, Calcutta, Oxford University Press, 1980, p. 247.

Chapter – 7

Feminist Ethics and its Concern

Asha Mukherjee

Feminism when takes reflective side of the movement takes the shape of understanding social reality of gender relations and tries to get rid of the patriarchal or male dominated culture. When feminists regard ending of sexual oppression and injustice as a moral imperative at the level of thought and practices it is called Feminist ethics. But it has a different logic from say Bio-medical ethics. It is possible to do ethics without being aware of the bio-medical issues of morality and it is not considered as a handicap. But, to study ethics without paying attention to feminism is certainly disadvantageous if not being handicap. The reason is this : it presupposes that we understand ourselves well enough as human beings — as *male* human beings. And this assumption is questioned by 'feminist ethics'. It does not modify ethics as medical, environmental or legal ethics do but it transforms *ethics.* It is about any kind of ethics. For feminist the experience of 'normal' female is the most important reality. "Feminism, in short, must construct an ethics which no longer relies on the concealment of power-relations but works actively to expose them" (p. 9 Introduction).

There is no unitary view of ethics that can be identified as "feminist ethics". Feminist approaches to ethics share a commitment to "rethinking ethics with a view to correcting whatever forms of male bias it may contain" (Alison M. Jaggar, "Feminist Ethics: Some Issues for The Nineties", *Journal of Social Philosophy*, 20, 1989, p. 91). While those who develop these approaches are "united by a shared project, they diverge widely in their views as to how this project is to be accomplished. Not all feminists agree that there are distinctive feminist virtues, values. Some are even skeptical regarding the traditional positive virtues such as willingness to nurture or an affinity with caring. Still, I think it is possible to get some important focal points evident in current feminist attempts to transform 'ethics' into 'feminist ethics'.

Feminism rejects *a priori* premise of male superiority. It argues that if women perceive the normative structures of ethical theory as inadequately grounded in their own experience, then the fault lies with the theory and not with the women. There is distinctive women's social experience, which is worthy of exploration. Feminist ethics has opened up a wealth of issues, which were on periphery such as issues of sexuality, the bodily self, moral connectedness, care, trust, friendship, mothering, nurturing, emotions, psychological fluidity and finitude, feminist thinkers about ethics have to discuss all this within the boundaries of socio-cultural reality. Thus, there is a kind of delicate balancing on the one hand the social reality of feminity which is a part of our own social being and on the other we must "avoid any naive celebration of 'feminine' characteristics which may be regarded as effects of oppression."

What features of 'normal' female experience are in question here? Within the phenomenon of gender difference the central is the contrasting relation of man and woman to the fact of embodiment. But, the proposition that moral autonomy is more difficult to women than men, or women cannot be full moral subjects, strikes most of us as self-evidently absurd. Women are obviously as capable as men of taking up the subjective viewpoint, of making moral judgements are, exercising will and controlling desire are. The adult women must all be competent of making life and death decisions about conception, birth, abortion, the care of the dying, etc. Yet there is massive contrast between male and female subjectivity in respect of the empirical conditions under which each is constructed. Male subjectivity enjoys the support of social institutions "which generate a sense of selfhood and personal importance and which do so — in part at least — by positioning women as the excluded 'other'" (M. Griffiths and M. Whitford (ed.), *Feminist Perspectives in Philosophy*, Macmillan, 1988, p.122). But, by contrast, men's absence from women's (traditional) grouping tends to be experienced, precisely, as an *absence.*

It might be pointed out that male selfhood is not really the ideal affairs just outlined. Men too, have to bow to contingencies, to choose and act within a complex social context always not of their own making. Why then are we presenting sex specific criticism of the ethical theories. We gladly accept that there is a kind of descriptive inadequacy in dominant models in relation to man and this is one of the points on which feminists are insisting. Moral and political theories have misunderstood not only *women's difference from men*, but also *men's difference from women*. They thought that men too are embodied and vulnerable; emotional and sexual life for them is a source of insecurity; and that they are caught up as women are, in social structures which they do not know how to alter.

Feminist theory is different from liberal theory not only in content but also in its outlook. It draws attention to certain defects of vision in liberalism, which result from its masculine bias. It calls into question the centre of the intellectual stage *he* who is pure and simple thinker, who is undisturbed by any of the perspective of his own (Critique of Rawls, 'Original Position'). Thus it is a male philosophical corpus.

Now the question arises how do the facts of gender affect the meaning for women of central ethical concepts such as rights, justice, duty, virtue, pleasure, guilt shame, etc.? Is it possible to sustain a 'normal' female identity while trying to conceive of one's own relation to other persons as suggested by liberal democratic thinkers? Thus 'otherness' becomes very important in Feminist Ethics. On the one hand, there is a rejection of "masculine" values as an ideal, "successful" man as role model, and on the other a refusal to be treated as *second sex.* There is dissatisfaction in the modern society over the formal 'equality' between man and woman. They have challenged the idea of "equality" which prevails in liberal theory as well as in feminism. Why to regard women's 'difference' or 'otherness' as a problem? Why should not a "different voice" formulate different truths and values, no less compelling than those of the dominant culture? (p. 13, Introduction).

The difference affirmation has also leads to many problems. The main risk remains, that we may be back with the same sort of qualities and roles, which has been the traditional male conservatives, have assigned. The other risk is of any idea of a universal "feminity" which would generate solidarity between women. Gender difference is central to our social experience, but it is only one of many systems of difference around which that experience is organized. Perhaps the most hopeful outcome of these difficult debates would be an appreciation that "otherness" extends beyond the phenomenon of gender, and a more generous conception of the ideal of *unity in difference.*

The other and most important question with which Feminist ethics is concerned. What would be of moral importance in post-patriarchal world? How the existing moral theories have to change if they are to follow our guidelines in constructing a new world order? To answer these questions many suggestions have been made. Non-contractual relations like between parent and child; of future-directed effort that is not an "investment"; of the possibility committed but non-possessive emotional experience; of reproductive freedom for women and banishing coercion; elusiveness of the sense of self. The important thing in implementing all this is that these are not "women's issues", if this implies a contrast with universal human issues. It is quite possible that women from their gender moral perspective succeed in finding out universal principle of the human frame.

It is often been suggested that in recent past a qualitatively new level of acceptance in the male world of business and government have emerged. This view is also questioned by the feminist ethics because it underestimates the continuing direct oppression of women by men. The real target of feminist critique has never been simply the empirical fact that various sorts of goods have been unequally distributed between sexes. Rather, it has been the very existence of the social system by which male and female individuals are assigned from birth to distinct classes whose identity is determined by their *relation to one another*—the relation of dominance in case of "men" and the relation of subordination in case of "women". This hierarchical relation cuts to the depth of our social being. It is just not a matter of time when the women's formal equality as citizens is achieved. We rather argue that gender difference—while it exists at all — must remain an object of suspicion, so that it ceases to exist and until this happens feminism cannot become redundant.

One may ask, at this stage, since the social fact of gender is the reality for feminism and subjectivity of specificity of experience is equally important, is it not possible that these experiences are conflicting? Or, to put it differently, can any way of negotiating social reality, any (every) way of interpreting our own sexual identity, in principle count as 'feminist'. The answer obviously is 'no'. Some patterns are objectively inconsistent—taking present social reality as given — with the deference of women's collective interest, consent to sexual abuse.

From a feminist point of view, moral theory along with almost all theories will have to be transformed to take adequate account of the experience of women. What are the fundamental aspects of the histories of ethics, which have not been gender-neutral? What are the issues where feminist rethinking is transforming moral concepts and theories? Let us try to answer these questions one by one.

The split between reason and emotion is one of the most familiar of philosophical conceptions. Reason has been associated with male endeavour and emotion with female weakness and of course this is not an accidental association. Maleness was aligned with active, determinate, and defining form; femaleness with mere passive, indeterminate, and inferior matter.[1] Feminist repeatedly show, if the concept of "human" were built on what we think about "woman" rather than what we think about "man", it would be very different concept. Ethics, thus, has not been a search for universal, or truly human guidance, but a gender-biased enterprise.

The other conceptual distinction between public/private as usually formulated, has been to privilege the point of view of men in the public domain of state and law, and later in the market place, and to discount the experience of women. Relegation of the private to the natural and the concept of the self as construed from a male point of view. Mothering has been conceptualized as a primary biological activity, even when performed by humans, and virtually no moral theory in the history of ethics has taken mothering, as experienced by women, seriously as a source of insight, until recently feminists have begun to.[2] Women were seen as emotional rather than rational beings, and thus were not granted full moral personhood. Women's behaviour was regarded as "natural" and driven by instinct and so was irrelevant to morality and moral principles. (It is worth noting that Rousseau, Kant, Hegel, all have ignored the reality of women, although they paid homage to the emotional power and aesthetic sensibility.) Annette Baier recently speculated about why it is that moral philosophy has so seriously overlooked the trust among human beings that in her view is an utterly central in moral life. She noted that "the great moral theorists in our tradition not only are men, they are mostly men who had minimal adult dealings with women."[3]

Now the question arises how to get away with this situation or how to change this traditional way of doing moral philosophy? To simply bring women into public and male domain of the polis will leave no one to speak for the household, will leave no one involved in the nurturence of children and cultivation of social relations. Nurturence and cultivation of social relations can be of greatest moral import. Therefore, there are very good reasons for women not to want simply to be accorded entry as equals into the enterprise of morality as so far developed. Women should certainly not agree, as the price of admission to the masculine realm of traditional morality, to abandon our own moral concerns as women. Although we do not have any feminist moral theory to offer as yet, we can suggest some directions to develop such theory. They may not be such "star" feminist moral theorists such as Rawls and Nozick as; we are in principal as feminists against self-presupposed star-centred male-dominated theory. "We experience it as a common labour, a common task".[4]

These are some of the questions about which everyone has to think for herself. All this is done as enquirer and not as 'expert'.

REFERENCES

1. Lloyed, G., *The Man of Reason: Male and Female in Western Philosophy,* University of Minnesota Press, 1984, p. 104.
2. Joyce Trebilcoe (ed.), *Mothering : Essays in Feminist Theory*, New Jersy: Rowman and Allanheld, 1984.
3. Annette Baier, "Trust and Anti-Trust", *Ethics*, 96 (1986), pp. 247-48.
4. Kathryn Morgan, "Women and Moral Madness" in *Science, Morality and Feminist Theory*, (ed.), Hanen and Nielsen, p. 223.

Chapter – 8

An Inquiry into the Ethic of Feminism and the Feminist Turn in Ethics

Sanjay Kumar

What is Feminism?

Philosophy has given and is still giving birth to progressive civilisations through various revolutions and reforms ignited by the intellectual exercises. Philosophy has been escorting humanity with unparallel exactitude and authenticity since time immemorial. Feminism is one of the modern upheavals in the philosophical domain with an atypical grit and perspicacity to eliminate male-biasness responsible for women's prosaic existence. Broadly speaking, feminism is an outcome of a cross-fertilisation of many ideologies rejuvenating in social, political and moral speculations. This movement promotes women's rights and issues, and seeks obliteration of gender inequalities, sexual objectification, patriarchy, stereotyping and institutionalised injustice. Feminism, essentially a brainchild of the West, morally militates against the dominated opinions, arrangements and institutions so as to create a better society. It faults everything that regards women as mean commodities. Women's unique individuality must be guaranteed social, economic, political and moral equality and justice along with self-respect and esteem.

Thus, feminism fulminates the poetic-justice so far apportioned to women by elite men, and thereby seeks complete abolition of entrenched discriminations and favouritism in the aeons of social history. It advocates women's autonomy over many issues, such as workplace and reproductive rights, and castigates specious arguments by traditional male-chauvinists. Since time began, women have been victims of sexist oppressions, be it cultural, social, political, economic or even linguistic. Stephanie Ross describes traumatic victimisation and marginalisation of women as, "A screw is hard and sharp; wood by contrast is soft and yielding; force is applied to make a screw penetrate wood; a screw can be unscrewed and reused but wood — whenever a screw has been embedded in it—is destroyed forever."[1] Traditional ethics and similar theories are Machiavellian and Androcentric, which tend to forget the above truth and relegate women to creepers. Feminism targets this dangerous evil concealing behind the beautiful bushes. Feminism is often accused to be a sexist philosophy. But it is not a sexist, rather it brawls against it. Feminism is not even gynaecocracy. It in an ideology, which promotes the equality of both sexes. We face a number of difficulties in defining feminism only because of its heterogeneity and also because of the fact that many thinkers, undoubtedly indulged in feminist works, do not identify themselves as feminists.

Feminism appears in many forms based on the individual prioritisation of certain issues. We shall succinctly deal with these forms. *Liberal feminism* wants to achieve freedom of voice and equality of opportunity through political and legal reforms, and not through sweeping measures. It maintains, with deep conviction, that women are able to conquer equality with their own actions without altering the structure of society. It does not instigate the women who are unobjectionably comfortable with traditional values. But, liberal feminists assert that there must be equal freedom and opportunity for those women who do not desire to live with traditional values and all kinds of codes. They will to free women from phallocentric cage to see through new horizons with the help of moderate measures. *Radical feminism*, unlike liberal feminism, dares to react drastically against penetrated and pernicious discriminatory practices against one half of the humanity, called women. It suggests overall reconstruction of the society since it believes that sexist oppression is an upshot of prejudiced authority and power structure. Few feminists, including Marcy Daly, argue that human society would be better off with dramatically fewer men. *Socialist feminism* is the Marxist interpretation of women's oppression. It encourages a paradigm shift in the social set-up. It opines that prostitution, domestic work, childcare, marriage and other institutionalised practices are diverse modes of exploitation of women by patriarchal system. *Black feminism* views sexism and racism closely interlinked. All the Black women have been victims of unethical racial discrimination and torture subjected to them since time immemorial by so-called superior races of the world. Elimination of sexist oppression should necessarily imply the abolition of racist oppression. Emancipation of black women is obligatory for universal uplift of the human society. Alice Walker used the term *womanism*, in her book *In Search of Our Mother's Garden: Womanist Prose*, to draw attention to the oppressions of black women caused by racism and classism. Womanism is rightly considered as an offshoot of black feminism. *Post-colonial feminism* expostulates the universalisation of women's experience by radical feminism and liberal feminism. It believes that the cultures influenced by colonialism are different, and should be handled as such. It cogently places gender oppression next to racial and class oppressions. *Post-structural feminism*, also called "French feminism", seeks multi-faceted explanation and eradication of exploitation and oppression by androcentric structure.

These various forms of feminism do not reflect a hiatus or schism among feminists. The spirit of feminism is inherently harmonious. There exists an enviable *esprit de corps* (deep loyalty) that unites the feminists against all challengers. The spirit asserts: A woman is not a woman. She is like a bonsai having all capabilities to grow into a big tree, but has been regrettably planted into a flower-pot. She is laden with infinite possibilities to transform the malicious structure of the society. She is not merely a creator and a preserver, rather an effervescent existence who can pave the path of enlightenment to humanity with her physical, intellectual and moral aptitudes. Feminism envisions women in this esteemed and valued form.

The Rise of the Feminist Movement

The irruption of feminist revolt became inevitable because of the subordinate status and accusatory remarks accorded to women since the inception of civilisations, in the name of security, religion, natural disposition and so on. Women's role and finesse directed towards achieving the prosperous progress of world have been by and large invalidated and flayed by the intelligentsia of every age. From every vantage, whether political, social, private, economic, moral or even linguistic, the validity of women's own interpretation of their experience and benefits has never been acknowledged in the gamut of sardonic views of androcentric thinkers and intellectuals.

History has witnessed the tumultuous and gory lives of women, who often became quarries of patriarchy, stereotyping, oppression, objectification, sexual-objectification, polygamy, gender-oppression and insane religious beliefs. Our heart-rending social codes incessantly underrated the significance and essence of women and labelled them as mere personal properties of men by doubting, surprisingly enough, whether women possess souls. Her pre-marital life was, and is, subservient to the parents and in post-marital life she acted as Stepford wife (irrationally obedient wife), and had to treat her husband as God and ignore his inexcusable sins, such as adultery and sadism, only because of the leviathanic social norms forbidding her to marry another as long as her spouse was alive. An old Bologna saying rightly describes the stigmatisation of women: "Woman is paradise for the body, purgatory for the soul, hell for the purse". And this world is not a completely distinct one. Still we can very often come across people who reiterate, in principle or in deed, this old adage.

Hopefully, three things alleviated the wounds of women, just like throwing somebody a bone, prior to the call for a paradigm shift by feminist movement: (a) Chivalry in the Middle Age eulogised the fair sex and contributed to the social equality of women to the detriment of their mesmerising beauty and hypnotising facade; (b) The social position of women was somewhat elevated during the period of the Reformation also, and (c) The Christianity significantly enhanced the honour of women by glorifying and insisting on monogamy with mutual love as the probable zenith of sexual union.

The East, often called the locus of the Enlightenment for humanity owing to its copious benevolent and emancipating religious messages, did not act on contrary to the West, and committed outrageous crimes, with same or even higher degree of alacrity, against the honorific sanctity of women. Ancient and medieval history of India is indelibly stained with incalculable and irreparable sins or offences executed on the bases of various dogmas and justifications. An orthodox Hindu woman was a fossilised embellishment for the house, especially for the bedroom, and an unpaid maid who never gainsaid the irrational and irredeemable commands of her foul-mouthed husband. Of late, the turmoil in the West for the women-oriented changes is bound to awake India and her women towards their inherent rights as capable individuals, on this planet called earth, and to alter their destined roles and duties by dint of an avalanche of calls and movements.

We know to our surprise, even in the twentyfirst century, that the women are experiencing highly unethical and unbridled violence, such as criminal violence (rape, abduction and murder), domestic violence (dowry deaths, wife-battery and sexual abuse) and social violence (female foeticide and eve-teasing). Implementation and enforcement of human rights and constitutional laws concerning the empowerment of women are just like a brave speech without action letting off useless steam.

No revolt is a product of an ephemeral and superficial languishment and wrath. The feminist revolt has assumed the present sense over a century, and has seen the unforgettable valour of a number of apostles slaving away all life for the furtherance of the cause of womanhood. John Stuart Mill (1806-1873), an audacious espouser of women rights, condemned legal subordination of women and vindicated their parity with men in his popular essay *The Subjection of Women* (1869). He bravely puts it as, "If, in addition to the physical suffering of bearing children and the whole responsibility of their care and education in early years, the wife undertakes the careful and economical application of the husband's earnings to the general comfort of the family, she takes not only her fair share, but usually the larger share, of the bodily and mental exertion required by their joint existence."[2] The period during and following Mary Wollstonecraft (1759-1797) was taking a note of feminist voices championing education for women. However, very soon women demystified the inefficiency of education against perpetual injustice of manmade laws and institutions, and took an oath to have a say in the councils of nations and attain equality before law, and not equality in function. Feminism, as an implicit movement, seems to be coeval with The Enlightenment with the thinkers such as Lady Mary Wortley Montagu and Marquis de Condocert, who backed women's education. The term *feminisme* was coined in 1837 by a socialist named Charles Fourier.

Feminism aims at the advancement of womanhood. But the very connotation and conception of advancement of humanity of women have been conceived differently by discrete blocs of feminism. A group, comprising Pankhurst and her associates, understands humanity of women in terms of their *political emancipation.* Other feminists, such as Swedish reformer, Ellen Key, take it in terms of complete 'freedom as mothers'. With others, it stands for selfish individualism seeking the furtherance of one's own interests as an asexual and non-maternal woman.

Few feminists, spearheaded by W. L. George, are champions of 'free love' as opposed to 'freedom of love' advocated by Ellen Key. As we all can easily foresee, W. L. George's advocacy shall inevitably lead to a chance eroticism of men and women where they can prefer to live in couples, obliterating the concept of wifehood. There is another hue of feminism, represented by Mrs. Charlotte Perkins Gilman, which down plays the sexual impulse as a primary issue in feminism and argues to achieve *complete economic freedom* for women that will consequently, and certainly, result in total destruction of home. Domestic tasks will be performed by trained professionals, such as chefs, maid-servants, baby-sitters and adroit nurses; and not by wives—traditional domestic workhorses.

A holistic approach to feminism cannot be possible unless we assimilate the different waves of feminist thoughts. The first-wave began in the late eighteenth century and lasted till early twentieth century. This wave primarily focused on legal issues, such as women's enfranchisement, women's rights to property and women's education. Mary Wollstonecraft, one of the earliest progenitors of feminism, wrote her magnum opus *A Vindication of the Rights of Women* (1793). Being a trail-blazer, she criticised many of the contemporary high-minded ideals of womanhood, including the view of Jean Jacques Rousseau (1712-1778) who, intoxicated with macho pride, advocated women's education only in order to make them pleasing to men, useful to men and conducive to be loved by men. She aired, with niceties, many arguments against Rousseau and the likes. First, she warns that if women are educated to be the ornaments to men, then at a point of time in the history, society shall have to bite the bullets. Second, she pleads that women are equally capable of attaining the so-called virile virtues of wisdom or rationality. And third, if women are designed and programmed to be the playthings of men, then they will have no inner resources to fall back on when men, bored and distracted of daily contact, skip them off once their charm fades. She puts her futuristic instinct as, "It is time to effect a revolution in female manners—time to restore to them their lost dignity— and make them, as a part of the human species, labour by reforming themselves to reform the world. It is time to separate unchangeable morals from local manners."[3]

She was not the sole exponent of feminist thought. Many utilitarian thinkers joined the battle against injustice and disparity. These thinkers, often called utopian philosophers, were inspired by the utilitarian principle—greatest happiness of the greatest number—preached by Jeremy Bentham (1748-1832) in his philosophical treatise *Introduction to the Principles of Morals and Legislation* (1789). Anna Doyle Wheeler (1765-1833), a utilitarian reformer, focused on most exploited, because unpaid, labour force involving women. She and William Thompson (1775-1833) collaborated on a famous essay (1825) stating that denial of rights to women is inconsistent with utilitarian principle—greatest happiness of the greatest number. Another tide supporting feminist wind in the utilitarian ocean was Harriet Taylor (1807-1858). She was a merchant's wife and was often known through her association with J. S. Mill. She shot many cogent arguments for women's suffrage and against discriminatory and unjust practices barring women from having voice in the government—which often victimises the fair sex.

The first-wave feminism produced many trend-setting effects regarding property rights and the right to vote. The passage of the Nineteenth Amendment to United States Constitution is one of such markable victories that rejuvenated the second-wave of feminism to conquer unaccomplished loftier ideals and goals. I must clarify here that the term first-wave was retroactively coined when few feminists preferred to call themselves second-wave of feminists.

The second-wave began in 1949 with the publication of *The Second Sex* by a sprightly lady Simone de Beauvoir (1908-1986). She says in her book, ". . . . woman has always been man's dependent, if not his slave; the two sexes have never shared the world in equality. And even today woman is heavily handicapped, though her situation is beginning to change. Almost nowhere is her legal status the same as man's, and frequently, it is much to her disadvantage. Even when her rights are legally recognized in the abstract, long-standing custom prevents their full expression in the mores. In economic sphere men and women can almost be said to make up two castes; other things being equal, the former hold the better jobs, get higher wages, and have more opportunity for success than their new competitors."[4] Unlike first-wave feminists who largely concentrated on the absolute rights, such as suffrage, second-wave feminists were concerned with the issues such as economic equality between the sexes, rights of female minority, inclusion of women in traditionally male dominated areas and obliteration of cultural and political discrimination and sexist structure of power. One thing, I completely agree, that makes the second-wave distinct is the recognition of lesbian women within the movement as legitimate and *bona fide* human beings, who claimed that heterosexual relationship automatically subordinated women, and the only true independence can come in lesbian relationship (Lesbian Separatism). Second-wave feminism is often linked with radical feminism, which we have already discussed.

Simone de Beauvoir, an unusually capable philosophiser, novelist and feminist, belonged to the traditions of existentialism and phenomenology, and focused on 'cultural and social' tools of exploitation as opposed to the first-wave feminists who descended from empiricist and utilitarian clans and concentrated on public world of laws. She, like other existentialists, immortalised her insights, concerning womanhood, from psychoanalytic and Marxist perspectives in her captivating work *The Second Sex* (1949), which became a fountainhead gushing inspiration for many feminists and commoners for decades. She analysed the concept of womanhood as the concept of *Otherness,* where women essentially find themselves as *Others*, alienated from all, even from themselves. She writes, "When man makes of woman the *Other*, he may, then, expect her to manifest deep-seated tendencies towards complicity. Thus, woman may fail to lay claim to the status of subject because she lacks definite resources, because she feels the necessary bond that ties her to man regardless of reciprocity, and because she is often very well pleased with her role as the *Other*."[5] She says that "one is not born, but rather becomes, a woman", because of a womanhood imposed by the civilisation. Vitriolic responses from many critics could not check her inexorable march to restore women their praiseworthy value. Post-1960 period enjoyed audacity of radical feminists and many classic works, comprising Robin Morgan's *Sisterhood is Powerful* (1970) and *Sexual Politics* (1970) by Kate Millett. Gloria Steinem brought the feminist movement to the notice of masses through her various articles. Millett and Steinem began a rancorous battle to ravage the ramshackle androcentric practices and to realistically reappraise the women's experience and uniqueness. Shulamith Firestone's *The Dialectic of Sex* (1970) demonstrates that the subordinate status of women is essentially social and political in nature, and not at all biological. The second-wave feminists are still active, but few feminists identify themselves as members of the third-wave feminism, which began in 1990s as a response to perceived failures of second-wavers to recognise the true importance of insectionality. This wave is all-inclusive and incorporates post-colonialism, critical theory, transnationalism and post-structuralist interpretation of gender and sexuality. It grew out of a deep conviction that the second-wave feminism over-emphasised the experience and views of upper middle class white women in the western countries and mistakenly glorified them as icons or representatives of the universal womanhood.

It may be the source of evil effects, but it has admirably contributed to the development of morality by instigating women, victims of noxious and inhumane practices, to their rights as moral personalities. Feminism, with all its inextricably interwoven waves, is like a beacon shining in the midst of obscurity. The rest is up to us to draw wisdom from this inexhaustible didactic reservoir.

What is an Ethical Inquiry ?

Ethics or moral philosophy is a branch of philosophy which deals with morality, moral problems and moral judgements. The term 'moral' is derived from the Latin word '*mores*' – meaning customs or habits; and 'ethics' is derived from the Greek word '*ethos*'— meaning customs. Then, ethics etymologically means a study of values, customs or conduct. It is all about moral judgements, their nature and applicability. Cautiously, we often say an action or motive "morally good" just to indicate that "good" can be used in non-moral value judgements also. The work of ethics can be conventionally categorised into three primary areas as per the tasks that it performs. These three areas of work are — normative ethics, meta-ethics and applied or practical ethics. We must have a short discussion to clarify the different tasks undertaken by them.

Normative ethics studies the norms, ideals, principles or standards which help in labelling something or somebody as good (if it conforms to a norm), bad (if it does not), right, wrong, virtuous, etc. Voluntary or willed and habitual actions are the objects of moral judgements, and are judged by looking into their motives and their consequences. The tasks of normative ethics comprise discussions on the good conduct and good habits that a moral agent should inculcate, the duties ought to be followed or the ramifications of our actions. The normative ethics that focuses on nature and execution of duties is called deontological ethics, i.e. Kantian ethics. Kant asserts that actions which are inspired by any sort of human emotions or feelings are undeniably immoral and do not have any morally praiseworthy value. Nevertheless, this Kantian doctrine is disapproved by feminist thinkers because they are hell-bent to book a morally honourable place for human emotions, like love, care, empathy, etc. And the normative ethicists who value the consequences of our actions on us or on others are called teleological ethicists. Utilitarians, Jeremy Bentham and J. S. Mill are noted normative ethicists. Richard B. Brandt, in his work *Ethical Theory*, argues that the touted general norms or first principles of morality, such as teleology and deontology, need not be taken as final because we may conceive of other norms of morality which are on face-value non-moral, for example, social, political and economic standards or norms for evaluating what is *good* or worthwhile morally. Another debate in normative ethics is about anti-normative or anti-theoretic stance taken by the virtue ethicists, who claim precedence of virtues than norms because the principle-adherence of say "duty" is preceded by the virtue of "dutifulness". However, others (*cf.* W. K. Frankena, *Ethics*) say that virtue ethics need not be anti-principlistic because the assumed precedence of virtues is in fact corrected by the normative asking that an idea of dutifulness, for instance, begs a norm that justifies the said virtue to be a virtue in reality.

Metaethics studies the nature and meaning of moral language and analyses the ethical discussion and verifiability of moral standards or ideals. It unravels the mystery that when somebody utters "X is good", then: What is the meaning of "good"? On the bases of various theories, it explains the meaning and connotation of value-laden normative terms. There are two main strands of thoughts in metaethics, *i.e.* cognitivism or realism and non-cognitivism or non-realism. Cognitivism acquires descriptive and informative nature wherein it declares that moral judgements are independent of moral agent's feelings. It regards all moral judgements or moral utterances as independently true and cognitively verifiable. David Hume, Bertrand Russell, Jeremy Bentham, Mill, John Searl, G. E. Moore and W.D. Ross are some of its steadfast upholders. It is divided into two main categories—naturalism and non-naturalism. Nevertheless, naturalism may further be divided into subjectivism, objectivism and neo-naturalism. On the other hand, non-cognitivism takes non-descriptive, non-informative and prescriptive nature wherein it claims that moral discussions are dependent on moral agent's feelings or emotions. It treats all ethical judgements or utterances as cognitively non-verifiable and non-factual, because they express feelings of the speakers. In lieu of the cognitive verifiability, it talks of non-cognitive verifiability of moral expressions. Moritz Schlick (1873-1958), A. J. Ayer (1910-1989), C. L. Stevenson (1908-1979), R. M. Hare (1919-2002) and Nowell

Smith are some of its stalwart espousers. Non-cognitivism splits into three forms—emotivism, prescriptivism and functionalism.

Applied ethics is a discipline of ethics that explores the possible use of our common ethical knowledge in society for moral progress of human and non-human existence. Applied ethics relates ethics to almost all domains of human activities. Ethics in politics and economics, for instance, interprets applicability of our moral knowledge in political and economic value-laden cases to resolve them, and to demarcate a line between ethical and unethical actions of people related to politics and economics. Environmental ethics seeks just, affectionate and sustainable exploitation of natural resources. Professional ethics reflects on a range of professions, such as education, medicine, journalism and so on to resolve their value-laden cases. Each branch of applied ethics deals with the issues in formulation and regulation of moral codes in that profession, and exposes its responsibilities towards human and non-human entities. Moving forward, ethics in health care encompasses medicine, nursing, pharmacy, genetics and other allied health professions. Likewise, there is a wing of applied ethics called ethics in psychology, which studies how moral behaviour is possible by moral reasoning through different stages of moral development. These fields of ethics will be discussed later from feminist perspective.

Freedom is the human disposition to act or not to act by choosing from various alternatives without any external restraints. This moral autonomy is called 'freedom of will', which is an essential presupposition or postulate of morality. And unless freedom is granted to women, normative ethicists cannot club their actions into moral or immoral categories. Feminist ethics crusades against the flawed and erroneous male-biasness primarily in normative ethics and applied ethics on the whole. It rightly discerns that the ears of traditional ethicists, oriental or occidental, have been attuned to male, and not to female voices. However, we cannot close the eyes to its tentative say in meta-ethics also. We must observe here that lines of distinction between normative ethics, metaethics and applied ethics are often shadowy, and there is no absolute trichotomy among them. For instance, the issue of "euthanasia" can be viewed as an applied ethical topic because it involves a particular type of value-laden behaviour awaiting practical resolution, and also as a normative ethical issue since it may depend on a general principle, say the right to self-regard. This issue can form a relationship with meta-ethics because it is directly related to a number of meta-ethical questions, such as, "Where does a right come from?"

The Ethic of Feminism

Feminism has been often discussed in the light of ethics by some thinkers. The Ethic of feminism is thus seeking ethical justification of feminism, which has got an important berth in modern feminist philosophy to sanction moral foundation to feminism. It is generally conceived that there are four morally justified conceptions underlying this feminist revolt. These are *freedom*, *independence*, *labour* and *individuality*.

Evaluation of the concept o*f liberty,* an offshoot of individualism, is one of the ways to establish feminism as a just movement. It should be made clear here that the terms freedom and liberty are interchangeably used in different disciplines. However, socialist thinkers prefer to use freedom. We all know and thoughtfully agree that liberty is inherently good and ethically desirable. English feminists pay attention to this basic ideal and interpret liberty as "freedom from all external constraints". Few philosophers of Hegelian tradition do not hail the concept of women freedom, only because of their obsession with andocentric thoughts. But, renowned English utilitarian thinkers, John Stuart Mill (*On Liberty*) and Bertrand Russell (*Roads to Freedom*) support women's freedom from all constraints, which immorally corrode their welfare. Here, the connotation of constraints is incomprehensible. If individuals are given absolute liberty, then they may treat it as a licence to ignore the feelings and needs of neighbours and society, and violation of feelings and rights of others will leave behind an unethical order in the society.

Therefore, the need for external constraints may arise, be it political, social, economic or moral. Even J.S. Mill advocates the intervention of state in regulating marriage and enforcing compulsory education. Here, may appear an apparent dichotomy between state and liberty. But, it is certainly not the case. There is no inherent conflict in their coexistence. Liberty is ethical in nature and it must be interpreted in terms of only moral actions. There is no use of freedom outside the domain of morality. And state, if not mistakenly understood, is endorsing liberty, necessary for the wholesome development of human race, of course, including women. Feminists and some other thinkers support the ideal state whose laws are gender-neutral and conducive to women welfare too.

As women are essentially moral personalities, so they must enjoy liberty. They, like men, can take, using their freedom of will, equally efficient decisions — social, economic, political, matrimonial and sexual. The degraded status of women has had in the past open legal sanctions, but now it is inconsistent with the new streams of ideas running in veins of observant women. In fact, feminists do not demonstrate that women will be sole rule framers in the society; rather they want to foster the milieu where even women have equal participation in decision-making process in every realm of human activities.

The concept of *independence* is closely associated with the concept of liberty and both share ancestry with individualism. Idealism, unlike individualism, treats things as concrete wholes, where part insignificantly depends on its whole. And the whole is always greater than the part. Individualism, like metaphysical realism, considers everything as existing in itself and for itself. Something, say an individual, can have relations with others but its distinct tenets remain unaffected for keeps. As per this view, an individual is an end, while state is only means to fulfil the interests of individual and check all sorts of encroachment on his liberty. State is a necessary evil; evil in the sense that it acts as a hindrance in the liberty of the individual, and necessary because in its absence an individual cannot achieve perfect and undisturbed liberty. This individualism is also known as *laissez faire* system from economic point of view. J. S. Mill, an exponent of liberty, holds that a man is sovereign over his body, mind and soul. Unlike him, the upholders of 'organic theory' of state, from Plato to Hegel, are criticised for the fact that this theory hatches up the seeds of 'totalitarianism'. And this criticism is quite germane. Hegel, glorifying state, asserts that state is the march of God on the earth; and state is the actualisation of concrete freedom.

Feminists find, in individualistic regime, a full-fledged vindication of their campaign against the monstrous and insidious social practices, which engulf the independence and liberty of women. The very idea of dependence is anti-individualist and if women want, as they do, independence in all respect, whether political, social, economical and moral, then there must not be any uproar over their genuine demands. Why should she look helplessly and pleadingly towards her husband to meet her monetary needs? Why cannot she choose her own spouse? Why cannot she be a bread-winner as opposed to home-maker? There cannot be any truly justifiable answers to these questions and the likes. And if women rebel against these inhuman codes or norms then, what is unethical in it? This inalienable independence should not be taken in its absolute sense. When feminists evince that women must be independent, it only entails that they want to be mutually, and not absolutely, dependent. For instance, in domestic affairs they should not be assigned an unalterably dependent role as home-makers, who never sense economic independence and freedom. Rather, a woman, as per her disposition, can be a bread-winner, can elect her spouse, can decide on a number of moral issues and can interdependently guide humanity towards prosperity and tranquillity.

Labour is the third inherent aspect of justification of ethicality of feminism. We need to contemplate over it. First of all, we must acknowledge that labour, physical or intellectual, done by women is essentially dedicated to the uplift of the entire humanity. And there is no unethicality involved in it. The origin and nature of sex-wise compartmentalisation of labour have been minutely discussed by many feminists, especially by Marxist and socialist feminists, including Friedrich Engels in *The Origin of the Family, Private Property and the State* (1884). Women's image has been revolving around the domestic works. That is why the denial of or diversion from the traditional image by modern women does not get ethical sanction. In these evilly and slyly designed male-biased social orders, women's work is often belittled and treated as farcical. According to this vainglorious set-up, women's labour is the labour from labour room to kitchen and back to the bedroom. Women's taxing household task remains by and large unrewarded. Women are not considered to be active contributors in the development of society. Susan Moller Okin delineates the condition of women as, "Central to this socially created inequality are two commonly made but inconsistent presumptions: that women are primarily responsible for the rearing of children; and that serious and committed members of workforce (regardless of class) do not have primary responsibility, or even shared responsibility, for the rearing of children. The old assumption of the workplace, still implicit, is that workers have wives at home."[6] Feminists demand liberty for women regarding choosing any work outside domestic realm. They refuse to be home-makers for ever and bread-winners for never. Traditions regarded women as natural mothers. Well, feminists justify this task with honour. But the vital question is: Cannot women contribute something, apart from fostering the races, to the society? Its obvious answer should be affirmative.

Many thinkers consider women as physically inferior and vulnerable. Even Aristotle avers that women possess biological and natural defectiveness. Feminists accept the natural truism that women are physiologically different from men. But, being different is not being defective. The physiological difference between men and women is analogous to the difference between fins and feathers. Fins can and should never be considered defective only because they do not assist in flying or gliding. Similarly, women are physiologically distinct. This difference is honourably unique, and must not be termed as defective. One might argue that women are physically weak and fragile, and cannot perform virile works. Even, this view is not flawless. Perhaps, the humanity has forgotten the intolerable physical labour involved in the throes of childbirth! This is the yardstick for their physical strength. It is high time for both commoners and law-framers to recognise the work of women as priceless and incredible. Her value is well articulated by Solomon as: "her price is above rubies, for she looketh well to the ways of her household and eateth not the bread of idleness."

The concept of *individuality* has been undisputedly the highest ideal of morality. Human individuality or personality and immaculate character have paved ways for the progress of dynamic civilisations. Every human being in nature is physically and intellectually unique, and the development of her/his personality lies in the realisation of the inimitable and spectacular potential of soul and body. It is an obvious verity of affluent nature, that its every stage of evolution is unrepeatedly variegated and worthy. Every person should march towards his/her perfect, complete and multifaceted well-being. Human individuality cannot be confined merely to the one half of mankind, called male. So, it becomes an inviolable right of female to develop themselves fully. She is as much entitled to it as her male counterparts. This logic of individuality is thoroughly noticed and analysed by the feminists. They assert that as men are free to choose their sphere of activities, so are women. Why should women be held as hostages within the walls by the male hooligans? There cannot be any legitimately convincing response to it. It is a gaffe to take discriminatory and brutal measures against fair sex. To buttress their supercilious attitudes with verisimilitude, few men argue that the personality of women can develop even within the walls too. Feminists find it rather ridiculous and inexplicable. They object this view and question: If women can develop her personality at home, why cannot men? Moral chauvinists face a fusillade of such unanswerable objections from fervent feminists.

Women are physically, mentally and morally as potent, even more, as their spouses, brothers or colleagues. Morally, they are the founders of *philosophy of care,* which is guiding substantially in the different fields of applied ethics. Development of all aspects of personality is impossible within the restricted ambiance of house. Women can enhance their individuality by joining social, national, international and even cosmological communities. Conservationists, as bystanders, opine in favour of channelling women's potential in certain direction. We understand this euphemistic opinion very well. To channel women's potential means, as it is traditionally conceived, to make them tools of procreation and corporeal needs. And if, at all, channelling the natural disposition is ethically permissible, then: Why cannot men's potential be channelled to make them all wrestlers, samurais or warriors? In a nutshell, a woman with all probabilities is moral personality and realisation of quintessential individuality is a must for her holistic well-being. Feminism is a self-evidently just movement and it does not need any feminist lore and furore for its justification. Philosophy, including ethics, has been inclined towards male-biasness and divorced from gender-neutrality. Feminists emphasise on rather distinct issues than those embedded in the traditional standard philosophy and ethics in order to take a meticulous account of women's experience and needs. Their move is ethically desirable in the interests of entire humanity.

The Feminist Turn in Ethics

Feminist ethicists have recently reconceptualised the standard or traditional moral theory to free ethics from androcentrism and macho attitudes. Feminist moral theory shapes itself with the help of numerous researches and developments undertaken by various ethicists and psychologists. It urges moralists to rethink and correct all kinds of inconsistencies evolved as off springs of male-biasness, by re-examining and deploring the patriarchal attitudes gushing out from philosophy as a whole and moral theory in particular.

Before we proceed to the feminist account of moral theory, we must have a glimpse of historical evolution of ethical thoughts and attitudes. Since time immemorial, reason and clarity of thought have been associated with male sex, and emotion and irrationality with female sex. Women have been deemed analogous to the nature and earth. And with gliding time, when *form-matter* distinction was articulated in philosophy, maleness was intentionally aligned with active, essential and defining *form*; and femaleness was deliberately associated with passive, unessential and inferior *matter*. Significance-wise, the *form* matters and the *matter* does not. Apparently, the very nature of all sorts of knowledge was implicitly confined to maleness only. It is quite exoteric fact to understand that only men would constitute intelligentsia and frame all sorts to rules. Second and equally noticeable matter is the distinction between the public and the private domains of activities. In the public realm, men create history, frame all sorts of laws and codes and safeguard society by transcending their animal nature; while women in private sphere of activities serve the fundamental and procreative needs. Therefore, this distinction positively contributed to men and reduced women to mere biological and emotional beings incapable of moral expressions. To our surprise, the so-called majestic philosophers, like Rousseau, Kant and Hegel, paid homage to women's emotions and familial concerns, but excluded women from the club of moral codes framers only because they lean to emotional and contextual elements of human activities, and not to rationality.

To form a wholesome approach to feminist ethics, it is essential to elaborate the above mentioned points and some more, if required. Let us start with dichotomy between reason and emotion. Two chief modern moral theories based on reason have tried to form and establish abstract and universal principles as the appropriate source of moral guidance. One is Kantian moral theory, which eloquently speaks of very general, abstract, deontological and universal moral principles, i.e. Kant's moral imperatives, and considers rationality or practical reason as the sole source of moral guidance. Very similarly, utilitarianism suggests rules of rational choice for maximisation of the happiness or satisfaction. Feminists aver that applying an abstract principle to particular cases and jettisoning the emotional responses in morality cannot be acceptable. These two theories and the likes are a ploy to disparage the experience and concern of women. And a genuinely universal and gender-neutral moral theory must not overlook the interests of women and the role of emotion in morality. Women very often prefer to value feelings of empathy and care in a particular context in which a moral problem emerges. Even the work of psychologists, such as Carol Gilligan *In a Different Voice* (1982), reveals that women tend to preserve actual human relationship and *care* while interpreting moral problems. This is the point where *'ethic of care'* deserves the due importance.

Feminists do have a number of empirical instances where authenticity of abstract principles as litmus test for morality is easily challengeable. In any case, feminist philosophers are in the process of re-evaluating the place of emotions in the moral judgements. Many think that morality requires the development of the moral emotions too. Annette Bair, in *Science, Morality and Feminist Theory*, vehemently discusses how abstract moral theory will be challenged if we pay attention to the roles of parents and other relationships, because these need the cultivation of desirable emotions, i.e. love, and not just rational insight. The feeling of love between a mother and a daughter cannot be excluded from morality only because of the fact that it does not involve some sort of highly rational principles. To be seriously noted here, the ethics which regards these forms of emotions as value-neutral, non-moral or immoral should immediately redefine its nature, objectives and tasks, because motherly and friendly feelings should have moral worth. Apart from the ethical desirability of emotions, they are useful in gaining moral understanding. Virginia Held, in her paper "Feminist Transformation of Moral Theory" rightly depicts the status of emotions by saying that "emotion will be respected rather than undermined by many feminist moral thinkers in the process of gaining moral understanding." She further adds that the experience and practice out of which feminist moral theory can be expected to be developed will include embodied feeling as well as thought. The caring relationship, essential to feminist morality, cannot be conceived in terms of abstract doctrines. Feminists demonstrate that achieving and maintaining a faithful and caring relationship can be different from acting in accord with rational principles. Since rational and abstract moral theory has miserably failed, at least in many practical cases, if not in all, feminists are rather optimistic that care, empathy and feeling towards others may be a better guide to what morality requires in actual contexts. Feminist ethics is often criticised as "relativistic situation ethics". But this criticism is like a sandcastle, as it forgets that some feelings can be as widely shared as rational beliefs. Nevertheless, feminist re-evaluation of emotion and reason requires to be further developed, but we can already notice that the views of non-feminist moral theory are severely untenable.

Coming to the traditional distinction between public and private realms, feminists revolt against the deep association of public realm, distinctively human realm, with man where he transcends his animal nature; while private realm, natural region, with woman where she merely reproduces the species. This association, implicit or explicit, is venomously pervaded in standard concepts and theories, especially in politics. Dominant pattern of thoughts have portrayed women primarily as mothers, and mothering as an essentially biological function which is analogous to the work done by other animals of the nature. Men engage themselves in political life, often called the truly human life. Virginia Held describes that "man creates government and law, and protects society by his willingness to risk death". In the household, it has been supposed that women merely "reproduce" life as mere natural and biological matter. And in this way, women are unavoidably excluded from the domain of public life. One thing must be clarified here, and elsewhere, that standard theory wrongly conceives essentially non-biological functions as biological ones. The functions which involve biological organs to be executed are not mere biological. Had it been so, then every human activity would be biological. Nursing and caring a baby is not a biological act, rather it is cultural and human. The act of human mothering, a non-biological function, is undoubtedly creative and entirely distinct from animal-mothering, because it shapes language and culture, and fosters progressive society and morality. It is the mother's care and love that creates a spiritual and moral human being out of bone and flesh. And this mom's act is not biological, not at all. A mother's task is not confined to private realm since it creates creative and morally capable individuals. Childcare should and must be at the centre of social, political, economic and moral thoughts, and never at the fringe. Thus, a reconceptualisation is necessitated to frame an ideal and probable model of human relationship and moral theory.

Apart from earlier mentioned two distinctions, feminist moral theory strives to review the concept of self also as embedded in standard moral theory. The concept of self as ego or as individualistic self cannot justify our ties with others, i.e. between mother and child, because it has been designed to maximise the satisfaction of an individual self. Our moral union with other members of the society cannot be analysed into individual gain or loss. Contrary to it, the universalistic concept of self grounded in "what would be right for all rational beings"? cannot satisfactorily and morally explain the particular context of moral activity. An all-inclusive ethics, as feminist ethicists conceive, should take the middle way to solve the problems arising out of individual self-interests and universal rules. Jean Banker Miller's work *Toward A New Psychology of Women* (1976) and Nancy Chodorow's book *The Reproduction of Mothering: Psychoanalysis and the Sociology of Gender* (1978) have substantially influenced the works done at Wellesley College, Massachusetts, USA, on a self-in-relation theory to establish how the female self develops.

Feminism has given a distinctive turn to our ethical thinking by showing that normativism needs a shake-up of that means monolithic norms like teleology and deontology are taken to be sacrosanct and omnipotent in an ethical or value related matters to find out ways out of crucial matters. Feminism objects to the application of any sacred norm unilaterally by ethicists to resolve our practical value-laden problems. It objects to the normative chauvinism made popular through the ages by a number of monistic normativists. This is not exactly same anti-theory stance of the virtue ethicists of early period such as Ms. Anscombe. Feminism, on the other hand, allows a thorough critique of normative monism and artificiality of normative chauvinism because inherent in such conceptions and practices are domination of overreacting theories and the tendency to crush the spirit of *care* for common ethical experience and knowledge in moral evaluation, moral resolution and decision-making. Feminism is a lesson for androcentric normative thinking that is "power-tracking" of professional ethicists — best understood as sophistical and casuistic power-tracking. Looking at the misconceptions buried in the standard moral theory, feminists are reconceptualising the standard or traditional moral theory. Carol Gilligan, a psychologist-*cum*-researcher on moral development of people, concludes in her popular book *In a Different Voice* (1982) that the development and reasoning of morality of women are characteristically different from that of men. Women concentrate on care and personal relationship in their moral deliberations, and not on abstract or general rights and justice. They express their understanding of moral problems through knowing the context and situation in which a moral dilemma arises. They interpret their moral responsibilities in terms of context and care for others. Gilligan observes that men and women cannot score equally on same moral development scale. Her view was highly inspired by the foresightedness of Nancy Chodorow, a psychoanalyst. Chodorow states that all sorts of metal and behavioural differences between men and women can be traced back to the child-fostering practices and psychodynamics at home. Nel Noddings, an apostle of 'ethics of care', suggests the reshaping of non-feminist moral theory in her work *Caring A Feminist Approach to Ethics and Moral Education* (1984). The concept of justice, central to ethics, is being rediscussed and redefined by many feminists. Susan Moller Okin, in her eye-opening work *Justice, Gender and the Family* (1989), exposes from feminist platform the inconsistencies embedded in many contemporary views on justice. The theories of John Rawls (1921-2002), Robert Nozick (1938-2002), MacIntyre and the likes are literally gender-biased and blind to female gender. Kate Millet and Okin crucify Rawl's theory of justice because it skirts the issue of female gender. Rawl, in his book *A Theory of Justice* (1971), has always used male references in lieu of gender-neutral references. The individuals described by him are only male members of society. It will not be wrong if we consider Rawl as the upholder of patriarchy. Like other patriarchal thinkers, Rawl also distinguishes between public and private domains, and believes that all political, not domestic, ideals, including the ideal of justice, come within public domain. And Rawl's "veil of ignorance", necessary to attain "original position" (a highly hypothetical position), ignores even sex of individual, which is an important aspect of justice. This is overwhelmingly challenged by feminist moral thinkers. Okin resolutely opposes the paradoxical "entitlement concept of social justice" by Nozick, a libertarian thinker, mentioned in his book *Anarchy, State and Utopia* (1974). Nozick maintains that a person justly owns whatever he or she produces or acquires through his or her endeavour and potential. It is very clearly reflecting from this view that women must own those they produce, i.e. human species. And if women are entitled to own what they produce, this will violate person's right on himself. So, his view is unable to explain or short out this problem.

The feminist turn in practical ethics may be traced in environmental ethics. Environmental ethics is meant for the analysis of ethical inquiries into human use of non-renewable and renewable sources or treasures of nature. It also comments on a desirable pre- and post-management of environmental hazards and ecological maladies. These crises and maladies, and their remedies, have been philosophically and ethically interpreted from various perspectives. Anthropocentrism relies on pure rational doctrines and places humans at the centre and non-humans at the periphery. But ecofeminism, feminist interpretation of environmental ethics, traces the root cause of these crises to patriarchalism. It always demonstrates that the exploitation and oppression of women and nature are inseparably linked. Ecofeminism has been supported by Val Plumwood, Karen J. Warren, Sallie McFague and Carolyn Merchant. Warren writes, "A responsible environmental ethic also *must* embrace feminism. Otherwise, even the seemingly most revolutionary, liberational, and holistic ecological ethic will fail to take seriously the interconnected dominations of nature and women that are so much a part of the historical legacy and conceptual framework that sanctions the exploitation of non-human nature. Failure to make visible these interconnected, twin dominations results in an inaccurate account of how it is that nature has been and continues to be dominated and exploited and produces an environmental ethic that lacks the depth necessary to be truly *inclusive* of the realities of persons who at least in dominant Western culture have been intimately tied with that exploitation, viz. women."[7] As women are inalienably dynamic constituents of environment, so their incisive wit cannot be overlooked in the course of discussing environmental issues. Ecofeminists are obdurate in their determination to become a rallying point for creating an environment conducive to wholesome welfare. Environmental ethics is also involved in the issues pertaining to the intrinsic values and rights to be given to different non-human entities of environment. It deals with the questions, like "What entities have moral worth?", "Do animals and plants have rights and interests?", "What all does an entity need to be entitled for moral standing?" and so on. Before we move to a detailed discourse on ecofeminism, let us clarify few terms used in environmental ethics.

Ecology is the scientific study of the interrelationships of organisms with each other and with the environment, biotic or abiotic. Ecosystem, an ecological concept, means that organism and environment are one interacting unit. F.R. Fosberg states that it is functioning and interacting system composed of one or more living organism and their effective environment, in a biological, chemical and physical sense, and is a concept applicable at any scale ranging from the planet earth as an ecosystem down to the smallest patch of moss and lichen on a rock surface. Environment refers to the sum total of the conditions within which an organism lives. Its factors, biotic, climatic, edaphic, etc., act collectively and simultaneously in a holocoenotic way, so that the action of anyone factor may be qualified by the others. Environment especially means natural environment, built environment, marine environment, continental environment, lagoonal environment, etc.

Now we shall first see the deep-rooted causes of inferiorisation and domination of women and nature, then a more feasible solution to these injustices and crises from feminist perspective. Val Plumwood expresses an in-depth analysis of devaluation of women and nature in her essay *Nature, Self, and Gender: Feminism, Environment Philosophy, and the Critique of Rationalism* (1991). Rationalism is flooded with dualistic concepts, such as reason-emotion, mind-body, enjoyer-enjoyable and masculine-feminine. Mind is superior to body and is an essential element of human self. It takes higher position as knower, enjoyer and regulator of non-mind or body. Body, doing biological and animal functions, is considered to be of lesser significance. This body incorporated the nature, i.e. the natural environment. Masculine is connected with the mind and rationality; and feminine with body or nature. Similar to nourishing nature, feminine owns traits like emotion, love, care, empathy, etc. It is transparent here that mind, male and reason rest on one platform; and body, female, nature and emotion on the opposite and inferior platform. Female sex and nature are bound to occupy subordinate status at the periphery of existential circle. Plumwood maintains that both feminism and environment philosophy are repairing the flaws committed by rationalistic culture. Another ancestry of this inferiorisation and degradation is the individualist conception of human self. As per it, an individual should be autonomous and at the centre of our speculation. An individual can and should enjoy others, including humans and non-humans, for its own egoistic and myopic well-being. This concept, like rationalism, drags nature to the periphery. In addition to ecofeminists, theologicians, liberal feminist geographers and post-modern geographical thinkers deeply regret the sexist, patriarchal and phallocentric practices; and advocate the inclusion of women in policy and codes framing for the resolution of various problems, including environmental ones.

Now it is well known to us that ecofeminism, promoting an all-inclusive development of entire existence, squarely rejects the rationalist, anthropocentric and liberal individualism. Debashis Guha, in his book *Environmental Ethics* writes, ". . . . the real chauvinism in ethics is male-centred so far as ecological decision-making is concerned. The dominant male attitude has affected the entire environmental set-up just for the sake of benefit of man. There has been against it a wave of "eco-feminism" which speaks of more caring and loving relation with the material nature and natural things. Its ethic is thus far moved from androcentric ego-phobia and hedonic overtone."[8] The rejection of anthropocentrism, more precisely androcentrism, does not entail anti-humanism. Ecofeminism is indeed all-inclusive and pluralistic. It welcomes all the hues of ecosystem, and advocates their more equitable and respectful coexistence. Nature is and should be equally honourable in the form of carer, nourisher and mother. This image of nature soon evades the spiritualism and mysticism with the metaphysical "Body of God" and "Gaia-God" interpretations. Ecofeminism allots a central and moral berth to the values of *care*, *love*, *empathy* and *trust* in dealing with our relationships to other, including the nature. It states that instead of purely rational approach to environmental issues, we should have a non-dualistic, loving, emotional, empathetic and *identical* relationship with every element of environment, humans or non-humans. And even in post-hazard management, the *ethics of care and love* should be our prime source of guidance while thinking about the rehabilitation of victims of natural or human hazards. We must harbour empathy inside us and extend it to others as a defining element of our existential values. The contemporary intelligentsia will have to recognise, albeit reluctantly, the admirable contributions of women in the uplift and preservation of environment. Ecofeminism reconciles and re-envisions environmental ethics and feminism.

Biomedical ethics, a field of applied ethics, is the ethical interpretation of biological science and medicine. Biomedical ethics is concerned with the ethical relationships among life sciences, biotechnology, medicine, caring management, philosophy and theology. Feminists examine and try to obliterate the male-biasness or androcentrism involved in biomedical ethics. Van Rensselaer Potter used the term 'bioethics' for the first time in his work *Bioethics: Bridge to the Future* (1971). Peter Singer, a noted pioneer of applied ethics, has written many books and articles, including *In Defense of Animals* (1986) and *Applied Ethics* (1990). He considers it as a branch of moral philosophy. However, it will be better to call it interdisciplinary. Biomedical ethics is not synonymous to bioethics, ethics of life. It deals with many ethical issues arising in treatment, nursing and management of sick people. Here "sickness" has physical, mental and social implications. The World Health Organisation conceives "health" in terms of a state of complete physical, mental and social well-being, and not merely the absence of diseases. As the issues related to bioethics are very diverse, many theologicians also comment on these issues.

Biomedical ethics in modern sense is only three decades old, but its root may be implicitly traced to ancient thinkers, such as Hypocrite and Charaka, who were interested in the ethical inquiry of medical issues. Biomedical ethics incorporates ethics of care and ethics of allocation and distribution of means of care. It also comprises ethics of experiment and research with numerous members of flora and fauna. It has to deal with a plethora of issues, such as abortion, animal rights, artificial insemination, artificial womb, human cloning, euthanasia, gene therapy, nanomedicine, etc. Feminists say that all these issues are directly or indirectly related to women. For example, the issue of abortion or reproduction is directly concerned with women. So, the ethicality of interpretation of abortion should depend on women's opinions, and not on phallocentric attitude and need. Ethics of abortion should take care of voice and experience of women. Medical termination of pregnancy, or at least of accidental pregnancy, at earlier stage may be ethically permissible. Whatever may be the decision, to go for abortion or continuation of pregnancy, the women's say must be the final and the most ethical. Women's own experience and interests should be the guiding stick in the discussion about abortion. Susan Sherwin unravels the flaws of non-feminist medical ethics, because the new reproductive technologies may further decrease the control of women over reproduction. Whatever may be the case, biomedical ethics should and will have to take account of feminist perspective while dealing with various biomedical problems. *Ethics of care* is highly useful in dealing with animal care, treatment and nursing. Since the pure abstract and rational principles have miserably failed, empathy as advocated by feminism can help in resolving various issues with different orientation. A gender-neutral biomedical ethics will be a munificent gift of feminism.

Educational ethics is another area of applied ethics where feminism can contribute substantially. Educational ethics primarily targets the ethical interpretation of teaching method and students' welfare. And in these both areas feminism can show the path with its philosophy of care and empathy. Pedagogy may drastically fail in its motives if it heedlessly degrades the importance of human feelings of love, care and empathy. The task of pedagogy is highly painstaking. Extreme dependence on abstract rules can cause ruckus in the loving relationship of teachers and students. When a teacher begins to teach his or her students, he or she must have faithful and empathetic ties with the students. Highly rational or abstract educational ethics does not honour the emotions, and promotes the formulation of very general doctrines as guiding principle of student-teacher bond. Feminists advocate the 'caring' and 'identical' ties among teachers and pupils. Another task of educational ethics is to throw light on the *welfare* of students. Feminism again states that educational ethicists should not neutralise the significance of care and empathy while speculating about students' well-being. It believes that women, lively symbolisation of value-laden feelings of love and care, can exceptionally ponder over method of teaching and welfare of students.

Conclusion

Feminist ethics has proved that it will budge when it comes to the interest of women. Feminist ethicists endeavour to rectify the faults and lacunae of androcentrism and ethical chauvinism that jeopardise the interests of women, and posit more viable resolution. The spirit of resolution of value crises in business, management, politics, legality and so on, that covers the realms of occupational and professional life forms is best undertaken in the spirit of care, the involvement of the ethicist and common men in moral matters without being biased with any one or more norms or theories of ethics. The *Intersubjective Corroboration* as feminist model of ethical application and non-normative chauvinism is highly viable model for resolution of ethical crises. Nevertheless, feminist ethicists must keep in mind that they should not recklessly begin to take their ethics as absolute and infallible, because this stand by them will make their views androcentric—a practice against which they have been crusading for centuries. Their ethics will turn monolithic, because of being unilateral, and ignore the importance of what other parties have to say. A monolithic feminist ethics is very likely to go against the interests of women, if it misleadingly universalises the experiences and theories of female feminist icons, and forgets the common ethical experience and knowledge we have in this biotic community. And in this way, feminist ethicist themselves will defeat their purposeful motives that have been fostered for a long time by clairvoyant thinkers.

Normative chauvinism refers to an absolutist monopoly of few ethicists or their theories, say teleology and deontology, regarding ethical reflections. It overlooks the significance of the opinions of others. This stand is not acceptable and desirable in ethics. The most appropriate stand that the feminist ethics can take should be relativistic or non-unilateral nature, wherein it pensively values the opinions of others and appreciates the ethical *involvement* of people. This will make it indeed an all-inclusive ethics free from all sorts of undesirable ethical chauvinism. Here we can say with all probabilities that the feminist ethics can itself be normative in status and still remain non-dominant. Feminist ethics is justified in its own right in ethical matters. Its non-sexist, because non-gynocentric, approach to ethical application makes it morally worthwhile. It wins for its normative non-dominance in resolution of value crises in our life. It wins for its care and empathetic model for ethical evaluation, resolution and decision-making.

REFERENCES

1. Ross, Stephanie, "How Words Hurt: Attitude, Metaphor, and Oppression", as appears in *Philosophy: The Power of Ideas*, (eds.) Brooke Noel Moore and Kenneth Bruder, Tata McGraw Hill Publishing Company Limited, New Delhi, India, 2005, p. 463.
2. Mill, J. S., "The Subjection of Women", as appears in *The Ethics of Feminism: A Study of The Revolt of Women*, A. R. Wadia, Asian Publication Services, India, 1977, p. 46.
3. Wollstonecraft, Marry, "A Vindication of Rights of Women" (1793), as in *Philosophy: The Power of Ideas*, (eds.), Brooke Noel Moore and Kenneth Bruder, *op. cit.*, p. 472.
4. de Beauvoir, S., "The Second Sex" (1949), 1974, as in *Philosophy: The Power of Ideas*, *ibid.*, p. 475.
5. *Ibid.*, p. 476.
6. Okin, Susan Moller, "Justice, Gender, and the Family", as in *Philosophy: The Power of Ideas, op. cit.*, 482.
7. Warren, Karen J., The Power and the Promise of Ecological Feminism, as in *Philosophy: The Power of Ideas, op. cit.*, p. 490.
8. Guha, Debashis, *Practical and Professional Ethics*, Volume 2, *Environmental Ethics,* Concept Publishing Company Pvt. Ltd., New Delhi, India, 2007, pp. 54-55.

Chapter – 9

Women Empowerment and Science

(Is a feminist science possible?)

Umesh Kumar Shrivastava and Rajesh Kumar Singh

The question of the possibility of a feminist science has gained special importance among the feminist thinkers, because it is thought that women hold subordinate status to men, partly because women lag behind men in the area of science and technology. Science and Technology is thought to be the power of the age. In spite of all efforts taken to raise women participation in science education, men are not only major inventors in the area of science and technology, but also are in great majority in the area of science research education, teaching and research. The liking and concentration of women is seen in the area of arts, literature, music, crafts etc.—generally termed as *womenly*. These area are known as the areas of *feelings*, *emotions* and *personal interaction.* These can generate a pleasure of living in harmony with nature, but cannot give the ability of controlling nature and generating wealth in which the real power lies. Many feminist philosophers of science feel that this is so because the nature and psychology of women is unfit and uncomfortable in doing science, technology and mathematics. This is because modern science is the projection and product of male outlook of the universe and its method is governed by male way of working.

The growth of this androcentric science has on the one hand valorised masculine nature, temperament and worldview and on the other hand, it has looked down upon female sensibility and cognitive temperaments as *emotional*, *personal*, *confused*, etc. Thus, this is a misogynist science, which creates a social atmosphere in which men not only look down upon women, but women also realise themselves as a defective personality.

So many feminist thinkers hope that parallel to this androcentric science, there is a possibility and great need of a feminist science springing from women's cognitive temperaments, values and way of working (methodology). This science will empower women (mentally and externally both); just as the present science is empowering men alone.

(i) Which Science?

Here the readers may feel confused, as the title *science conceals multiple ambiguities*. Not only do the sciences consists of many distinct fields, but the term "Science" can be used to refer to a method of enquiry, a historically changing collection of practices, a body of knowledge, a set of claims, a profession, a set of social groups, etc. And as the sciences are many, so are the scholarly disciplines that seek to understand them : Philosophy, history, sociology, anthropology, psychology etc. In this essay, the title is about the possibility of theoretical natural science, that is feminist and from the perspective of a philosopher.

(ii) Feminist Science and Objectivity Claim

Critics argue that a science which is feminist is self-defeating and hence an obvious impossibility. A science is science, because it is objective, universal, inexorable and value neutral. But a science which conceals in itself contents and practices, like a particular (feminine) world view, sensibility, cognitive temperaments and aimed at achieving feminine values, etc. will make it a bad-science or non-science.

A real scientific enquiry must guarantee that the method of inquiry is free from values and all value related considerations. It follows the logical positivist model that (i) the phenomena of natural world (the empirical data of science) are received in empirical obnservation, (ii) they are interrelated in a fixed, consistent and coherent manner, and (iii) the process of scientific theorisation (hypothesis) is a process of linking them through a formal rational process (though not mechanical) of searching the coherence between them. So the method of science is a method of discovery not a new creation, through value imposition. But feminist thinkers do not agree with the view that science is a value neutral discipline which liberates men and women equally. Rather, they say it is a weapon in the hands of men, which brings about subtle and deep rooted subordination of women. This is why we can observe that the more scientifically technologically advanced a society is, the more gap between the status of men and women lies.

If we look at the little of the science books or articles of the science magazines, we can easily discern how subservient to social and cultural interest the scientific enquiries are.

Here some thinkers reply that the object of scientific enquiry may be subservient to social, cultural and economic values or interests, but the nature of scientific enquiry cannot be polluted by these values. To understand it more clearly, we can distinguish between two kinds of values relevant to the science :

(i) Contitutives Values

Which constitute the internal rules, or way of working or the method of science.

(ii) Contexual Values

Which indicate the social and cultural context in which science is done. The value neutrality of science lies in the fact that its consititutive and contexual features, are clearly distinct from and independent of one another. The contexual values plays no role in the inner workings of scientific enquiries. Thus the results (or theories) of scientific enquires cannot be poluted by any bias such as gender, race, culture, etc.

(iii) Feminist Critique of Value Neutral Science

The success of feminist stand lies in proving that the above seperation of constitutive values from contextual values cannot be maintained.

Helan Lognino, in her article "Evidence and Hypothesis" says, that the process of hypothesis formation is an effort of linking the datas (received from empirical observation) and the problem through an imagined theory. There is no formal mechanical method of hypothesis formation. Hence all hypotheses are liable to overthrow or replaced by some better ones. Thus we can see that there is some room for personal considerations in the creative process of conceiving or selecting hypothesis; within the limits of scientific standards.

Again the whole process of hypothesis formation is guided by some basic assumtions (regarding the concept of truth, reality and knowledge) upon which that science is based. These assumptions are laden with values metaphysical, epistemological, social, cultural, economic, etc. We will discuss some of these afterwards. Thus assumptions of science which constitute the constitutive values of that science cannot be totally seperated from the contexual values of the science; though, it may be able to screen out personal ones of the scientist.

(iv) Modern Science : A Projection of Patriarchal Values

(a) Helen Longino says that modern psychological researches prove that human behaviour and cognitive performances are greatly influenced by sex harmones (like the levels of androgens and estrogens). They are primarily responsible for sex roles in animals and humans.

Researches in neurobiology, psychology, etc. show that sex roles do effect the way, how the datas are described or explained and how we interpret or react towards a situation. Thus Longino says that "not only are we, as scientists, victims of the truth, but, we are the prisoners of our bodies. "We can further see the gendered nature of modern science ahead.

(b) *Modern Science :* "Man of Reason" and "Women of Emotion" : The age of enlightenment trumpeted by Becon and Descartes was an age of renaissance or rationalism.

They emphasised that reason and emotion are not complementary to each other, but subversive to each other, Descartes emphasised that pure reason (or intution) is both source and method (deductive), of real knowledge (both logical and scientific), which must be objective, universal and certain. Reason was associated with the mental, the cultural, the universal the public and the male quality. Whereas emotion was associated with the irrational the physical, the natural, the particular, the private and of course, the female quality. Thus reason (the masculine or *purusah*) must be seperated from and dominated upon the emotions (the feminine or the *prakriti*). Even the British Empiricism maintain that our data and interpretation should be free from the impurities and deviations of emotions, values, dogmas etc.

Feminist Reply : Some successes of reason and science motivated the "Man of Reason" to identify manliness in rationality. Thus they overlooked the importance and inevitability of emotions.

1. Emotions are an inevitable part of our personal and social behaviour. Children are taught appropriate emotional responses to situations like enjoy food, music or learning, fear strangers or respect teachers, etc.
2. Objective or scientific truth and reality are themselves

one of the values of man. Again values are nothing, but emotional responses of approval or disapproval.

3. Plato says knowledge is a higher level of love.
4. Knowledge starts from perceptions, a selective or valuational process.
5. Knowledge is the evaluation of perceptual data which is based upon values (or emotional attitudes).

Thus, we see that the Cartesian dream of seperating reason from emotions and values is untenable and the possibility of value neutral science is unachievable. The question is that if science even if based upon masculine values can be a good science; why a science based upon feminine values and emotions, not be a good science?

(c) *Modern Science :* As man's Aggression, Desire to control and exploitation : Bacon the father of modern philosophy and scientific revolution promised to create "a blessed race of heroes and superman who would dominate both nature and society". Bacon's experimental method create a dichotomy between male and female, mind and matter (nature), objective and subjective, facts and values, rational and emotional etc.

It was not a neutral method, but man's project of knowing through controlling (as experimenting) nature for exploiting maximum benefit out of it.

In the field of economy it looked at nature only as source of raw materials. Vandana Shiva says that "for Bacon, nature was no longer Mother Nature, but a Female Nature, conquered by an aggressive masculine mind." His model of scientific method is that of aggression and rape. This ruined the balance of ecology and poisoned the earth, water, air, crops and vegetables. Forests are being cleared and millions of useful species living in them and treasure of our biodiversity are vanishing day by day. Scientific growth (based upon division and domination) is threatening our very survival.

Modern science developed an industrial capitalist sophisticated society, in which women were automatically excluded from the industrial production and capitalist marketing system. The only business left for them was that of a housewife or small jobs like steno, sales girl, etc. The old system of their equal participation in economy in the hunting society or agricultural society was lost. Harding called the modern science a "western, white, bourgeois, masculine project", which enslaved nature, women and the black equally.

This new science gave birth to reductionist view in which the rhythmic teleology of universe, the spiritual meaning of life, values, beauty all were reduced to mechanical, material and monetory entities. Ancient intutive apprehensions lost in the theory of "Real is Rational".

(v) The Model of Feminist Science

Now once we are able to discern the androcentric values as the constitutive value of science, we can understand the possibility of alternative science based upon alternative values.

The ancient science of Indian Ayurveda, Yoga, Buddhist Reikie and other tribal communities are good examples of better alternative sciences. The vedic epistemology of knowing through being, living in harmony with nature (as the tribals knew about coming of Tsunami in the Nicobar island) and intuitive apprehension —had given good medical and other sciences. The wisdom of ancient India, gave better family and social cultural order based not upon division but union of *Shiva* and *Shakti* (male and female), way of living with ecological balance of nature and meaningful spiritual values (which kept them away from psychological disorders of today).

Vandana Shiva finds Vedic sciences and the sciences of the tribals more inspiring upon which feminist model of science can be built. She says that the feminist science will aim at union of man and woman (*Purusa-Prakriti or Shiva-Shakti*) and its world view will be characterised by (a) creativity, activity, productivity (against scientific view as inert and passive), (b) diversity in form and aspect (not universality, uniformity and mechanistic), (c) connectedness and interrelationship of all beings including man (against seperated and fragmented), (d) continuity between human and natural and (e) sanctity of life in nature (against nature as separated from and dominated and exploited by man).

(vi) Pre-requisite of Feminist Science

But doing science differently requires more than just the will to do and it would be disingenuous to pretend that our philosophies of science are the only barrier. Scientific enquiry takes place in a social, political and economic context that imposes a variety of institutional obstacles to innovation. For example, the nature of university carrier ladders means that one's work must be recognised as meeting certain standards laid down by the university. Success requires that we present our work in a way that satisfies those standards than to strike out in a new direction. Thus in male dominated society, feminist science in order to be conceptualisable, understandable and acceptable, should satisfy the androcentric outlook. So only a slow and gradual shift and effort may do. Again any new science to develop needs a change of outlook, philosophy and political and economic support. Thus to do feminist science we must gradually change the social and political context in which science is done.

Conclusion

So, is a feminist science Possible ? If this means : is it in principle possible to do science as a feminist?, the answer must be yes. If this means : can we in practice do science as a feminist?, the answer must be; not until we change present conditions.

Chapter – 10

Women Empowerment through 73rd Amendment: In the Political Context

Deepali Singh

> *'Today women are playing an important role in rural development after getting elected from village panchayat to district level organizations. Although this is new field for women and they are facing still resistance from men in the male dominated society. But women have proved themselves to be a better and more sensitive administrator in a short span of time.'*

Women the word sounds so powerful. Since eternity, women have played a role more important than men and that is no exaggeration. The world would not have been the same lovely adorable and livable place without wonderful contribution so selflessly made by women. It has been said that, you teach a female and you build up a nation and truth can't be closer than that. Women have always carried the burden of being a wife, mother, sister all on their own and we need not to explain how magnificently they have carried this position.

Men and women complement each other. If men were supposed to handle outside stuff then women were more responsible for internal affairs. The only difference in this notion is, today women are equally competent behind the veils and outside world. They are more confident and one can find them in every possible sphere of human's life. No male bastion is untouched by females and thats' a wonderful sign of strides made by women.

After independence, in 1948, India opted for a democratic political system. In an attempt to democratize, a decentralized system of government was established with power divided between the federal, state and local government. The village panchayat is the basic local government unit in rural India. The functions of the village panchayat include civic, welfare service and other socio-economic functions. The Panchayati Raj system of the pre and post-independence period differed on the topic of representation. Before independence, members of the upper class and caste dominated the system of local government. Women were also generally excluded from formal representation. In the 1950s, several laws were passed which increased women's representation in local government through regular elections and meetings and also increased its strength by widening the scope of their functions.

Women's involvement in local government becomes an issue at the same time that efforts were underway to strengthen the Panchayati Raj. Although women's involvement in local government since independence has been low, this is not to suggest that women have been totally excluded from the local government system.

The principle of gender equality is enshrined in the Constitution of India in its Preamble, Fundamental Rights, Fundamental Duties and Directive Principles. The Constitution not only grants equality to women, but also empowers the State to adopt measures of positive discrimination in favour of women. Women's rights and issues have always been a subject of serious concern of academicians, intelligentsia and policy makers. From pastoral society to contemporary information and global society, the role of women has changed drastically. The role of a typical "*Grihini*" (house wife) who catered to all the requirements of the households including the rearing and upbringing of children in various sub-roles of daughter, daughter-in-law, wife, mother, aunt etc. has been played quite efficiently. The continuity of changes in socio-economic and psycho-cultural aspects of human living has influenced the role of women. With the process of industrialization, Modernization and Globalization showing its deep impact on the human society all over the world, the role and responsibilities of women has attained new definition and perspective. Further this has also led to addition of responsibilities and widened the role of women who also shares the financial responsibilities.

Empowerment of women involves many things—economic opportunity, social equality and personal rights. Women are deprived of these human rights, often as a matter of tradition. In rural areas, women are generally not perceived to have any meaningful income generation capacity, and hence, they are relegated mainly to household duties and cheap labour. Without the power to work and earn a good income, their voices are silenced. Even in matters of sex and child bearing, women often do not have the ability to oppose the wishes of their men. Within the framework of a democratic polity, our laws, development policies, plans and programmes have aimed at women's advancement in different spheres. From the Fifth Five Year Plan (1974-78) onwards has been a marked shift in the approach to *women's issues from welfare to development*. In recent years, the empowerment of women has been recognized as the central issue in determining the status of women. The National Commission for Women was set up by an Act of Parliament in 1990 to safeguard the rights and legal entitlements of women. The 73rd and 74th Amendments (1993) to the Constitution of India have provided for reservation of seats in the local bodies of Panchayats and Municipalities for women, laying a strong foundation for their participation in decision making at the local levels. Women rights and women empowerment are most of the times looked from an urban perspective, whereby the situation relatively appears to be in favour of women when compared to their rural counterparts. *The 73rd amendment establishes Panchayati Raj:* a system of local democracy through local council known as *panchayats.* The amendment mandates that resource, responsibility and decision-making power be devolved from central government and placed in the hands of rural grassroots people, with elections every five years. *The most revolutionary aspect* of the amendment is that one-third of all panchayat seats are reserved for women. Rural women—who for centuries have lived in conditions of malnutrition, illiteracy and powerlessness —are now taking leadership roles in addressing these very issues.

- *Reserved seats.* The 73rd Amendment reserves seats for the most powerless members of society on a revolving basis, as determined by the Election Commission. One-third of all seats—including one-third of all panchayat presidencies—are reserved for women. In addition, seats are also reserved for members of Scheduled Tribes and Scheduled Castes proportional to their population.
- To provide reservation of seats for Scheduled Castes, Scheduled Tribes and women (not less than 33%).

The Constitutional Amendment ensures a three tier structure at the zilla, block a village levels, an election commission to hold election periodically, a state level finance commission to find out ways and means to increase resources for local bodies. Reservation of 1/3 of seats in all the position of the three tier for women, reservation of seats for SC/ST in proportion to their population in all the positions of the three tiers, establishment of Gram Sabha for enhancing people's participation for their own development, and establishment of planning committee for local bodies; and an earmarked list of 29 items under Eleventh schedule. Now, the world's most populous democracy has the constitutionally mandated 2,32,332 village *panchayats*, 6,000 intermediate *panchayats* and 534 zilla *panchayats*. The three tiers of these elected bodies consist of as many as 27,75,858 village *Panchayat* members, 1,44,491 members of intermediate *panchayats* and 15,067 members of *zilla panchayats*. This is the broadest representative base which exists in any country of the world (Panchayati Raj Report 2001, NIRD). Besides breadth, depth of these figures can be gauged from the fact that more than fifty per cent of these grassroots representatives are from the downtrodden and marginalized sections of the society, namely women (one-third of the total), the SCs, STs and OBCs (as per their proportion of the population). This kind of constitutional provision has created a scope for accomplishing development with social justice, which is mandate of the new *Panchayat Raj* system.

Relevance to Present Day

The women representatives at the Panchayat will in turn to get an opportunity to become empowered. There is lot of impediments for women if they wish to freely exercise their rights, and play their own role in social-political field. But in a society where even stepping out of the house is not considered decent for women, a new revolution of change has definitely started in the rural set-up. If has now become imperative although difficult to break the barriers of illiteracy, poverty and traditions. At least in the initial stages, the powerful people for their own vested interests are half-heartedly promoting the women to contest elections. This system of reservation for women has initiated a silent solution era to the different problems faced by women. This will definitely conclude in bringing positive results in the years to come.

Women's empowerment in light of the enactment of the 73rd Constitutional Amendment, *Panchayati Raj*, in the Constitution of India in 1992. It begins with the assumption that women's empowerment implies progressive on women's empowerment differs from ideas about women's development in some important ways. Women's development is primarily a socio-economic concept while women's empowerment is essentially a political project. It is argued here that women's empowerment is indeed a precursor to women's development. The constitution of India ensures equal rights to both men and women and has special provision for the welfare of women to enhance their status in the society. But still, after 66 years of independence, women representatives in politics have been negligible. To fill this vacuum, the Government of India amended the Constitution to empower women at local levels. The purpose behind this move is to provide more opportunities for women to participate in decision making and thereby to increase the possibilities of accruing more benefits of development of rural areas.

The status of women in India has been undergoing a sea-change. Supported by Constitutional guarantees to ensure dignity and equal opportunities, their active participation in all walks of life including education, politics, sport etc., has been growing. Taking note of women's role in the nation-building activities, the Government had declared 2001 as the year of Women's Empowerment by adopting a National Policy to offer "*Swashakti*" to women. Several laws have also been adopted to empower women socially, economically, legally and politically. Considering the role of rural India, the country's backbone, the Government had taken several measures to strengthen Pachayanti Raj System with the active participation of women. This gave a boost to increase the number of women being elected to the Lok Sabha and State Assemblies, an indication to suggest their political empowerment.

Today women are playing an important role in rural development after getting elected from village panchayat to district level organizations. We have seen this in although this is new field for women and they are facing still resistance from men in the male dominated society. But women have proved themselves to be a better and more sensitive administrator in a short span of time. Now political parties are compelled to offer more and more respectable posts to women. There are three aspects of rural development-economic, social and political which are dependent on each other. Women contribute the most towards economic development. In rural area women perform almost double work as compared to men. Whereas a man puts in ten hours of work everyday and in same time a women labours for sixteen hours everyday. But since her contribution to direct income is less, it does not receive the desired importance which she deserves. Today thousand of question are being raised regarding the condition of women in panchayat, but this opinion is absolutely wrong; that women are not ready to take up any responsibility or they are incapable of taking decision. The fact is that till now women have been deprived of their rightful claims and there have been attempts to create hindrance in their path of progress, if they wish to excel in socio-political field. There is lot of evidence that shows, that whenever opportunities were provided, women have fully utilized them in the panchayat elections in different states whereas one-third women have been elected at every stage of panchayat in some states even more than one third women have been elected there in no doubt that a sea change is taking place in the society; women are slowly becoming aware, their inclination towards education is increasing veil (*parda*) system is on its way out and the voice of women is becoming strengthened day by day but the journey is long.

REFERENCES

A Journal of Local Administration Overseas: Henery Maddick, *Panchyat Raj*, Rural Local Government in India", Vol. I, 1962.

History and Results of Indian Local Government system with Focus on Constitutional, Legal Democratic and Administrative empowerment, Director George Mathew, Institute of Social Sciences , New Delhi.

Jyoti, Panchayati Raj: Two alternative approaches, *A Development Journal of Yojana,* Vol . 33, 1989.

C.V. Raghavalu and C.A. Naryan, "Reforms in Pancayati Raj," *IIPA,* New Delhi, 1991.

Bandyopadhyaya & Amitava Mukherjee, *New Issues in Panchayati Raj*, published for Task Force on P.R. Rajiv Gandhi Foundation, Concept Publishing Company, New Delhi, 2004.

Women's Empowerment, Issues, Challenges, and Strategies: A Source Book, Hajira Kumar and Jaimon Varghese, Publisher Dya Books, 2005.

Latika Menon, *Women Empowerment and Challenges of Change,* Kanishka Publishers, New Delhi, 1998.

S.P. Punalekar, "People and Panchayat", *IASSI Quarterly,* Vol.19, No.3, 2001.

Nirmala Buch, " Panchyats and Women", *Employment News,* Vol. XXVI, No. 19, 2001.

Chapter – 11

Feminist Ethics

Yamini Sahay

Feminist are of the view that traditional ethics depreciates and devalues women's moral experience, so that there should be every attempt to revise, reformulate and rethink the traditional ethics. In particular, the feminist Alison Jaggar has found five ways in which the traditional ethics has devalued women and let them down. And before going into them in detail, the ways, it should be asserted that this was the particular reason that the need for feminist ethics arose and feminist philosophy took shape in demand of the feminists or feminist philosophers. The feminists felt as well that the traditional ethics and some particular notions of them should be reconceptualized evading the previous based ones altogether. All such notions which are tilted in favour of masculine gender or even written from their point of view should be absolutely quashed giving place to new conceptions unbiased and unprejudiced.

Now, coming to Alison Jaggar's views, her ways she found to fault traditional ethics are important, more so because they also give a clue so as to how the newer unbiased ethical conceptions should be formulated in feminist ethics. The traditional ethics is faulty in the five following ways :

First, it shows less concern for women's as opposed to men's issues and interests. Second, traditional ethics views as trivial the moral issues that arise in the so called private world, the realism in which women do housework and take care of children, the infirm and the elderly. Third, it implies that, in general, women are not as morally mature or deep as men. Fourth, traditional ethics overrates culturally masculine traits like "independence, autonomy, intellect, will, wariness, hierarchy, domination, culture, transcendence, product, asceticism, war, and death, while it underrates culturally feminine traits like interdependence, community, connection, sharing, emotion, body, trust absence of hierarchy, nature, immanence, process, joy, peace and life." Fifth, and finally, it favours "male" ways of moral reasoning that emphasize rules, rights, universality, and impartiality over "female" ways of moral reasoning that emphasize relationships, responsibilities, particularity and partiality (Jaggar, "Feminist Ethics", 1992).

Based on these five ways traditional ethics has failed or neglected women, feminists have developed a wide variety of gender-centered approaches to ethics. Some feminist ethicists emphasize issues related to women's traits and behaviours, particularly their care giving ones. In contrast, other feminist ethicists emphasize the political, legal, economic, and/or ideological causes and effects of women's second-sex status. But be these emphases as they may, all feminists ethicists share the same goal; the creation of a gendered ethics that aims to eliminate or at least ameliorate the oppression of any group of people, but most particularly women.

1. Feminist Ethics: Historical Background

Feminist approaches to ethics, as well as debates about the gendered nature of morality are not recent developments. A wide variety of thinkers like Mary Wollstonecraft, John Stuart Mill, Catherine Beecher, Charlotte Perkins Gilman, and Elizabeth Cady Stanton raised topics related to "women's morality". These thinkers raised questions such as : Are women's "feminine" traits the product of nature/biology or are they instead the outcome of social conditioning? Are moral virtues as well as gender traits connected with one's affective as well as cognitive capacities, indeed with one's physiology and psychology? If so, should we simply accept the fact that men and women have different moral virtues as well as different gender traits and proceed accordingly? If not, should we strive to get men and women to adhere to the same morality: a one—size—fits—all human morality?

In answer to the questions raised above, Mary Wollstonecraft concluded that morality is the same for one and all, for men and women alike. In other words moral virtue is unitary. Though Wollstonecraft did not use terms like "socially constructed gender roles" and no less found women less virtuous than men but she agreed they were of weak moral characters pre-eminently due to deprived of sufficient opportunities to develop their rational powers. She said that due to societal reasons, women wind up being over-emotional, hypersensitive, narcissistic, self-indulgent individuals. Wollstonecraft said further that there was nothing wrong about women, including their supposedly weak moral characters, that could be cured by a rigorous education that is the kind of education that aims to develop students' rational powers. Men receive a proper education and so, they have concern, causes and commitments over and beyond petty, self-interested ones. Give women men's education, said Wollstonecraft, and women, no less than men, will become morally mature human beings (Wollstonecraft, '*A Vindication of the Rights of Women,*'[1] p.105).

Wollstonecraft said that it was reason rather than sentence the characteristic trait which distinguishes humans from non-human animals. Similarly manners are different from morals. Manners are mindless automation which one might master, but morals are such which require critical thinking. Whereas parents teach boys morals, they teach girls manners. More generally, society as a whole encourages women to cultivate negative psychological traits like "cunning", "vanity" and "immaturity", all of which impede women's moral development. What is worse, society twists what could be woman's virtues into vices. For instance, women's positive psychological traits of gentleness is quickly transformed into the negative psychological trait of obsequiousness "when it is the submissive demeanour of dependence, the support of weakness that loves, because it wants protection and is forbearing because it must silently endure injuries; smiling under the lash at which it dare not snar."

Wollstonecraft reasoned that the best way for women to become full-fledged moral agents was to start thinking and behaving like men. Only then they could evade negative psychological traits which Wollstonecraft found much prevalent especially in upper-middle class women. However, she does not question whether men's morality was in fact human morality. Only she says that on the face of it men's morality seemed better than women's morality and so was a superior candidate for the title "true human morality".

Wollstonecraft emphasized that the women of her times needed a better education, but she fails to provide a definite rationale for providing women with men's education. Her opinion differs and gives mainly two reasons for that. First, she opines that the purpose of educating women is simply to supply men with "rational fellowship", that is with more observant daughters, more affectionate sisters, more faithful wives, more reasonable mothers". Secondly, she suggests that women needed to be educated like men so that they can become rational, responsible, independent adults, she noted that if women were to be "really virtuous and useful", they needed to be economically independent of men.

'What made a human being good?' was such a topic which did not end with Wollstonecraft. Rather, the discussion continued into the next century. What would be more ironical, was that by the nineteenth century, women were now considered as more moral (though less intellectual) than men. However, John Stuart Mill, the Utilitarian philosopher was much disturbed by this view, As he viewed society was mistaken to set up an ethical double standard, according to which women's morality was to be assessed differently than man's morality. Reflecting on women's alleged moral superiority, Mill concluded women's morality was simply the result of systematic social conditioning. He said that to laud women on account of their "complex abnegation of themselves",[2] is merely to compliment society for inculcating in women those psychological traits that serve to maintain it. Women are taught to live for others; to always give and never take; to submit, yield and obey; to be long suffering. They are also taught to demur to men because they are not as smart and strong as men. This being the case, women's virtue is not the product of autonomous choice. Rather, it is the consequence of social programming. At the root, there is but one virtue—human virtue—and women as well as men, should be pushed to adhere to its standards. Then, and only then, will society be as just as possible.

J.S. Mill and Mary Wollstonecraft thus hold one and the same standard of morality for both sexes. However, other nineteen century thinkers object to this. They think that male and female virtues are simply different. They give expression to a separate and unequal theory of virtue according to which female virtue is fundamentally better than male virtue. Importantly, this diverse group of thinkers disagree among themselves about how to assess the characteristics (nurturance, empathy, compassion, self-sacrifice, kindness) typically associated with women. They asked whether these "female" or "feminine" characteristics are : (1) genuine moral virtues to be developed by men as well as by women; (2) positive psychological traits to be developed by women alone; or (3) negative psychological traits not to be developed by anyone?

Catherine Beecher belongs to this group of thinkers. Unlike some of her contemporaries, she thought that women's place was in the home. Women's work, such as, creation and maintenance of strong families, in which moral virtue thrives, was essential for society's well-being. In order to esteem women's housework, Beecher developed the discipline of "domestic science"[3]. She stressed that women's housework required as much intelligence and organizational and occupational skills and it may be as demanding as to manage a small business properly.

Beecher also emphasized that women's most important work was to make the member of her family noble and gentle like Christ, who died a painful death so that humankind could be redeemed from its fallen, sinful state. Insulated in the private realm, where they are supposedly deaf to the siren calls of worldly wealth, power and prestige, women are supposedly better situated than men to cultivate the Christ like virtue of "self-denying benevolence" and to serve as role models for their families. The more pure and perfect women are, the better society will be. Beecher is convinced that women are responsible for morally perfecting men and children. However, Beecher never asks herself as to why God had burdened women rather than men with this responsibility, imposing on women the task of specializing in the virtue of self-denying benevolence. After all, given that Christ was a man, should not God have selected men as the keepers of society's virtue?

Elizabeth Cady Stanton, a contemporary of Beecher also saw differences between women's and men's morality. However, her view is far different from Beecher. Stanton is not certain whether men's and women's virtues and vices are the result of social manipulation or biological imperative, but she has a low opinion of men's morals though it has set the standard for behaviour in the public world. The solution to this regrettable situation, says Stanton, is a relatively simple one: push women and their superior morals into the public world. Humankind cannot afford to leave women, as Beecher would, in the private world, exerting their good influence there and only there.[4]

Stanton is also reared up in Christian faith like Beecher and so she values women's self-denying benevolence. But Stanton believes that there is an even higher virtue foı women to develop; namely self-development. In the course of interpreting a biblical passage in which a poor widow is praised for her charitable actions, Stanton agreed that the woman's generous gesture of giving was, on the face of it, indeed praiseworthy. Nonetheless, Stanton cautioned women that women's generosity—their willingness to do more in the way of caring and giving than men

—may be contributing to women's second class status. Although acts of self-sacrifice are morally required in the abstract, ought implies can in the concrete. Women cannot be always afford to be totally other—directed, says Stanton, sometimes they have to be self-centred, so that they can care for themselves and make progress towards securing the same political, social and economic rewards and power men have.

Charlotte Perkins Gilman another contemporary feminist of Stanton, takes a different line of thought. She imagines an all female society, Herland in which women and their daughters (produced through parthenogenesis) are able to practice a superior morality. Herland is women-centred society of mothers in which the lines between the private realm and the public realm have been radically redrawn. The women of Herland would be just as visible in courts of law and centres of trade as they are in the nurseries and schools. Competitive, individualistic approaches to life would disappear in Herland, where women would be able to relate cooperatively because they feel no need to dominate on each other.

No wonder, then, that three male explorers—Terry, Jeff and Van—who reach Herland do not know what to make of it. Before they arrive, they make light of the mythical land, assuming there must be men in it, since women could not possibly be competent enough to run a nation without men's help. When they see how successfully Herland is run, however, only one of them, Van is honest enough to recognize that its all—female population is a group of extraordinarily accomplished human beings. As he sees it, the women of Herland cultivate both the best feminine virtues and the best masculine virtues—the virtues that joined together are co-extensive with human virtue. Thus if a society in the real world wants to be virtuous, it should embrace Herland as its ideal[5].

To be sure, Herland is a *fictional utopia* in which imaginary social, economic, political and cultural conditions permit women to develop in morally good as well as psychologically healthy ways. But Gilman admitted, that conditions are quite different for women in the non-fictional, real world. In '*Women and*

Economics' (1966), she wrote that so long as women are dependent on men for economics support, women will be known for their servility and men for their arrogance. Women need to be men's economic equals before they can develop truly human moral virtue, a perfect blend of pride and humility: namely, self-respect.

2. Care-Focused Feminist Approaches to Ethics

These eighteenth and nineteenth century feminist thinkers like Wollstonecraft, Mill, Beecher, Stanton, and Gilman contributed to the development of a wide range of feminist approaches to ethics that focused on the similarities and differences between "*male masculine*" ethics and "*female/feminine*" *ethics*. In doing so, they inaugurated a discussion of the different ontologies and epistemologies that underpin these type of ethics. In the main, they challenged the ontological presupposition that the more separate the self is from others, the more fully developed that self is. They also questioned the presupposition that the more universal, abstract, impartial and rational knowledge is, the more closely it mirrors reality. In place of these presuppositions, decidedly present in most traditional ethics, they instead suggested the ontological assumption that the more connected the self is to others, the better the self is. They also offered the epistemological presupposition that the more particular, concrete, partial and emotional knowledge is, the more likely it represents the way in which people actually experience the world. Thus it is not surprising that "communal woman" gradually began to replace "autonomous man" in eighteenth and nineteenth century feminist approaches to ethics.[6]

Building on the legacy of many of the thinkers who preceded them, a prominent group of twentieth century feminist ethicists have continued to use "communal woman" to develop a variety of care-focused feminist approaches to ethics. Unlike non-feminist care-focused approaches to ethics, feminist ones are highly attune to gender issues. Feminist care-focused ethicists are quick to notice instances of female subordinatiôn and the tendencies of patriarchal societies not to properly esteem women's way of thinking, writing, working and loving.

1. Feminist Care Ethics: The Different Voice

Proponents of feminist care ethics, including Carol Gilligan and Net Noddings stress that traditional moral theories, principles, practices and poiicies are deficient to the degree they lack, ignore, trivialize or demean values and virtues culturally associated with women. Freud, the well-known psychologist developed the notion that whereas men are morally well-developed, women are not. Women's supposed moral inferiority, Freud attributed to girl's psycho sexual development. Whereas boys break their attachment to their mothers forbear of being castrated by their fathers if they fail to do so. However, girls remain tied to their mothers because the threat of castration has no power over them. As a result of this theorized male-female difference, girls are supposed by much slower than boys to develop a sense of themselves as autonomous moral agents, personally responsible for the consequences of their actions; as persons who must obey society's rules or face its punishments. In other words, boys and men come to respect law more than girls and women do.

Gilligan finds more than one traditional thinkers who view women as morally inferior to men. Freud is only one of them. Educational psychologist Lawrence Kohelberg puts forward extended criticism of women. Kohelberg claimed that moral development is a six-stage process. Stage one is the "punishment and obedience orientation". To avoid the pain of punishment and/or to receive the pleasure of a reward, children do as they are told. Stage two is "the instrumental relativist orientation". Based on the notion of reciprocity—scratch my back and I'll scratch yours—children meet others, needs only if others meet their needs. Stage Three is the "good-body nice girl" orientation. Adolescence adhere to prevailing norms to secure others' approval and love Stage Four is the "*law and order orientation*".

Adolescents develop a sense of duty, defer to authority figures, and maintain the social order to secure others' admiration and respect. Stage Five is the "*social contract legalistic orientation*". Adults adopt a utilitarian moral point of view according to which individuals may do as they please, provided they do not harm other people. Stage Six is "*the universal ethical principle orientation*". Adults adopt a Kantian moral perspective that transcends all conventional moralities. Adults are no longer ruled by self-interest, the opinion of others, or the fear of punishment, but by self-imposed universal principles.[7]

Although Gilligan concedes that Kohlberg's moral ladder appeals to many people schooled in traditional ethics, she points out that wide acceptance of a moral development theory is not necessarily the measure of its truth. She questions whether Kohlberg's six stages of moral development are indeed universal, invariant and hierarchical. In particular, *she asks why, in the Kohlbergian scheme of things, women rarely climb past stage three, whereas men routinely make it to stage Four or even Five*? Does this gender difference mean that women are less morally developed than men are? Or instead, does it mean there is something wrong with Kohlberg's methodology—some bias in it that permits men to achieve higher moral development scores than men?

Thus Gilligan concludes that *Kohlberg's methodology is male-biased*. Its ears are tuned to male not female, moral voices. Thus it fails to register different voices Gillian claims to have heard in her study of twenty-nine women reflecting on their abortion decisions. This distinctive moral voice, says Gilligan, speaks a language of care that emphasizes relationships and responsibilities. Seemingly, this language is largely unintelligible to Kohlbergian researches who speak the dominant moral language of traditional ethics, namely a language of justice that stresses right and rules.

Although Gilligan notes that it is not that all women speak only the language of care and all men speak only the language of justice, so that the above dichotomy is not perfectly true. In her abort on study, she shows only women moving in and out of the three moral frames of reference that together constitute her relational ethics: Level One in which women overemphasise the interests of their selves; Level Two in which women over-emphasize others' interests; and Level Three in which women weave their own interests together with those of others. Thus a woman at Level One would make her abortion decision in terms of what is best for herself, at Level Two in terms of what is best for others, and at Level Three in terms of what is best for herself and others considered as a relational unit. Women at Level Three display a kind of thinking that is fully and properly feminist.[8]

Gilligan's care ethics has been widely applauded and adopted, but it is also not free of criticism. Some critics claim that Gilligan's levels provide no more an account of human moral development than Kohlberg's Stages. Kohlber's Stages focus on men's moral experience and Gilligan's focus on women's. Gilligan takes this objection seriously and she has launched several studies of men's moral experience. Her central aim is, however, to explore the ways in which U.S. society, for example, may muzzle boys' and men's moral sensitivities, encouraging them to be less than fully nurturant human person so that they can succeed in a highly competitive public world. Gilligan stresses that today's women can speak the moral language of justice and rights nearly as fluently as the moral language of care and responsibilities, but to our dismay, today's boys and men still find it very difficult to articulate their moral concerns in anything other than the moral language of justice and rights. The primary aim of Gilligan's new studies is to demonstrate that Level Three thinking is after all, the kind of thinking that should guide moral deliberation.

Some critics insist on that even if care is a *bona fide* moral virtue, it is a less essential moral virtue than justice. These critics claim that it is better to act from a general moral principle like "aid the needy" than a particular caring feeling for a specific person. Constant principles are more reliable action guides than ephemeral feelings, they say. They also put forth the view that, when justice and care conflict, considerations of impartiality should triumph on considerations of partiality: my children's fundamental rights and basic needs are neither more nor less important than anyone else's children.

Yet some other critics claim there is nothing really new about the "different voice" Gilligan hears. They emphasize that benevolence (i.e. care) is no less present than justice in traditional ethics. From benevolence flows ideas like maximizing aggregate good, not harming anyone, and not interfering with individuals' liberty. From benevolence flows ideas like maximizing aggregate good, not harming anyone, and not interfering with individuals' liberty. From justice flows the notions of equality of respect for persons and equality before the law. But, in defence of Gilligan it can be said that what some traditional ethicists mean by "benevolence" may not be what Gilligan means by "care". Philosopher Lawrence A. Blum asks us to consider the specific principle, "Protect one's children from harm", a principle that flows from the general principle of benevolence. As Blum sees it most parents subscribe to this specific principle, but only those parents who are caring—that is sensitive to and aware of their children's unique interests and needs—will know when and how to meet its terms.

Now, here also, there is a divergence of opinion among critics. Although most traditional philosophers agree with Blum that caring parents are more likely to actually act benevolently than uncaring parents are, they do not agree with him that only caring parents are capable of acting in such a way. Instead they insist that a formal sense of duty, whether or not it is accompanied by caring feelings is sufficient to generate moral action. Blum follows the view of some ethicists who have developed versions of care ethics. In conformity with their views Blum believes that people who would be moral must do more than merely obey the letter of the law. They must also be infused with the appropriate emotions, sentiments and feelings to perform an entirely morally worthy action.

Gilligan is faced by non-feminist criticisms as well as feminist criticisms. Of these criticisms the most powerful one stress that even if women are better carers than man, it may still be epistemically, ethically and politically imprudent to associate women with the value of care. To link women with caring may be to promote the view that women are in charge of caring or, worse, that because women can care, they should care no matter what they cost to themselves.

Sandra Lee Bartky in her book 'Feminity and Domination' argues that women's experience of building men's egoes and binding men's wounds ultimately disempowers women. She claims that the kind of "emotional work" practiced by women in some service-oriented occupations causes them to disconnect from their own base of feelings and sentiments. For example, paying a person to be always upbeat even when customers, patients, or clients are rude, nasty or abusive means paying a person to act nice even when she does not feel nice. But a person pretends to be nice only so long before she imperils her ability to recognize the difference between phony niceness and real niceness.

Here Bartky points out yet another view of importance. She concedes that some women feel energized rather than drained by the emotional work they do. Many wives and mothers claim the experience of caring for their husbands and children, even when difficult, is meaning-giving. The more they care, the more they view themselves as persons who hold everything together for everyone else. But, says Bartky, such subjective feelings of empowerment are not the same as the objective reality of actually having power. Many women get upset, for example when they fail to please the men in their lives. Yet, the men in their lives may not notice how much pain their words and deeds sometimes cause the women in their lives. Men seem to worry less about women's feelings than women worry about men's feelings. Thus, according to Bartky, women's care of men may account to a "collective genuflection by women to men, an affirmation of male importance that is unreciprocated."[9]

Another concern Bartky expresses about women's caring of men in particular is that women may sacrifice their moral integrity in the process. Bartky gives the example of Teresa Stangl, wife of Fritz Stangl, Kommandant of Triblika. Aware of the fact that husband was sending thousands of Jews to their death in his concentration camp, she nonetheless continued to attend his needs dutifully, even lovingly. In doing so, says Bartky, she became complicit with his evil, for a woman cannot remain silent about evil and still expect to keep her goodness entirely intact. Because evil perpetrated by a loved one is still evil, women need to analyze "the pitfalls and temptations of care giving itself" before they embrace an ethics of care wholeheartedly.

Mullet, another feminist, *distinguishes between distorted caring and undistorted caring*. Mullet views that, a woman is not in a position to truly care for someone if she is economically, socially, and/or psychologically forced to do so. In other words, authentic caring cannot occur under conditions characterized by male domination and female subordination. Only if women are truly equal to men, can women care for them without fearing that men will take advantage of their loving acts, feeling no need to reciprocate them. So long as women do more than their fair share of care giving work, both sexes will remain morally deprived. However, to care too much is to risk being servile. To care too little is to risk being so selfish that one's heart freezes along the way. To care appropriately is to care reflectively and well.

All care-focused feminists find Bartky's and Mullet concern about care worthy of attention. But Gilligan view is even more important. It holds that even if it is risky for women to care in a patriarchal society, care remains part of any credible ethics. Care's contested status calls for the development of a more robust feminist ethics of care that includes men as well as women; certainly it does not call for the rejection of care.

Net Noddings, yet another feminist, has developed an ethics that valorizes the virtues and values traditionally linked to women. Noddings is of the view that ethics is about particular relationships between two parties: the "one-caring" and the "cared-for". True care does not consist in proclaiming one's universal love for all humankind. Nor does it consist in sending aid to victims of war, famine or natural disasters. Realistically, a mother in the United

States cannot care about the children in Sudan as much as she cares for her own children. Real care requires actual encounters with specific individuals; it cannot be bestowed from afar upon individual in general.

Next, Noddings *differentiates between natural caring and ethical caring*. Noddings claims that as children we act from a natural caring that motivates us to help others simply because we want to help them. Later, when we get so "busy" or "important" that we think we do not have time to care, the deliberateness of so called ethical caring supplements the spontaneity of so called natural caring. We try to be available for someone even when our calendars are full of meetings and appointments. We tap into our memories of those days when caring was easy for us, when we always had time for those who loved us or needed us. For Noddings, whatever the value of ethical caring may be, it is not as basic as natural caring. Natural caring is the condition of possibility for ethical caring; Sociopaths cannot care ethically because they cannot care naturally. Presumably, they are born into the world without the hardwiring to develop caring behaviour.

Some critics of Noddings think that she valorizes women who care to the point of imperiling their own identity, integrity, and even survival. This is due to the reason that although Noddings insists that men can and should be carers, she most often uses women in her examples of care giving people. Noddings protests that her critics misunderstands her. She is of the opinion that she also thinks that the one caring for others should also care for herself, so that she can care for others better. Preserving relationships, in so far as it is possible to do so, is a high priority for Noddings. To break a relationship without working hard to find someway to hold it together is a cause of concern for her. Noddings suggests that when a person breaks a relationship, particularly a close one, he or she risks being ethically diminished.

In '*Starting at Home: Caring and Social Policy* (2002)', Noddings extends the principles of her feminist care ethics into the arena of public policy. There are some critics who criticized Noddings' feminist care ethics as a "fine domestic theory" which is unable to address the moral complexities of wider social issues and policies. In response to them, Noddings insists that having a robust sense of social justice is predicated on the lessons learned in the private sphere. If we are to develop truly effective social policies about matters such as homelessness, mental, illness, and education, we have much to learn by "starting at home" where the origins of care have their roots.

Fiona Robinson takes Nodding's general point about the relationship between private and public ethics farther. According to Robinson, in the realm of international relations, no real progress can be made to address a problem like poverty without a critical feminist ethics of care. Robinson points that despite all the efforts traditional right – based and duty – based theorists have made to motivate nations to rid the world of its huge income gaps, poverty remains a bigger problem than ever before. Robinson thinks that traditional ethical approaches to specific problems like poverty are too abstract and generalized to motivate enough action to eliminate the actual suffering caused by poverty. Ethics must make consciousness of poverty a part of the everyday lives of people who are anything but poor. Robinson claims that we need a critical feminist ethics of care that helps privileged people understand the ways in which their affluence is related to non – privileged people's poverty. Unless privileged people give up some of their advantages by fostering certain economic, political and social changes the charitable contributions they make here and there to alleviate human misery are mostly about making themselves feel good.

2. Care- Focused: Paradigmatic Moral Relationships

About human relations, Sara Ruddick, Virginia Held and Eva Kittay have much in common with Gilligan and Noddings. They are of the view that human relationships are not between equally informed and equally powerful persons but between unequal and interdependent persons. When a parent relates to a child, or a self-confident and well adjusted adolescent to a depressed and distraught friend, for example, they do not relate as two business persons do during a contact negotiation, but as two, differentially empowered people, trying to resolve an issue of mutual concern. Ethics, they say, should be built on a model that fits life as most people experience it on an everyday basis. Not the concepts, metaphors, and images associated with the practice of contracting, but those associated with practices like parenting/mothering best express the dynamics of moral life, in the opinion of Ruddick, Held and Kittay.

In her feminist ethics of care, Ruddick claims that society should properly value what she terms maternal practice. Like any human practice, maternal practice has its own form of thinking with a vocabulary and logic peculiar to it, and its own aims and goals. In the case of maternal thinking, these aims and goals consists in the preservation, growth and acceptability of one's children.

Preserving the life of a child is the first aspect of Ruddick's maternal practice. No human being is, on the surface, more vulnerable than an infant. Infants cannot survive unless someone feeds, clothes, and shelters them. To show just how dependent infants are on their caretakers, Ruddick provides the example of Julie, an over-extended young mother with a very needful infant. Finding it increasingly difficult to care for her baby, Julie imagines herself killing her baby. Horrified by her own thought, Julie boards a city bus with her baby. She spends the night riding the bus, reasoning that as long as she and her baby remain in the public eye, she will not harm her baby.

Ruddick tells Julie's story to emphasize that mothering is not easy. Not every mother finds herself as distraught as Julie; but most mothers have days when they wish, however secretly, they were not mothers. Ruddick says that in order to be able to treat their children well on these lead days, mothers need to cultivate virtues like scrutiny (the ability to see things in perspective), humility and cheerfulness. Equipped with these virtues, people who mother will be able to roll with the punches that life delivers to children and adults like.

The second aspects of Ruddick's maternal practice is fostering children's growth. To foster a child's growth does not mean to impose some sort of ideal life script on one's child. Mothers should try to make their children perfect. Rather mothers should help their children realize that what is important in life is trying to be a better person despite one's weaknesses and foibles.

The third and final aspect of Ruddick's maternal practice are training. Typically, mothers work diligently to socialize their children—to help them become law abiding citizens. But there are times when conscientious mothers refuse to conform to society's needs or expectations. For example, a conscientious mother may refuse to get her son ready to fight for an unjust cause, or to diet her down into size 0 designer jeans. She may find herself caught between the values of a competitive, power obsessed, individualistic society on the one hand and her own conviction that these values are fundamentally flawed on the other. If a mother trains her son in the ways of the world, he may gain success in it. But he may also become an arrogant employer who runs roughshod over his employees. In contrast, if a mother raises her son to be a "nice guy", he may grow up a "loser" in society's eyes. Like all mothers, says Ruddick, a conscientious mother must decide whether her values or those of the larger society should guide her child-rearing practices. Is it more important that her child adhere to social norms or critically question them?

Ruddick's ultimate hope is to being maternal thinking into the public to get more men and women to think through issues "maternally". She points out for example, that people who think like mothers are apt to understand what was means in the concrete rather than what war means in the abstract. For maternal thinkers, war is not about making sure that one's nation comes out on top no matter what happens. Rather war is about risking the life of child whom one has spent years preserving, nurturing and training. For a maternal thinker, war is about death—about cancelling out the "product(s)" of maternal practice; it is about losing that which is most precious to one.

Like Ruddick, Virginia Held finds the relationship between

mothering persons and children an excellent paradigm for human relationships. Held speculates that were the relationship between two rational contractors the paradigm for a good human relationship society might have looked different. Yet, life is more about cooperation, consensus and community, about meeting other people's needs rather than conflict, competition and controversy. Held continues that it is to our dismay that traditional ethics not only discounts women's morality but presents to what amounts to men's morality as *gender neutral* morality. She claims that if traditional ethics were really gender neutral, it would not favour paradigms—for example, the contract model—that speak for more to men's experience than to women's (In Held's estimation too many traditional ethicists bless a human relationships as moral to the degree it serves the separate interests of individual rational contractors).

Held, however, admits that, mothering person-child relationship is not fool proof. A father-son or mother-daughter relationships can be just as oppressive as employer-employee relationships. Indeed, some intimate relationships can be far more abusive and cruel than some professional ones. It is usually easier to walk away from an abusive employer than an abusive husband.

However, Held does not advocate wholesale rejection of traditional ethics. She says that just because a feminist care based ethics can handle issues that exceed the "moral minimum" of respecting individual's rights does not mean it should trivialize this moral minimum". Mothering persons must be just as well as caring, critical thinker as well as emotionally sensitive persons able to make generalizations about human relations as well as to tease out their unique characteristics. Like principles, relationships are subject to evaluation as good, better or best (bad, worse or worst). If bad principles should not be followed, then bad relationships should not be maintained.

For Held, like other feminists, care is the fundamental and central value to feminist care ethics. Asked whether it is care or justice that is most fundamental value, Held does not hesitate to answer that it is care. As she sees it, care can exist without justice but justice cannot exist without care. Held says that before the police came into existence, these were families. Some of them were very unjust in that men were privileged over women, or that the old were favoured over the young. Still these families survived because there was enough care within them for their members to tend to each others' basic human needs and protect each others' paramount human interests. Were this caring behaviour non-existent within families, the police—with its rules, contracts, and scales of justice—would never have come into existence. Says Held, "There can be no justice without care or without care no child would survive and there would be no person to respect."

Like Ruddick who speaks of maternal thinkers and Held who speaks of mothering persons, Eva Feder Kittay also seeks to avoid the charge of female essentialism. Her feminist care ethics refers to "dependency relations" and "dependency workers" rather than "maternal relations" and "mother". For Kittay, the paradigm dependency worker is a close relative, friend or paid worker who assumes daily responsibility for a dependent's survival. The dependency worker's labour is characterized by care, concern, and connection to the dependent, and she typically suffers negative personal and/or professional consequences as a result of doing the essential work she does. According to Kittay, the dependency worker is obliged to the dependent because she is best suited to meet the dependent's needs. For example, the source of a mother's moral obligation to her infant is not the rights of the dependent person as a person, but rather the relationship that exists between the one in need and the one who is situated to meet the need. The defining characteristic of this largely socially constructed relationship is that it is not usually chosen but already given in the ties of the family, the dynamics of friendship, or the terms of employment.

Importantly, Kittay claims that the dependency relation paradigm can and should guide public policy about human equality. On her view, we are all equal because we are all the product of one or more mothers'/dependency workers' labour.

Because everyone is some mother's child, everyone has the experience of being dependent on someone—indeed radically dependent on someone for mere existence. It is only fair that society takes care of all its dependency workers, including its official mothers. For society to do anything less than this for dependency workers is to wrong not only dependency workers but also those who depend on them. It is to gradually unweave the entire fabric that binds society together. Thus, if society wants to keep itself together, Kittay insists the first goal of public policy must be to empower society's dependency workers.

3. Status-Oriented Feminist Approaches to Ethics

Status-oriented feminist approaches to ethics is asking questions about power, that is, domination and subordination, before moving on to questions about *good* versus *evil, care* versus *justice,* and *maternal* versus *parental thinking*. It is not that status-oriented feminists are more or less feminist than care-focused feminists. It is just that their emphasis is different than the emphasis of care-focused feminists.

Status-oriented feminist ethicists approach the systematic subordination of women to men in many different ways. Liberal, radical, Marxist/socialist, multicultural, global, and ecological feminists have each offered a different sets of explanations and solutions for women's "second sex" status. So, too have existentialist, psychoanalytic, postmodern and third wave feminists. Proponents of these schools of feminist thought maintain that the destruction of all systems, structures, institutions, and practices that create or maintain invidious power differentials between men and women is the necessary prerequisite for the creation of gender equality. In someways, then seem to think that, contra Held, justice precedes care.

1. Liberal, Radical Marxist / Socialist, Multicultural, Global and Ecological Approaches

Liberal feminists have their historical roots in Mary

Wollstonecraft's "Vindication of the Rights of Women", John Stuart Mill's "The subjection of Women", and the women's suffrage movement of the nineteenth century. Among the organizations with which contemporary liberal feminists are most aligned is the National Organization of Women (NOW). Liberal feminists maintain that the primary cause of women's subordination to men is a set of social norms and formal laws that make it hard for women to succeed in the public world. Unless women have the same opportunities that men have women will not be able to achieve their full potential in the academy, the forum, the market place, the operating room, and so forth. Although many people think that liberal feminism is passī and that the ethical issues that preoccupied it have been resolved, truth be told as of 2009, the Bill of (Women's) Rights proclaimed by NOW in 1967 in the United States, for example, has yet to be fully implemented. U.S. Women's reproductive rights are still not secure and the Equal Rights Amendment has yet to pass. Moreover, as of 2009, the average U.S. female worker still earns about 20 per cent less than the average male worker (Maher, *The Wall street Journal,* 2008); only 17 of 100 U.S. Senators are women (Confessore and Hakim, *New York Times,* January 21, 2009). and as of December 2008, only 13 fortune 500 CEOs are women. (CNN Money.com, 2009). If the goal of liberal feminism is to push women full force into the public word and catapult women to its higher orbits, then its work is far from done. Women tend to do mostly dependency work—the work upon which Eva Feder Kittay focuses—and, in the public world, that care giving work is some of the lowest status, lowest paid work to be had.

Radical feminists think that the liberal feminist agenda is wrongly focused on weak "affirmative action" remedies like Equal -Pay-For-Equal (or comparable)-work and Maternity leave. Women will remain the second sex, in their estimation, until that day and time when women gain full control over their reproductive powers and sexual desires. At first, radical feminists were rather "libertarian" in their attitudes towards sexuality and reproduction. They encouraged women to experiment with all types of consensual sex including ethically controversial ones like sadomasochism. They also urged women to bear children as painlessly as possible. Why go through an uncomfortable pregnancy and painful childbirth experience when you can instead use a surrogate mother—even better, a hypothetical artificial womb—to have your child for you? Finally, "liberatarian" radical feminists pushed women to become as androgynous as possible. The less women tried to embody the traits of "Woman" as society has constructed her, the more free and equal to men would women be.

Later some radical feminists began to have doubts about libertarian prescriptions for women. This group of radical feminists, sometimes referred to as "cultural feminists", cautioned that heterosexual sex was far more harmful and compulsory than beneficial and consensual for women. They maintained that heterosexuality, viewed as an institution has as its purpose to control and objectively women's sexuality for the gratification of men. Cultural radical feminists also maintained that artificial/ technological means of reproduction were a threat to women, meant to gradually deprive women of their exclusive power to bring new life into the world. Deprived of this power, women would be of value primarily as "sex-objects". Finally, challenging the "androgynous" ideal of the fully good human person, they rejected "male" / "masculine" ways of being, thinking, and acting as defective. Why try to be like a "man" – that is an aggressive, hyper-competitive and war-mongering individual—when you can instead be a "woman", that is, a cooperative, caring and peace-making individual?

Although these are problems with extreme forms of libertarian radical feminism on the one hand and extreme form of cultural radical feminism on the other hand, radical feminist thought has managed to generate some very useful ethical work. So called lesbian ethics is a particularly rich, though controversial addition to feminist ethical theory for example. Its contested nature stems from the face that it has been developed primarily to serve women-centered women and, in some versions, only lesbian women.

According to philosopher Sarah Lucia Hoagland, one of the most well-known developers of lesbian ethics, the quintessential moral question for lesbians is "Does this contribute to my self-creation, freedom and liberation?" rather than, "Is this good?" or "Am I good?" (Hoagland Lesbian Ethics, 1989). About Hoagland's point, Mailyn Frye claims that "traditional ethics is preoccupied with questions about goodness because its proponents have a vested interest not only in being good, but also in making others good." For example, a white / Christian / middle class heterosexual American male bases his conception of himself as an authority leader, or boss upon his conviction that he is in the right—that he knows what is good for others as well as himself. So long as women continue to accept this conception of moral agency, says Frye, they no less than men, will continue to think that ethics is about knowing what is best for everyone and then imposing this best on them no matter how painful or harmful doing so proves to be. (Frye, "A Response to Lesbian Ethics: Why Ethics?" 1991).

Claiming that lesbian ethicists have no interest in imposing their good upon anyone but themselves, Hoagland and Frye theorize that in so far as lesbians are concerned, the act of choosing, in and of itself, makes the object or action of choice good. More than any other tenant of lesbian ethics, it is this one that provokes as comment from critics. They doubt that just because a lesbian freely chooses to do something, it is thereby morally justified for her to do so.

Hoagland has a response to this challenge. She notes that society has imposed so many limitations and boundaries on lesbian choice that perhaps for now choice is of more moral importance to lesbians than the things chosen. Yet Hoagland is not prepared to claim that there are absolutely no limit on lesbian choice. At one point in her analysis of what constitutes moral agency and interaction, for example, Hoagland observes that in choosing for herself, a lesbian chooses for other lesbians, who in turn chooses for her. Lesbians do not weave value in isolation from each other, they weave value together. Ethics is not an individualistic quest with moral value emerging from somewhere deep within one's self or from far outside of one's self. On the contrary, moral value—that is, personal meaning—emerges from what Hoagland terms "lesbian context" an energy field capable of resisting oppression. A lesbian approach to ethics, is then about lesbians becoming the kind of human beings who refuse to dominate or to be dominated (Hoagland, Lesbian Ethics, 1989).

Marxist/Socialist feminists disagree mainly with liberal feminists. They claim it is difficult, perhaps even impossible, for oppressed persons (especially women) to do well in a class system. The only effective way to end woman's subordination to men, is to replace the capitalist systems with socialist systems in which both women and men are paid fair wages for their work. Women must be men's economic equals before they can be as powerful as men.

Significantly, contemporary Marxist/ Socialist feminists are far less beholder in the traditional Marxist view that women's relatively low social status is only a function of whether or not women are part of the paid, productive workforce. Over the years and largely as a result of incorporating many radical feminist ideas into their own theory and practice, Marxist/Socialist feminist have increasingly produced works like Juliet Mitchell's "Women's Estate" in which she argues that four socio-economic structures over determined women's status; specifically, women's role in production, reproduction, sexuality, and the socialization of children. Women's role is all of these structures must change if they are to be men's equals. Furthermore, as Mitchell adds in *Psychoanalysis and Feminism,* women's interior world – their psyches—must also be transformed, for unless women are convinced of their own value, change in their exterior world cannot totally liberate them.

Multicultural Feminists affirm much of what other schools of feminist though say about women's status, but they fault them for not being fully attentive to the inseparability of structures and systems of gender, race and class. As they see it, feminists should not focus exclusively on women's oppression as women or as workers or as members of a disadvantaged racial or ethnic group. Rather. they should understand that everything about a woman— the colour of her skin, the fatness of her purse, the direction of her sexual desires, the age on her birth certificate— explains her status in society. Even if they are separable in theory, racism, sexism and classism are not separable in fact. Many women are the victims of "multiple jeopardy" and "interlocking system of oppression" (Bell Hooks, Yearing : *Race, Gender and Cultural Politics*, p. 59), For example, an undocumented Hispanic woman in the United States working as a low paid domestic helper for a white woman who is high paid lawyer, is multiply oppressed. Viewed as an interloper, an alien, an intruder, one of those people who have no "right" to be in the United States, she may start to feel badly about herself. Her identity and view of herself as someone who is acting responsibly as possible in trying circumstances may be eroded. Multiple oppression takes a spiritual/psychological toll as well as material toll on people.

Although global feminists and post-colonial feminists largely praise the work of multicultural feminists, they nonetheless regard it as a somewhat incomplete discussion of women's oppression. They emphasize that women in so called First World countries (located primarily in the Northern Hemisphere) need to better appreciate the status and situation of women in so called Third World countries (located primarily in the Southern Hemisphere). All too often, feminists focus in a nearly exclusive manner on the gender politics of their own countries. Thus, while U.S. feminists struggle to formulate laws to prevent sexual harassment in the workplace, women in other countries are stoned to death for adultery or subjected to genital cutting (including infibulations in some instances). Similarly while U.S. feminists protest against pharmacists who, because of their conscientious objection to abortion, make it difficult for some U.S. women to secure emergency contraceptive pills, many women in other countries have been little or no access to family planning services and die from botched illegal abortions or, as the result of poorly managed pregnancies and childbirths. Postcolonial feminists do more than call attention to the fact that women in the First World Typically have more material goods than women in the Third World typically have. They also underscore the fact that some of the privileges First World women have are bought at the expense of Third World women, many of whom are exported to the First World to work as low paid homecare aides, domestic servants, or nannies.

Ecofeminists agree with global and postcolonial feminists that it is important for women to understand how women's interests diverge as well as converge. However they fault them and most other feminists for not paying attention to human beings' responsibilities to non-human animals. Some eco-feminists, for instance, have developed *Gilligan's ethics of care as a foundation for animal defense theory.* Similar to feminist ethics, feminist animal care theory arose as a critical response to utilitarian and right based animal ethics (Singer – Animal Liberation, 1974; Reagan, The Care of Animal Rights, 1983). Critics argue that these rationalistic frameworks are inadequate because they maintain an anthropocentric importance (i.e. the more non-human animals are similar to us the greater moral consideration they enjoy) and as a result fail to see non-human animals on their own terms with unique preferences, needs and realities. Another concern with justice-oriented approaches lies in their explicit denial or suppression of the role of emotions in our moral deliberations about the abuse of non-human animals. When one considers the lack of emotional response to animal suffering as a major reason why abuse continues, it seems antiethical to exclude care when addressing the proper treatment of non-human animals. (Donavan and Adams, Feminist Care Tradition in Animal Ethics, 2007). That is not to say we ought to dispense with the utilitarian and right based models. They present useful arguments for the ethical treatment of nonhuman animals. The point is, according to Josephine Donovan, "it is not only possible—indeed, necessary—to ground that ethic in an emotional and spiritual conversation with non human life forms. Out of woman's relational culture of caring and attentive love, therefore, emerges the basis for a feminist ethic for the treatment of animals. We should not kill, eat, torture, and exploit animals because they do not want to be so treated, and we know that. If we listen, we can hear them (Donovan, Signs, p. 375). The care approach to animals ethics consists of an empathetic way of understanding the plight of individual animals in patriarchal and capitalistic institutions. Proponents maintain that sympathetic responsiveness, compassion, and care can and should inform our ethical understanding as to why we have a responsibility to free non-human animals from human domination. Our treatment of the natural world is another matter. Part of the reason why our world is characterized by injustice, lack of care, and huge socio-economic disparities between different people is that we treat the natural world with difference and sometimes even contempt, say ecofeminsts. We stock pile of weapons of mass destruction, consume energy resources, if they were infinite, dump waste into our waters, and slaughter animals for meat, we really do not need to eat. In so doing, we manifest our belief that it is our right to control nature to create a better world for ourselves. But we are suffering from a delusion in our feverish attempt to dominate nature, says Ynestra King. Nature is rebelling and the human species is setting its own annihilation in motion as it, deters forests and extinguishes animal species.[16]

2. *Existentialist, Psychoanalytic, Postmodern and Third Wave Approaches*

Departing from modes of feminist thought that stress the material consequences of second sex status, existential feminists focus on the psychological consequences. In 'The Second Sex', Semone de Beauvoir writes that, from the beginning, man has named himself the Self and woman the Other. If the other is a threat to the self, then women are a threat to men. If men wish to remain free, they must not only subordinate women to themselves, but also convince women they deserve no better treatment. Thus, if women are to become true Selves, they must recognize themselves as autonomous agents who are free to chart the course of their own destinies. Women should refuse to define themselves in terms of men and simply go their own way.

Like existentialist feminists, psychoanalytic feminists seek an explanation of women's status in the inner recesses of women's psyche. As they see it, as children are reared almost exclusively by women, boys and girls are psychosocialized in very different ways. Boys grow up desiring to separate themselves from others and from feminine values culturally linked to their mothers and sisters. In contrast, girls grow up like "little women" replicating their mothers' behaviour and wanting to remain connected to them and others. Moreover, because of the ways in which patriarchal systems and structures shape human beings' values, boys and girls come to think that allegedly masculine values such as justice and conscientiousness, which they associate with culture, are more fully human than allegedly feminine values such as caring and kindness, which they associate with nature.

Seeking to free women from a psychosexual dreams that causes women as well as men to view women as of less value than men some psychoanalytic feminists reason that the source of this wrong-headed view of women is rooted in society's reliance on women to do its care giving tasks, and men to do its world building tasks. They claim that were men to devote as much time to fathering as women devote to mothering and were women to work just as hard in the world of enterprise as men do, then children would no longer identify home with women and work with men. Instead, they would grow up thinking of their parents as two human beings who value, in relatively equal measure, the benefits of both home life and work life.

Significantly, not all psychoanalytic feminists think that a dual parenting/dual working arrangements is the remedy for the infamous Oedipus complex described above. In passing through this complex, the boy is fully integrated into culture. In exchange for giving up his first love object, his mother, the boy not only escapes castration at the hand of the father, he gets to rule over the irrational powers of both nature and women unable to get through the Oedipus complex nearly as well as boys do, girls, who have no penises to lose, do not completely separate from their mothers. As a result the girl's integration into culture is never full. Women exist at society's peripheries and margins, as they are who do not rule but are instead ruled. Thus, in the estimation of some psychoanalytic feminists, the only way to change women's states in society is to reject the view that human beings will remain in the state of nature unless they pass through the Oedipus complex. Lucy Irigaray and Julia Kristeva advice women to stay in what they term the Imaginary, the place in which mother and infant are symbiotically united. To leave this place to enter the so called symbolic Order that is, men's world of language, rules, and laws making little sense for woman. Instead of entering this world in which they are inevitably oppressed and suppressed, women should stay in the Imaginary where they can take joy in their difference from men and live life on their own terms. Civilization will not collapse if women stay in the Imaginary but patriarchy will crumble.

Finally, as postmodern and third wave feminists see it, all attempts to provide as single explanation for women's oppression is flawed. There is no entity, "Women," upon whom a label may be fixed. Women are individuals, each with a unique story to tell about her particular self. Moreover, any single explanation for "Women's status is simply another instantiation of so called "phallogocentric" thought: that is, the kind of "male thinking" that insists on telling as absolute truth one and only one story about reality. Women must, in the estimation of postmodern and third wave feminists, reveal their differences to each other so that they can better resist the patriarchal tendency to centre and congenial thought into a rigid truth that always was, is and for ever will be. To become themselves, women must embrace conflict, even self-contradiction; they do not have to follow any script, including a self-imposed one, throughout their lives.

4. Conclusion

Care-focused and status-focused feminist approaches to ethics do not impose a single normative standard on women. Rather they offer to women multiple ways to understand the ways in which gender, race, class, and so forth affect their moral decisions. Because feminist approaches to ethics tend to be genocentric as well as gender sensitive, non-feminist critics of them have complained that these approaches are "female-biased". Ethics insist these critics, cannot proceed from a specific standpoint in this case, from the standpoint of women and still be regarded as an ethics. Indeed, traditional ethics has proceeded on the assumption that its values and rules apply to all rational persons equally. Yet, most traditional ethical theories seemed to be based on the moral experience of men—usually powerful ones as opposed to women.

Feminists developing care-focused and status-focused approaches to ethics may safely argue that they are trying to do what traditional ethicists should have done in the first place, namely pay as much attention to women's moral experience as men's. In the same way that historians have ignored the stresses, strains, and struggles of the private world of children, church, and kitchen to focus on the economic revolutions, political upheavals and military conquests of the public world, traditional ethicists have all too often focused on men's moral interests, issues and values to the neglect of women's. Therefore, when proponent of feminist ethics insists on highlighting women's morality, she may simply be doing some remedial work adding women's moral experiences to a male-biased ethical tradition sorely in need of them.

However, she may be doing more than this. She may be suggesting that it is not enough for traditional ethics to incorporate women's interests and issues, and to recognize women moral agents who must be taken seriously. On the contrary, she may be urging traditional ethics to rethink the ontological and epistemological assumptions upon which their thinking is based; and to consider the possibility, that far from being sources of human liberation, their principles, rules, regulations, norms, and criteria actually serve to support patterns of domination and subordination that demoralize everyone.

If ethics is about human beings liberation, then Abison Jaggar's summary of the fourfold function of feminist ethics can not be improved upon in any significant way. According to Jaggar, all feminist approaches to ethics seek to (1) articulate moral critiques of actions and practices that perpetuate women's subordinations; (2) prescribe morally justifiable ways of resisting such actions and practices; (3) envision morally alternatives for such actions and practices; and (4) take women's moral experience seriously, though not uncritically (Jaggar, "Feminist Ethics", 1992). Feminist ethicists should aim, first and foremost, to improve the overall condition for women in particular and also for other vulnerable people like children, the elderly, the infirm, the disabled and disadvantages minorities.

Although feminist, ethicists' different interpretations of what constitutes a voluntary and intentional choice, an illegitimate or legitimate exercise of control and a healthy or a pathological relationship reassure the intellectual and moral community that after all, feminism is not a monolithic ideology that prescribes one and only one way for all women to be, this fashion of thinking is also the occasion of considerable political fragmentation among feminists. Asked to come to the policy table to express the feminist perspective on a moral issue, all that an honest feminist ethicist can say is that there is no such perspective. Yet, if feminists have no clear, cogent, and unified position on key moral issues, then perspectives less congenial to women may fill the gap.

Although it is crucial for feminist ethicists to emphasize, for example, how a policy that benefits one group of women might at the same time harm another group of women, it is probably a mistake for feminist ethicists not to endorse polices able to serve the most important interests of the widest range of women. For this reason, many feminist ethicists believe they have an obligation first to listen to women's differing points of view and then to fashion a consensus view form them. Whether it is possible to achieve this goal is uncertain, however. Nonetheless, feminists ethicists remain committed to the task of pulling all women towards the goal of gender equality with men. The twenty first century will, no doubt, see new advances in feminist ethics as it meets the challenge of living in a globalized world.

REFERENCES

1. Mary Wollstonecraft : *A Vindication of the Rights of Women*, p. 117.
2. J.S. Mill: *The Subjection of Women*, p. 32.
3. Beecher and Stowe: *The American Woman's Home,* 1971.
4. Buhle and Buhle, (eds.) *The Concise History of Women's Suffrage.*
5. Gilman: *Herland*, 1979.
6. Tong: *Feminine and Feminist Ethics*, 1993.
7. Gilligan: *In a Different Voice*, 1982.
8. Bartky: *Feminity* and *Domination*, 1990.
9. *Ibid.*
10. Ynestra King: *Healing the Wounds: Feminism, Ecology and Nature/ Culture Dualism*, 1995.

BIBLIOGRAPHY

1. Beasley, Chris: *What is Feminism?: An Introduction to Feminist Theory*, London: Sage Publications
2. Bubbeck, Chilla : *Re-Orienting Western Feminisms: Women's Diversity in a Postcolonial World*, New York, Cambridge University Press.
3. Firestone, S: *The Dialectic of Sex*; New York: Bantam Books.
4. Gilman, C.P (1979) *Women and Economics*, New York: Harker and Row.

Chapter – 12

Women in Islam and Hinduism – An Analysis in Indian Context

Damodar Singh

The place of women in society is one of the indices of civilizing processes of human mind and behaviour. In an essentially patriarchal society, wherein the male is the dominant partner who takes advantage of females, the women are automatically relegated to a secondary position, if not made victims of oppression and discrimination. This makes women's status one of the most controversial and serious issues of our time. The reader may find himself perplexed owing to the large number of books that treat this subject, for the most part, superficially and partially. Some cover achievements for the woman, maintaining that several religions, not to exclude Islam and Hinduism, had, in fact, given women their due rights and honour, while others blame all the disadvantages in the position of women on their respective religions. In this paper, I intend to discuss the status of women in Islam and Hinduism. Since Hinduism is predominantly found in India, I shall confine myself to the Indian society.

In pre-Islamic Arabia women were a possession to be used by males, abused, and even inherited. There was no clear-cut idea of incest, and sexual abuse of women was frequent, sexual liaison outside the tribe only was considered adultery. Women did not possess any rights whatsoever, and did not function either socially, economically or juridically. They were considered instruments of pleasure and procreation and in the pre-Islamic Arabic society, an individual child was the child of the tribe, juridically. This attitude of women was not peculiar to pre-Islamic Arabia, but was common in almost all civilized countries, more so in the Western world, which has been approved by Plato[1] and more definitely by Aristotle[2], considered to be the prime mentor of Western civilization.

On the other hand, the pre-colonial India was invaded by several racial groups—Shakas, Huns, Kushanas etc., who ruled over the acquired area and, in due course, barring the Muslims / Turks, all of them were assimilated into the Indian society. In consequence, the country has been an admixture of different racial groups during the various stages of development. However, there are some common streaks which impart characteristics of "Indianness" to the various aspects of life in India. As regard to women, an average Indian view, echoing the usual male chauvism, is that she is a *bhogya*, i.e. a vehicle to impart pleasure to man, an attitude in keeping with man's atavistic mind. This has been responsible for the brutalities inflicted on womankind in war and peace in all countries and in all ages. But then differentiation when one considers domestic life; for a Hindu woman becomes *bharyya*, that is a companion. She becomes a civilizing factor, a partner in life, and, as the Aryans put it, *sadharmini*, an equal participant in the religious and spiritual life of man, a real helpmate in the battle of life; "united in life and thereafter", as marriage vow says. As *Silappadigram*, a Tamilian classic, as well as Sanskrit works like *Mrichchhakatika* show, women in Ancient India had wit, intelligence, grace and poise; she was not merely a housewife or a domesticated being, but had a public character of her own. But, then she basked in a reflected glory in what was essentially a man's world: a joint and an aid, sometimes a playmate but more often than not a plaything" as the poet Bhartrihari says. It should also be remembered that no nation has excelled the Indians in producing erotic literature. *Anang-*

Rang and *Kamasutra* are manuals for the art of love which for sensuous details, and for a psychological insight in the erogenous zones of the body of both men and women remain unparalleled. These works do not show the Ancient Indians exactly as ascetics or abstemious, as the common supposition is, but rather as men and women bent upon drinking the cup of sensual pleasures to the last drop. The Indian womanhood, however, had another character, that of a *pujyya*, one to be worshipped as "Mother" for, after all, she was the procreator of the race, at once the cause and effect of the continuity of mankind. The *Tantras* says that a woman's feet are to be worshipped as those of a *guru* or preceptor. In short, the Indians interpreted womanhood in three forms, as a beloved, as a wife and as a mother; the treatment to be given to them differed according to the character they lived.

Islam, however, has no use for such sophistry. It does not view women in conjunction with man. She is considered an independent entity, with her own rights and obligations defined both as an individual and in reciprocal relationship with man as well. Such a view was no doubt revolutionary, and a precursor to modern ideas about women's place in society. The advent of Islam brought a great deal of emancipation of woman from the bondage of man. At earlier civilization, she was considered, an instrument of pleasure and procreation' as in old Aryan view; and a 'mere chattel and possession' as in pre-Islamic society. Islam attempted to change the said notions. No matrimonial alliance was valid in Muslim law without express consent of the bride. No father had the right to dispose her off as he liked, as she was considered to have a will of her own recognized and sanctioned by Islamic injunctions. This may be contrasted with the old Hindu view in regard to the fate of the daughters. The basic assumption in Hinduism is that a daughter never belongs to the family of the father, as Yaska[3] declares: "they gave away to other the female children. There exists *dana*, *vikraya*, and *atisarga* of the female but not of the male." In other words, a daughter was to be given in gift (*dana*), or in sale (*vikraya*) or simply abandoned (*atisarga*). The Vedic Indians who formulated such ideas for social organization appear or have excessively with notions of purity of the race, as well as with the fertility syndrome. Purity of race was the prime consideration, but then they appear to have been aware of the principle of eugenics that cross-fertilization is necessary for healthy and abundant procreation; constant fertilization within the same social group results in dwindling of numbers as well as lopsided development of progeny. Hence, the conception of *dana*, gifting of the daughter for purpose of marriage outsides the clan (*gotra*), but within the racial group (*varna*). Thus, Vedic marriages were both endogamous as well as exogamous, ensuring purity of race and cross-fertilization. *Vikraya*, sale, was a less reputable device, but was still recognized if it became necessary for both sides. Giving of daughter by the king to another king as part of diplomatic alliance was also a form of *vikraya.* One comes across several instances of diplomatic marriages alliance between Rajput kings and Mughal Emperors.[4] *Atisarga* (abandonment) was, of course, the most despicable mode of disposal, and was rarely practiced. Kalidas, the great Sanskrit poet, has risen to great heights in depicting the situation when Sakuntala, having come from the *ashram*, where she had been brought up and where she had got married to the king Dushayant after a romance with him, is disowned by him. Her dignified disdain of the king as *anarya*, un-Aryan, a term of contemptuous abuse is illustrative of the wounded pride of a forlon and abandoned woman.[5] It is, therefore, clear that irrespective of sanctity attached to *dana* of a daughter as a sacramental form of marriage in Hindu conception and practice, the personal feelings of women as an individual is of much less importance than her position or utility on the social plane.

The stand of Islam, on the contrary, is one of equality of sexes. Marriage is a contract between two contracting parties of opposite sex, entered into willingly, to live together according to Islamic injunctions, the right of dissolution of the contract inherting both the parties. The contract is also subject to payment of a fixed amount of dower by the male to the female, fixed at the time of contract, a kind of jointure, enforceable under law and custom. Lord Buddha had advocated equality of sexes, and admitted women to the ascetic order; so had the Jains. But then, with no clear-cut social formulations, equality of sexes both among the Buddhist and the Jains had remained pious wishes. The admission of women into ascetic order only provides the equality of abstinence and austerities, and does not extend to equality of life and comfort. It was a kind of *atisarga*, abandonment, than the conferring of any privilege on womanhood. Islam, however, does not admit of any ascetic order, male and female. It, as a matter of fact, does not admit any special class among the faithfuls, and inequality, in any form, is repugnant to Islamic teachings. Even then, complete equality between the sexes could not be achieved even in such egalitarianism. For example, in case of adultery (all extra-marital relationship are fornications in the eyes of Islamic laws), the dice is heavily loaded against women in comparison to men in respect of proof of guilt and punishment for guilt as well. This could not be the fault of Islamic teachings; the drawbacks, if any, are the result of human infirmities, and the then Semitic ideas and practices which Islam, in spite of itself, could not shun completely.

Islam, significantly, ensured economic independence for women by giving to daughters, along with sons, a share in the inheritance of the property of the father, and to widow, a share in the estate of her husband along with her sons and daughters. Dower was actually a promised share to the wife in the estate of her husband, and could be collected. She is, above all, a person with legal status in the eyes of Islamic laws.[6] However, in old Hindu law, rights of women to inherit property either as daughter or as widow was denied, but not her right to posses her property, called as *stridhana*, which included gifts and bequests received at the time of marriage, and property acquired either from the income of *stridhana* or out of savings from the maintenance allowance to which she was entitled as a widow out of her husbands's property. She was, therefore, not such a helpless creature as in some European/ Christian countries. It may be noted here that in Hindu polity, from the king to the commoner, the right to possess or inherit property was not absolute even for Hindu males; it was limited to possession, and to enjoying their fruits of the property, but not to the property itself which was considered to be in the nature of trust. It would be interesting in this context to note the views of a modern philosopher Schophenhaur. He assigns definitely a loser position to women, who are inclined to extravagance because they live only in the present. He says: "Women think that it is men's business to earn money, and theirs to spend it. I am, therefore, of opinion that women should never be allowed altogether to manage their own concerns, be it of father, of husband, of son or of the state, as in the case in Hindosthani and that consequently they should never be given full power to dispose of any property they have not themselves acquired."[7]

One common charge against Islamic law in regard to women is that Islam sanctions and practices polygamy, and, therefore, cannot be called such a champion of women's rights as it is made out to be. However, a careful scrutiny of relevant *Qur'anic* precepts would exhibit that though possession of more than one wife in special circumstances was allowed, polygamy by itself does not appear to have had a general sanction. The Holy *Qur'an* says:

> And if you are apprehensive that you shall not deal fairly with orphans, then of other women who seem good in your eyes marry but two, three or four, and if you still fear that you shall not act equitably then one only.[8]

As stated earlier, in pre-Islamic society, the child was a charge of the whole tribe. At the time of advent of Islam, wars had ravaged between believers and non-believers, involving large killings, and many children of the tribe were left orphaned. It was to provide for such orphans that the *Holy Qur'an* allowed marriages—two, three, four so that the orphans might get fatherly affection. This was the special circumstances in which marrying more than one wife was allowed; but then again, the rider was a difficult, if not an impossible one. All the wives were to be treated equally. If one was not sure that he would have equal affection for all his wives, he was debarred from marrying more than one wife even to meet special situation. Polygamy is allowed in Islam only to meet an exigency and to fulfil a social duty, not for satisfaction of lust. On going through these injunctions one would see that marriage a second, third or fourth time was to be with widows and mature women, as the prime consideration was welfare of orphans. The principle of Islamic equality prevails here, in the care and consideration Islam had for women.

Citing the personal example of Prophet Muhammad the *Holy Qur'an* clarifies:

> O Prophet! We allow thee thy wives whom thou hast dowered, and the slaves whom thy right hand possesseth out of the booty which hath granted thee, and the daughters of thy uncle, and of thy paternal aunts who migrated with thee to Medina, and any believing woman who hath given herself up to the Prophet, if the Prophet desired to wed her – *a privilege to thee above the rest of the faithfuls.*[9]

Thus, the privilege ganted to the Prophet applies to him only and to no other. There is a Perisan saying "*Khuda ra khuda danad*" — "God only knows God's way" and this applies appropriately to such special privileges.

It is true that constant interpretation, re-interpretation and codification of the *Qur'an* and the *Hadith* by various Muslim jurists and divines, coloured by their personal inclinations and pre-possessions, as also the customs and the usage of the different countries and the changing times they lived in, did produce a great deal of variations not contemplated originally. The 8th and 9th centuries were periods of consolidation and expansion of Islam in various countries. Abu Abd Malik Ibn Anas (716-795), founder of the Malik School of Law, favoured the historical approach to *Shariat*, but being a practical jurist, he often went beyond *Qur'an*, and strove for agreed solutions based on common sense and exigencies of circumstances. However, Abu Hanif Al-Niman Ibn Thabit (700-767), who was among the earliest of jurists, and founder of Hanifi School of Law, was more acceptable. Ahmad Ibn Hanbal (780-855) was a stickler for form, Imam Bukhari (Abu Abdullah Ibn Ismail) (810-870) collected 7,00,00 *Hadith*, but applying stricter rules of reliability, actually accepted only 7,000 of them. It was, however, Abul Hassan Ashiruddin Muslim (817-825), better known as Imam Muslim, who divided the *Hadith* under different heads. However, Shia Muslims do not accept all the 7,000 *Hadith*, and are said to believe in only about 6,000 of them, arranged in four books, known as *Kutub-i-Arbna*. In such circumstances, there was bound to be clash and confusion of views. It was left to Abu Hamid Md. Al-Ghazzali (1058-1111) to reconcile many of these conflicting views and interpretations. His method and approach was intuitive; he went more by faith than reason, and prayed to God to send him just thoughts in His wisdom. "Inner light is a surer guide than the outer, physical light", he says. No wonder he has been called *Hijjatul Islam*, the Proof of Islam. If, therefore, we find any deviation from the original Islamic position in regard to women it is due to the fact that both Semitic and customary law, as the case may be, were allowed to operate in many of the countries, including India, where Islam was adopted as a religion.

In India, the position, to say the least, was curious. Muslim invaders came to India in waves not to proselytize—not like the Ansars[10] of the old—but to find home, hearth and fief. Most of the conversions they effected were born of military, political or social necessity. It was, however, the Sufi saints who generally spread the light of Islam on an extensive and almost countrywide scale, laying stress more on the substance of faith than its form. Foreigners coming from Central Asia and the Middle East brought along with them their local variations. Added to this, there was the mental make up of the Indian converts. As habit to an individual is on the personal plane, so is custom on the collective plane. In regard to chastity and fidelity of women, Indians had very strong views; this persisted with the Muslims too. Divorce, though sanctioned, was rarely resorted to. Again in regard to incestuous liaison, the prohibited degrees were wider and more extensive in India than those in the Islamic laws, and generally the Indian Muslims observed their old taboos in this regard customarily, and marriages among first cousins were rare among Indian converts. The practice in Islam had grown to keep four wives; there was no such limit in Indian society. But, generally, the common masses of people could not normally afford more than one wife, and polygamy, if at all, was practiced mostly among the rich and princely classes, both Muslims and Hindus.

One evil practice that the Muslim rulers, in an attempt to imitate the Persian court, adopted was the keeping of a seraglio or *harem* which was sometimes copied by the Rajputs and other Hindu royal families. Under the *Shariat* law, the Muslim kings were permitted to have only four wives, as against the pre-Islamic norms in Persia wherein there was no such restriction to the rulers. However, *harem* was habitually maintained by the wives of the king, which—quite similar to the royal court of the King—invariable served as an inner court, conducted by the chief queen with her own retinue of female officials, eunuchs, and female followers. It was, one would say, a female kingdom where writ of the chief queen ran and the king rarely intervened. There were intrigues galore, and dramas of passion and profligacy, kindness and compassion were enacted frequently. Sometimes the inner court also interfered and exercised undue influence in affairs of the state. Taking a queue to it, the Muslim nobles and *Amirs* of the court also kept *harem* on smaller scale. However, it should be noted that far from being only a social phenomenon, this practice had far reaching and disastrous consequences for the abilities and character of the people in positions of power. For one thing, a rival seat of power of the court did not allow a polity of nobles to emerge who could take independent and healthy decisions in moments of crisis and advise and act accordingly; secondly, it sapped the energies of the ruler to manage two kingdoms—one real and the other pseudo. The *harem*, most of all, exercised a deleterious effect on the upbringing of the princes of the realm, and with exceptions, made them unfit, by training and inclination, to be efficient administrators. This was indeed one of the most potent causes of decline of the Mughal empire in India, and later on, of the Turkish empire in Europe. As Stanley Lanepool said, "the Muslims in India had grown effete; a race of conquerors had become a jostling crowd."

Islam prescribes *hejab* or modest in dress and manners. The Hindu also considered modesty to be an ornament for the women. However, due to historical reasons, as also the fact that in a male dominated society beautiful women were considered a possession and were likely to be carried away by the enemies, if unguarded, in those turbulent days of unsettled conditions in Middle East, Central Asia, and Northern India, the practice of wearing a veil or *purdah* came in vogue. The nobility did not allow unfamiliar males to gaze upon their ladies; the portraits of royal ladies are more a product of imagination than of reality. This also resulted in cloistering the ladies of noble birth, stunting their growth intellectually and spiritually, even though there were some remarkable exceptions and a few of them became historical figures. However, this was not the case of women of working classes, either Hindus or Muslims, but then, certain social evils, like child marriage, and female infanticide in some Hindu communities crept in. The tribals were mostly unaffected by these social changes, and in some tribal communities of central India, Kamrup, and hilly regions, it was mostly the women who dominated socially and economically, the males being generally so many wastrels.

The real difficulty in regard to inheritance by women arose from the law of inheritance in an agricultural country, like India where all social institutions, customs and economic activities were woven around an agricultural almanac. Islam enjoins a well-defined scheme of proportionate share in property of the deceased, for sons, daughters, widows etc. Now, the main property in India consisted of agricultural lands with rights of tillage and possession and could be inherited. Mere title to land was of no great consequence, as the utility of land consisted in its tillage and not in its mere possession, and agricultural occupation were the joint effort of the entire family. Parcelling of land resulted in uneconomic holdings. Daughters married elsewhere without a habitat in the village itself could not be expected to carry on the agricultural operations properly, at least in small holdings. These were the practical difficulties in ensuring strict observance of the Islamic law of inheritance, and Indian converts. Generally, chose to follow their old customary law of inheritance. Since *Urfi* law or customary law is also recognized in Muslim law, the Muslim divines chose to ignore these deviations from Islamic practice, and the rulers, on demand, enforced customary law in respect to Indian converts. Then again, many of the Hindu chieftains who turned Muslim continued to observe the law of primogeniture, and chose to claim the right to impartible estate to themselves. However, the nobles of foreign extraction generally followed the Islamic inheritance law, though, in their case too, deviations were not rare.

This state of affairs continued right through the British rule. It was only in 1937 that, in the heat of communal passions, enactment was made for uniform application of *Shariat* law to all Muslims irrespective of any customary law to the contrary. An opportunity was thus lost to maintain a common code of inheritance for all Indians, Hindus, Muslims and others in the light of these historical developments.

REFERENCES

1. Plato states: "The courage of a man and that of a woman are not, as Socrates supposed, the same; the courage of a man is shown in commanding: that of a woman in obeying, as the poet says 'silence is glory'" – *see* Plato, quoted in Aristotle, *Politics,* I.13.
2. Cf. Aristrotle, *De Gen Animalium*, II.3; Aristrotle, *Hist. Animalium,* VIV. 1; Aristrotle, *Politics,* I.5. The author considers that a woman is to man as the slave to the master, the manual to the mental worker, the barbarian to the Greek. His definite view is that woman is an unfinished man, left standing on a lower step in the

scale of development. The male is, by nature, superior, whereas woman is of weak will, and, therefore, incapable of independence of character or position, her best condition is a quiet home life in which, while ruled by the men in her external relations, she may be allowed to be supreme on domestic affairs. Women should not be made more like men, as in Plato's *Republic*, rather the dissimilarity should be promoted; whatever is different is also attractive.

3. Yaska, *Nirukta,* p. 208.
4. For recent valuable study on matrimonial relations between Mughals and Rajputs, *see* Harbans Mukhiya, *The Mughal of India*, Oxford, 2005; I.A. Zaidi, "The Pattern of Matrimonial Ties Between The Kachhwaha Clan And The Mughal Ruling Family", *Proceedings Of Indian History Congress*, 35th session 1974; A.Z. Khan, "The Mughal Marriages: A Politico-Religious And Legal Study", *Journal of Pakistan Historical Society*, 1985; Afzal Hussain, "Marriages Among Mughal Nobles As An Index of Status And Aristocratic Integration", *Proceedings of Indian History Congress*, 33rd session 1972.
5. Kalidas, *Abhijnan Sakuntalam,* V: 23.
6. Notably, in Christian societies, a daughter could get bequests and gifts but a wife's property became her husband's at marriage. In England, the Married Women Property Act put an end to this unjust law only late in Victorian Period, i.e. in the closing years of 19th century.
7. Schopenhaur, *Essay on Women*, cited in Wallace, *Life of Schopenhaur,* p. 80.
8. *Holy Qur'an,* IV:3.
9. *Holy Qur'an,* XXXIII:39.
10. Ansar is an Islamic term that literally means "helpers" and denotes the Medinan citizens that helped Prophet Muhammad and the Muhajirun on the arrival to the city after the migration to Medina that took place between June 21 and July 2 in 622 CE and waged war for the cause of Islam.

Chapter – 13

Buddhist Nuns – Past and Present

Abha Singh

Buddhism[1] began with the Awakening of the Buddha (whose title means "Awakening. One"), an event that took place in sixth century B.C. at Bodh Gaya (Bihar). Soon after the Buddha's enlightenment, many people, attracted to this serene, wise, and compassionate man and his teachings, sought to become his disciples. Some became lay followers, maintaining their lives as householders with a family, while others became monastics. In the process, according to Theravada tradition, the *bhikkhuni* order of nuns came into existence five years after the *bhikkhu* order of monks; and historical evidence indicate that this order (i.e. Buddhist nuns) survived and thrived in India for fifteen centuries and, during the period, played some effective role in the religion as well. In this paper the position and role of the Nuns—during the days of Buddha, as well as, in the different branches of Buddhism presently functioning—shall be scanned.

In pre-Buddhist India there was a tradition distinguished as 'going forth' which advocated people—preferably belonging to higher stratum of the society—to live according to the four *ashramas*, viz. *Brahmacharya*, *Grihastha*, *Vanaprastha* and *Samnyasa*. These practices were, however, reserved for men only. Women were banned from learning and practicing like this, especially studying the Vedas. It was regarded as a secret scripture whose wisdom was only for men.

Just around this time Gautam Buddha[2] appeared on the spiritual horizon, Many women, who of course did not have right to practice spirituality in such a way, were drawn towards the Buddha, who had just appeared on the spiritual horizon, advocating openness and equality, as well as recommending the renuniant path as the most effective means of attaining liberation. Naturally, many women too were attracted to this path. This led to the emergence of a need for a separate order of Buddhist nuns.[3]

However, Buddha was initially quite reluctant to ordain women into the *sangha*. His aunt and foster mother Mahaprajapati Gotami, made repeated requests, on behalf of herself and five hundred other ladies of the court, to admit women to the *sangha*, but the latter did not heed to the former's request. At this, his attendant and half-brother Ananda[4] relayed a final request. He begged the Buddha to allow women to become nuns and realize their spiritual yearning and give them the option too, of renouncing domestic life. Anand's intercession was quite effective.[5] Resultantly, even though hesitant initially, Buddha eventually conceded that women too were capable of following the aforementioned path and achieving liberation. Thus, within a few years of the founding of the *Bhiksu Sangha* emerged the *Bhikusni Sangha* (Order of Nuns). Led by the able and astute Mahaprajapati, this community of nuns soon started flourishing and thousands of women went on to become *arahants*, purifying their minds and liberating themselves of suffering and rebirth.

Even though Buddha believed and preached that women and men are equals in terms of the capability of achieving liberation, the standards of monastic discipline were made significantly more stringent for women than those for men. Eight *gurudharmas* (vows of respect) were formulated for the nuns. The vows that the *Bhiksunis*[6] were supposed to follow were as follows: during the rainy season retreat, no nun shall reside in district wherein no monks are present; at the end of the rainy season, a nun shall invite criticism from both nuns' assembly as well as that of the monks'; a nun shall have to undergo penance before both the assemblies; nuns shall have to schedule their Observance in line with that of the monks; a female candidate shall have to undergo a compulsory two year apprenticeship and only then shall she seek ordinance, which shall again have to be sought from both the assemblies; a nun shall never abuse a monk verbally; even though a monk may rebuke or reprimand a nun, she wasn't allowed to do the to the monks; and finally perhaps the most significant of the rules that a nun shall always honour a monk even if she has been ordained for a hundred years, and he, for a mere one day, i.e. the period for which they have had been ordained for shall have no impact on their formal relationship, the contexture of which shall be defined solely on the basis of their gender. In essence, these stringent rules technically made the *Bhiksunis* (fully ordained nuns) subordinate to the *Bhiksus* (fully ordained monks). It is believed that this strict subordination of nuns was provided for by Buddha for he believed that when women retire from the household, religion is not able to endure for long.[7] He had predicted that True *Dharma*, in its present unadualterated form[8], shall be able to continue for only five hundred years in comparison to the thousand years for which it could have continued for had women not been admitted.[9]

For women of those times, following the renunciant life not only helped them in achieving spiritual liberation, but also helped them in attaining freedom from the compulsions of family life which involved, among other things, obedience to their husband and in-laws, suffering of repeated childbirths and toiling endlessly performing household chores. In everyday life, the nuns managed their own communities themselves. These *sanghas* were, therefore, able to bring in the much-needed and the very welcome social liberation for women.

Buddha believed that the orders of the monks and the nuns needed to be kept separate and yet the extent of separation had to be such that all contact wasn't lost between the two orders. He wished to keep the degree of this separation in check and maintain its balance. It is for this reason perhaps that when Mahaprajapati requested him, on the basis of the argument that the order of the nuns had been able to achieve institutional maturity, to allow nuns to blend in their lines of seniority with those of the monks, he refused to grant permission for the same. He did so because doing otherwise would have automatically led to the cancellation of the vow of respect which the nuns had to show for the monks. It would have become difficult to keep them separate. The merging of the lines of seniority and the dissolution of the boundaries between the two orders would eventually have led to them jeopardizing the vows of their celibacy even. However, he did not want to keep the orders radically separated as well for such separation might have led to the fostering of divergences in the interpretations of the teachings.

Even though a widespread belief does exist that Buddha advocated absolute equality for all members of the *Sangha*, such was not the case. Buddhist views of hierarchy help shed some light on the reasons behind the subordination of the Order of Nuns to the Order of Monks. He did believe that everyone had an equal potential of attaining *nirvana*. However, this spiritual sense of equality did not reflect in the organizational structure. For effective and efficient functioning of the minor issues within the order, Buddha recommended a clearly defined hierarchy. Monks were of the view initially that such a hierarchy should be on the basis of merit. However, the question of how to measure and effectively compare merit led to a lot of controversy. A neutral criterion of obtaining such a hierarchy was missing. Buddha, therefore, *decided that seniority be chosen as the criterion for deciding hierarchy*. Due to this basis, one's *position was no more a reflection of one's worth and capability*. Also, the customary acts of showing respect like bowing down to an individual were not to be interpreted, therefore, as a sign of submission to an individual. They were to be seen as a mark of respect for the customs of the Order. Similarly, even though the Order of the Nuns was formally subordinate to the order of the Monks, this *organizational subordination was not to be interpreted as any kind of spiritual inferiority*. Throughout the Hinayana tradition, women were recognized to have attained full *arhantship*, which was a state of liberation equal to that achieved by the Masters.

The same is reflected through the *Verses of the Women Elders* (the Pali Canon's *Therigatha*), which was a garland of seventy-three poems composed by the elder nuns and memorized by the monks and the nuns alike.

Also, steps were taken in the direction of keeping the monks in check as well. It was necessary that the nun's position be protected and the hierarchy may not go on to become a medium of abuse. Nuns were given every right to outrightly publicly boycott any monk who treated them in an unseemly manner. Also, the monks were forbidden to even request the nuns to perform menial tasks for them. Such steps helped maintain the necessary check and balance.

Such a formalized relationship between the monks and the nuns may seem quite contrary to, and even offensive to our modern sensibilities which are flush with ideals of social and gender equality. However, social and religious arrangements were missing during most of the ancient and the medieval period. Throughout history, through the advent and downfall of several civilizations, women had been relegated to the lower rungs, excluded from religious hierarchies, from positions of social power and kept at an inferior status. Such formalized organizational structure however prevented the same from happening here as well.

Buddha also took care to provide for both categories for his female disciples, viz. nuns and lay women with opportunities of spiritual advancements. Pali *sutra*[10] encouraged education for female lay disciples. Its impact can now be seen in the female literacy rates of South-East Asian counties, which are amongst the highest in the world.

Amongst the Buddhist nuns, the name of Uppalvana Theri (female elder) is enshrined as being one of the chief disciples of Buddha, being foremost amongst the nuns in psychic powers. Kisagotami Theri excelled in the frugality of her lifestyle. Khemi Theri, the former queen of King Bimbisara, was ranked foremost amongst the nuns in terms of her acumen of judgement. The ability to teach Dharma was excelled in by Dhammadinna. Bhadda

Kapilani Theri, who married Pippala, did not consummate her marriage because she and her husband had experienced great compassion after seeing ploughing resulting in the killing of several ants and insects. She went on to become an arhant and was declared to be the foremost amongst nuns who could recall past lives. Bhadda Kundalakesa was known for the swift intuition. She had fallen in love with a handsome man, but on discovering his intentions of stealing her jewellery and killing her, pushed him down a cliff and went on to join a sect of extreme ascetics, She left this sect when she came in contact with Buddha and subsequently obtained *arhantship*. Mahaprajapati, the aunt of Buddha and the seniormost amongst the nuns gained awakening after hearing a sermon from Buddha about the distinguishing characteristics of Dharma and Vinaya. She is known for having performed several miracles. Other Theris were known to be experts on Vinaya and meditation, and a few were famous as Preachers of Dharma and had a following of their own as well.

However, very less is known about the nuns who came up after the death of Buddha and in the Mahayana times. Such a silence on account of the nuns is perhaps due to the subordination of the nuns to the monks. This undermined the ability of the nuns to attract material support and large following of students. However, stone inscriptions, such as those at the great stupa at Sanchi do list nuns among the major donors towards the building of such centres, which would not have been possible without them have having at least some following of their own. Hence, it seems perhaps the main reason behind the lack of names of nuns is the tendency of history to focus more towards the politically influential scholars and missionaries. Nuns had, however, focused more on the aspects of meditational practice, and hence such political influence had been missing from their being, thus relegating them to the shadows of history.

Even though the *Bhikshuni Sangha* did not flourish in India, it did go on to last for around sixteen hundred years, which is no mean an achievement for any human institution.

A bird's eyeview at the Buddhist nuns today tells us that

their lives vary widely depending in the country they are in, the traditions they are following, and the person that they are. The colour of their robes ranges from being grey, black and purple in East Asia to maroon and yellow in and around Tibet to white orange and brown in Theravada countries. Their lifestyle ranges from medicant practices of daily alms in Sri Lanka to vegetarian feasts in Combodia. While some try to remain away from money economy, others are engaged in nine to five jobs. While some are vegetarian, others freely eat anything that is given to them, including meat.

However, in spite of these differences that exist, a few connecting links of commonalities do exist among these nuns and the lives that they lead. Keeping their heads shaved, wearing monastic robes and following an ethical code of discipline are the foremost and the most important ones amongst these common connecting links. They refrain from taking life, stealing, lying and taking intoxicants. They lead an entirely celibate life, thus managing to keep themselves free from the duties that a household might demand.

Two major branches of Buddhism that are recognized are Theravada and Mahayana. In some classifications, a third branch is also talked about, and is recognized as the Tibetan tradition. The lives of Nuns can be seen in the context of tradition they fall under and follow.

Nuns practicing the Theravada tradition can be found in Laos, Vietnam, Cambodia, Myanmar, Sri Lanka and the nearby places. The nuns in theses traditions try leading a life similar to that led by the nuns in the early Buddhist traditions. They dress up in simple cotton robes. They remains dependent on the local community to provide them food in the form of alms. They avoid taking solid food after midday. The follow eight to ten precepts and refrain from singing, dancing and wearing any ornaments. They chant Pali *suttas* and meditate daily for an hour in the morning and another hour in the evening. Till very recent times, complete *bhiksuni* ordination wasn't available to the nuns in these traditions. While this practice had died out in some countries, it had altogether failed to start in others. They were, therefore, not regarded as members of the Sangha and were given less respect than that given to monks. Both educational and material support were lesser. Since 1988, however, they started seeking complete ordination. Over the years, their work in the field of social work has been commendable.

The followers of Mahayana tradition are found majorly in Korea, Japan, Taiwan, Indonesia, Malaysia, Philippines and Singapore. The lifestyle of the Nuns in these traditions was adapted to meet the climatic and cultural requirements. Instead of going about looking for alms, they receive donations of vegetarian food. This food is cooked by them and is supplemented with vegetables that are grown by them. The *bhiksuni* tradition has been strong in these regions. Every morning and evening, the nuns of these traditions gather together and chant *sutras* in Chinese, *mantras* in Sanskrit and prayers in their local language. On specific dates, *dharma* gatherings for several Buddhas and *Bodhisattvas* are held by them. The establishment of educational institutions providing four to five years training programme in Buddhist studies has helped the nuns herein become very active in society on account of the comprehensive education and training imparted to them. The nuns have expanded the range of services to include health care, elder care, prison outreach, hospice work and the like.

The nuns of the Tibetan tradition can be found, apart from Tibet, in Bhutan, Mongolia, Nepal, parts of Soviet Union, Himalayan border regions of Ladakh, Lahaul and Spiti and other nearby countries. The nuns herein are recognized as members of the *sangha* even though the tradition of full ordination was never established officially. Majority of these nuns are involved in meditation and *tantric* ritual practices of the Vajrayana tradition. The practice of visualizing themselves as a *Bodhisttva* or fully enlightened Buddha to achieve enlightened qualities was carried on by the nuns as well. Also, what is important here is the fact that a number of popular Buddhas and Bodhisattvas, such as Tara and Vajrayogini, were female, thus emphasizing the importance of nuns in this tradition. The nuns were free to receive Buddhist teachings privately or in public gatherings, but did not have the access to systematic study of Buddhist texts. Consequently, rarely did they acquire religious education or recognition as Dharma teachers. However, in the past twenty years, study programmes and practice centres for women have been established throughout the region. Increased education and encouragement has given them the self-confidence, recognition and respect that they deserved.

Throughout Buddhist history, the predominant patriarchal society has had its impact on the status of Buddhist nuns as well. A new awareness of the inequalities between nuns and monks has been recognized in the past two decades and efforts have been made to correct these inequalities. The year 1987 marked a turning point for Buddhist nuns for in that year was held the first Skayadhita International Conference on Buddhist women[11], and nuns were kept as the focal point of this conference. Issues of lack of adequate healthcare, nutrition and education were brought to the forefront. The conference had a strong impact and resulted in the opening up of several institutions and programs like literary programmes, schools, meditation centres, women shelters and health clinics to benefit the nuns.

Buddha is often regarded as a model of *social equality and yet a glaring disparity between the sexes within Buddhism itself has existed throughout its history. The social realities in Buddhist societies need to be brought in line with Buddhist teachings.* Thorough and genuine transformation in attitude is required. Efforts hitherto undertaken, especially in the last two decades, have been heartening. Yet, a lot more remains to be done in order to achieve the ideal of social equality.

REFERENCES

1. Interestingly, the term *Buddhism* comes from the thinkers of the 18th century European Enlightenment and their quest to subsume religion under comparative sociological and secular history. Only

recently have Asian Buddists come to adopt the term and the concept behind it. Earlier, while referring to their religion, the terms used by them were much more limited in scope: *the Buddha's message*, *the Buddha's way*, or *the Dhamma*. In other words, they conceived of their religion only as the teaching of the Buddha, what the Buddha called *Dharma-Vinaya* (Doctrine and Discipline). It may, however, be noted that *Dharma-Vinaya* is meant to be perspective, advocating a way of life and practice, and *Buddhism* is descriptive in that it only denotes actions of people who follow a vision of *Dharma-Vinaya* without suggesting to accept that vision or follow it, too.

2. For recent valuable study on Gautam Buddha and his teachings, see Akchaya Kumari Devi, *Gauṭam Buddha: His Life and Religion*, Calcutta, 1930; Bimla Charan Law, *Concepts of Buddhism*, Holland, 1966.
3. According to *Oxford English Dictionary* (Vol. X, p. 599), a nun is a woman who has taken vows committing her life to her religion. She may be a woman who decided to dedicate her life to serving all other living beings, or to be an ascetic who voluntarily chooses to leave mainstream society and live her life in prayer and contemplation in a monastery or convent. The term "nun" is applicable to Catholics – both eastern and western traditions – Orthodox Christians, Anglicans, Lutherans, Jains, Buddhists, Taoists, and Hindus.

   While in common usage the terms "nun" and "Sister" are often used interchangeably (especially as the same title of "Sister" for the individual member of both forms), they are considered different ways of life, with a "nun" being a religious woman who lives a contemplative and cloistered life of meditation and prayer for the salvation of others, while a "Religious Sister", in religious institutes like Mother Teresa's Missionaries of Charity, lives an active vocation of both prayer and service, often to the needy, sick, poor, and uneducated.
4. Among Buddha disciples, Ananda was considered to be closest. He succeeded Buddha andplayed a major role in longevity of Buddhist Sangha.. For the spiritual biography of Ananda, *see* Ratneshwar Mishra and Damodar Singh, 'Ananda', in *Atulya Bihar*, Patna, 2012, pp. 132-145.
5. *Cf*. John Strong, *The Experience of Buddhism: Sources and Interpretation*, Wadsworth, 1995, Sec.2.4.1.
6. *Bhiksunis* refers to a fully ordained Buddhist nun, i.e. a woman who

has taken higher ordination (*upasampada*) in the Buddhist monastic community. *Bhiksunis* of the *Theravada* tradition observe the 311 precepts. They live a simple life, equal to that of a *bhiksu* or monk, but quite different from that of other women. A *Bhiksunis* wears orange robes, shaves her head, lives near the *sangha* (a monastic community), learns and practices the Buddha's teaching and listens to *Dhamma* talks every 15 days.

7. *Cullavagga*, X.I.6.
8. The five-hundred-year mark corresponds to the period when the first Mahayana Sutras and the Theravadin commentaries were being composed, an issue about which both the groups were very touchy.
9. *Samyutta Nikaya*, XVI.13.
10. *Ibid.*, XXXVII.34.
11. Further information on Sakyadhita and the global Buddhist women's movement available online at www.sakyadhita.org.

Chapter – 14

Maham Anaga and Mughal Court Politics

Sunita Sharma

Maham Anaga, occupies an important place in the political history of the Mughals, as a person who played a proactive role in the early years of Akbar's reign. The study seeks to explore through the personality of Maham Anga, a person who belonged to the low rank but on the basis of her self-sacrifice rose to high position to become a close confidante of the ruler. Her consequent transition from the private to the public domain and indulgence in state affairs raises two pertinent issues. First, the issue of the extent of feminist influence over state or political affairs. Secondly, an equally important facet, that the age of Akbar was a period of institutionslisation of the empire for the establishment of his paramountcy – a process which began during the time of Maham Anaga. In tracing the political assertion of Akbar, the brief political role of Maham Anaga is of immense importance. In fact, her political advice were taken with serious considerations by Akbar and had its consequent impact on court activities. Her emergence as a political adviser and confidante drew the attention of contemporary chroniclers as Abul Fazl and Badauni, who have written about her at great length and provided us access to authentic information about her role, which though, apparently looked as advisory but nonetheless bore important consequences. Generally, only stray references are found about woman from nobility, but Maham Anaga, being only a wet nurse occupies larger space in the contemporary writings, which is also a pointer to her important political role. Her persona thus *deserves more attention in history as well as gender writing*. A close study of contemporary texts, particularly *Babur Nama*, *Humayun Nama* and *Akbar Nama*, brings to our notice an interesting cultural aspect of Mughal house that much significance was accorded to lineage of a person which was not confined to royal antecedents. Perhaps lineage[1] from the saintly family was accorded much more reverence and importance. Therefore, it was also Maham Anaga's lineage which facilitated her rise. Her descent from Ahmad-i-Jam a revered saint of the 11th and 12th centuries gave her an elevated position over any person with a royal lineage.[2]

The importance of the descent from Ahmad Jam can be traced from Maham Begum, the wife of Babur who enjoyed the status of Chief Queen. Hamida Bano's descent shows how her lineage remained a matter of pride in the later generation of the Mughals. Hamida Bano was also related to Bano Agha, wife of Shihabuddin Ahmad Nishapuri[3] and was a close relation of Maham Anaga.[4] These two ladies were privileged to act as wet nurse of Akbar probably because they hailed from this saintly family which was looked upon with reverence, therefore, their descent from Ahmad-i-Jam allowed them to enjoy many prerogatives unlikely to be given to a person of humble origin.

Maham Anaga[5] did not remain as just one of the three nurses of Akbar, the other two being Pichah Jan Anagah[6], and Jiji Anagah[7] who remained in oblivion. It was only Maham Anaga who came to enjoy the distinct honour of being addressed as "*Walida*".[8] This great honour was bestowed upon her not primarily as a wet nurse. In Muslim tradition much regard is given to the custom where a child when nursed in infancy by a lady is considered as a foster mother. In fact, the custom carried with it a religious sanctity as Prophet Mohammad was nursed by Halima who came to be considered as his foster mother. This tradition to accord high regards was maintained by Akbar and is reflected in the writings of Abul Fazl, who says that petitions were made referring to Maham Anaga as 'Walida'. It was also the greatness of Hamida Bano to allow Maham Anaga to share this honour on account of the loyalty shown by her and also because of their common descent. Maham Anaga and Shihabuddin elevation as prime minister was partially related to the fact that they belonged to the same saintly family of Ahmad-i-Jam. Thus their unprecedented rise can be understood in this context. The selfless sacrifice offered by her to save young Akbar's[9] life. In 1547 Humayun besieged the fort of Kabul, which was in the possession of Kamran. Finding himself unable to fight with Humayun, Kamran heartlessly ordered to lace Akbar upon the ramparts of the fort, so that the little child Akbar could become the target of Humayun's artillery. At that Maham Anaga came forward and made her own body a shield to Akbar was an act of spontaneous unstinted loyalty. It became a momentous event in her life which won the trust, confidence and respect of Akbar till her last. The beginning of the politicisation of the domestic sphere can also be seen in the political activities during the early years of Akbar's reign. Hamida Bano's silent bearing towards Maham Anaga in the later phase, only strengthens the fact of common descent shared with Maham Anaga.

It is thus often perceived that Maham Anaga later tried to over reach her authority and turned ambitious on account of the trust reposed in her by Akbar. It is alleged that later on Maham's aim became promotion of her son Adham Khan. In *Ain-i Akbari*, in course of providing information of nobles of the time Adham Khan has been referred as an illegitimate[10] son of Humayun and thus a presumption of his being a political contender though in a concealed manner can also be considered. The rise of Adham Khan was possible in the wake of the ruin of Bairman Khan. Therefore, Maham's role assumes significance in the fall of Bairam Khan and assumption of significant powerful position by her during the early years of the reign of Akbar.

Abul Fazl informs that after the fall of Bairam Khan "Maham Anaga, by whose mechanizations that result was brought about, became *de facto* (if not *de jure*) prime minister, while the ostensible minister was Munim Khan." One of Maham's relative.

We find a host of information on Maham's political role but very little information can be traced about her early life as she did not belong to the rank of aristocracy. However, it is known that she was wife of Nadim Kuka and mother of Baqi Muhammad Khan[11] and Adham Khan. Maham Anaga because of his background was perhaps more ambitious for him.

Maham Anaga got an opportunity to fulfil her political ambitious to upstage her son in the event of growing dissatisfaction of Akbar with Bairam Khan who wielded immense authority. Meanwhile Akbar was keen to assert his own political authority. Maham took this opportunity and made every effort to turn the fissures between Akbar and Bairam into a complete breach. She made every effort to convince Akbar that till Bairam Khan remained at the helm of affairs he would not allow any authority. She further provoked Akbar by bringing up her personal apprehension of facing Bairman Khan's wrath for aligning herself with Akbar. Since she had been advising Akbar to act independently on the basis of which Akbar made a visit to Delhi without seeking prior permission from Bairam Khan could have evoked his anger on Akbar's associates and thus through such provocation she helped in throwing off the overbearing guardianship of Bairam Khan. Akbar did not apprehend the growing political ambitions of Maham Anaga for herself and her son. Maham's position was further secured since her relatives Shahabuddin[12] occupied the important post of the governor of Delhi and Baqi Khan of Aligarh, through whom the negotiations with Akbar were carried out and Akbar's visit to Delhi was made possible. Maham Anaga in league with Shahabuddin advised Akbar to a great extent and succeeded in changing Akbar's mind that he would not be able to act as the real sovereign[13] till Bairam Khan wielded authority as his regent. Her advice had deep connotation as she was considered as a "marvel for sense resource and loyalty"[14] as conceded in the writing of Abul Fazl.

On the one hand, the antagonistic approach of Maham and Shahabuddin towards Bairam Khan led towards his removal and, on the other, Bairam's own overbearing personality to overshadow in political affairs compelled Akbar to turn towards Maham Anaga. To allay Maham's apprehension of being reprimanded by Bairam, Akbar wrote a letter informing him of his arrival at Delhi without seeking his approval. A reason which made his attendants utmost fearful. Therefore, Bairam was asked to be amicably inclined towards them, in fact this was Akbar first assertion of authority against Bairam Khan at the insinuation of Maham Anaga.

Bairam's favourable reply that Akbar's wishes would not be overlooked and his attendants who had discharged duties would be treated with kindness and favour,[15] failed to appease Akbar as his mind had been prejudiced by then Bairam's message did not receive approval and his messengers were sent back. This small victory against Bairam Khan then imbued Maham Anaga and Shahbuddin to wield supreme authority and the loyalty of the nobles of Delhi then shifted towards the newly risen powers providing them the first taste of power. Shahabuddin took steps to fortify Delhi in case of civil disturbance. The office and dominion of Bairam Khan was filched from him. A man who had supported Humayun in his adversity and was credited for Humayun's restoration was thus rewarded. This was a political event which proved to be the turning point in the political fortune of Maham Anaga.

Bairam Khan had been outmanoeuvred and thus resolved to move towards Makkah but the humiliation suffered by him provoked him to defy certain orders of Akbar. He desired his recall to office by fomenting disturbance in Punjab. With this hope Bairam left Agra for Alwar on 8th April, 1560, halted at Bianah and released and despatched two state prisoners to court. On receiving information of his act Maham Anaga induced Akbar to send an army to Punjab, so that any attempt of revolt could be crushed by the state. Her advice was followed and at the same time Akbar acted as an astute statesman and sent Abdul Latif his trusted tutor to convey his sense of acknowledgement for the service of Bairam Khan to re-assure Bairam Khan that the emperor acknowledges his honesty and fidelity but at the same time Akbar's determination to take the reign of government in his own hands. Bairam Khan was asked to move towards Makkah upon which he had long been intent. A suitable *jagir* was offered to be assigned for his maintenance. Bairam[16] thus gave up his banner, kettle drums and all other insignia of rank. On provocation of Pir Muhammad Bairam Khan turned bitter and in a state of despair be carried out a futile revolt for which he sought clemency.[17] This was generously granted by Akbar as Bairam was considered the "benefactor of the family" and was allowed to move towards Makkah, but he was not destined to reach the holy city and was murdered at Patan by an Afghan.[18] Maham's rivalry against Bairam Khan and effort to wean away Akbar from Bairam's overbearing influence is also a significant development in the course of independent assertion of power by Akbar. The consequent fall of Bairam who has largely been credited for the restoration of Mughal empire was to a great extent engineered by Maham Anaga in which Hamida Bano also played a vital role with Maham Anaga towards deposing Bairam Khan as Hamida Bano's objective was to pave way for political assertion of her young son.

Bairman Khan's death sealed his fall and his opponents thus rose out of this political void although the period was brief as Akbar realised his own potential and perhaps limitations and prejudices of his advisers.

According to some historians, the period of Maham Anaga and influence was merely for two years,[19] i.e. 1560-62 which ended with the tragic death of her son Adham Khan, but Vincent Smith gives a prolonged period.[20]

One view is that after the fall of Bairam Khan Maham Anaga enjoyed and shared power with her partisans whereas, others hold the view that no evidence of nepotism can be established. In fact Maham Anaga, appointed the relatives of Bairam Khan on high posts but neither her son nor her relatives were given any important post during this period.

To strengthen their own position as also to consolidate the changed circumstances at the earliest opportunity Maham and

Shahabuddin[21] spread the news of change of Akbar's mind and gave hopes of *jagirs* and titles as baits to the influential nobility.

Munim Khan[22] was then given the title of Khan Khana and the office of *wakil* but in reality power was wielded by Maham as Akbar's prime confidante. Traces of her ascendancy were soon perceptible, since Bairam Khan's death brought momentous change in civil and military administration. The strong administration of Bairam Khan gave way to undisciplined administrative machinery. It is alleged that since then Maham Anaga was less concerned for the welfare of the young sovereign as her own ambitions overpowered her and that selfless sense of sacrifice appeared to have waned away. Retention of her power and influence, the forwarding of her interest and promotion of her son who had then been entrusted with the re-conquest and government of Malwa in 1561.[23] With appointment of Pir Muhammad as Adham's Counsellor, an inconvenient rival from court had been removed. Adham Khan was successfully defeating Baz Bahadur[24] after a feeble resistance and forced him to flee towards Khandesh.[25] Adham Khan then took into his possession all property, the treasure and the seraglio.[26] The success made Adham Khan vain. Instead of sending the booty to the Emperor he sent only a few elephants and kept for himself the women and some choicest articles of the spoil.[27] The Malwa expedition proved his ability as a general but the fact that he concealed most of the spoils from the battle from the king brings out his inherent weakness, selfishness, treacherous ambition and lack of loyalty which made him a suspect in the eyes of Akbar. This misconduct of Adham Khan annoyed Akbar who quietly left Agra with a small escort to inspect the matter personally. This incident is of immense importance as it brings forth the insincerity of Adham Khan which Maham tried to conceal and Akbar despite knowing this lapse overlooked as his regard for Maham remained unmoved. Hearing about Akbar's departure, Maham sent two swift couriers to warn Adham but Akbar reached before them and took Adham by surprise. Adham was confounded at Akbar's arrival and failed to assuage his wrath. Meanwhile, Maham Anaga, who had accompanied Akbar reached Sarangpur and took care to shield Adham. She rectified the wrongs of Adham and in a way prodded Adham to hand over all booty before Akbar. Her presence may have prompted Akbar to accept Adham's submission as he always remained grateful towards her. After his brief stay of four days at Sarangpur, Akbar found at the time of his retreat that Adham Khan had still concealed two beautiful women of Baz Bahadur's harem.[28] This act of infidelity and law of honour of women compelled Akbar to stay on for further probe.[29] Maham Anaga perceived that if these two captive women were found her son's treachery would be exposed.[30] Maham Anaga got them murdered in order to conceal the hideous act of her sons. She wanted to prevent Akbar from hearing the truth of the abduction and thus indulged into this monstrous act of cruelty as "a severed head make no sound." Akbar was informed of this gross outrage but he in a way pardoned Adham's audacious act but she had certainly put Akbar in an awkward position.

Despite these acts of deceiving Akbar in order to shield her son, Maham Anaga's loyalty and wisdom allowed her to retain her influence and control over the affairs of the state.[31] She was still considered to be the prime confidante of Akbar. The appointment of Shahabuddin and Khwaja Jahan only helped her to manipulate the appointment of her partisans as Bahadur Khan, the brother of Ali Quli Khan, who was elevated to the office of vakil but in reality the work was still carried out by Maham Anaga[32] in collaboration with her relatives.[33]

Despite such difficulties created by her son which displeased Akbar, she was not outrightly decried by Akbar as he restrained himself from taking any stern action.

Maham had offered excellent services, and exceeding devotion but to regard herself as the substantive minister was a fact which actually disappointed Akbar, and by the coming of 1561, he preferred to place a person of distinguished career to improve the administrative structure. Shamsuddin Muhammad Atka Khan, who had received the title of Azam Khan as the prime minister.[34] His wife Jiji Anaga was also a wet nurse of Akbar, thus the loyalty of Atka Khan was time tested. He soon undertook the management of affairs, political and financial and disposed matters relating to the army and to the civil population according to his own sound judgement. Even Munim Khan was inwardly aggrieved and their combined grievance manifested in the assassination of Atka Khan at the instigation of Adham Khan. Abul Fazl mentions that instead of regarding Shamsuddin as a providential helper they were aggrieved and vexed[35] as their power was affected. This firm decision of Akbar to appoint a person with a distinguished career to this high post was not only a second act of political assertion but also allowed the coming rulers of the dynasty to institutionalize the administrative system based on the system of merit. This political decision of Akbar makes it clear that Akbar was never completely under Maham's influence.[36] Within a period of two months her influence disappeared from the administrative forum.

The recall of Adham Khan from Malwa was a strong indication of Maham's waning influence.[37] The vain attitude of Adham Khan led towards the marginalization of Maham Anaga. The rise of Atka Khan had turned Adham Khan envious who conspired to put Atka Khan to death in connivance with Munim Khan and Shahabuddin Ahmad, as they too suffered from this malady and instigated Adham Khan against Atka Khan. On 16th May, 1562, the tragic occurrence took place. Atka Khan while transacting public business was assassinated in an outrageous manner by Khusham Khan Uzbeg, one of the followers of Adham Khan. The incident caused a great uproar in the palace but Adham Khan oblivious of this and encouraged by his past audacity presumptuously advanced towards the harem. The sudden dreadful clamour and the sight of blood stained body of Atka Khan and Adham Khan's audacity made Akbar indignant who had been thrown over the terrace. Akbar had the conviction that Adham Khan had overstepped and so his punishment was being thrust back again and this act of retaliation by Akbar was thus considered a sublime justice for Adham Khan for his atrocities. Maham Anaga's political aspiration for Adham were doomed, it was perhaps this shock which at first did not make her realize that Adham Khan had been put to death. Her attempt to secure high position for her son and later save his life could not be realized. When she knew for certain that her son had been put to death, but by virtue of her wisdom, she retained her respect for Akbar and did not complain or lament but she was deeply shocked at the unexpected turn of event. Akbar in regard to her long service and close association spoke comforting words to her and consoled her somewhat, and did not allow her to see the body of the deceased son to save her some further sorrow. Her illness grew worse and because of inner grief she lost her health rapidly. Forty days after this occurrence she died of grief. Akbar was touched by this sad fate and expressed great sorrow. The body was sent with much respect to Delhi and Akbar escorted it for some paces. A fine monument was erected in her memory.[38]

Maham Anaga was considered as a person with wisdom and courage in "perfection", "suitable and trustworthy"[39] for political advice. But all this confidence reposed in her made Maham conscious of her importance and this importance she wished to perpetuate.

Therefore, the views of some historians that Maham's profound influence over Akbar and his deep sense of gratitude towards her enabled her to exploit this sentiment for her personal gain. But there is a different aspect to this theory. It is stated that it was Akbar who took advantage of Maham Anaga's position and talent but did not allow himself to be dominated as he could foresee the limitations of Maham and infact on several occasions condoned her acts of audacity.

The political fortune and gradual marginalization of Maham Anaga can be seen in the broader context of Akbar's political astuteness for whom state interest was paramount. His ability to discern the advantages for the state. Therefore, in his effort to establish institutions, for the creation of a strong stable administrative structure, he took the first decisive step towards this direction like, the appointment of able officers, as Atka Khan, clemency granted to Bairam despite Maham's antagonism, as

Akbar could not overlook the services of this benefactor. He overlooked the audacious acts of Adham Khan, to a certain extent due to his respect for Maham. Once Adham had overstepped, Akbar did not hesitate at first for his recall from Malwa, and ultimately considered killing him not in rage but what he considered as an act of sublime justice. She remained his prime confidante till she appeared to work in the interest of the state but once Akbar realized that like Bairam Khan, Maham's influence was causing political adversity and position of the sovereign was being undermined, he replaced her without hesitation from political positions but struck the balance by maintaining the interpersonal relation which did not undergo a change as he was always conscious of his indebtedness towards Maham Anaga. This aspect brings to light both the political acumen of Akbar as also the humane side of his personality and the case study also tries to bring forth the political ambitions of Maham Anaga.

REFERENCES

1. Abul Fazl, *Akbar Nama* (hereafter cited as *A.N.)*, vol. I, tr. by H. Beveridge, 1972, p. 51.
2. *Ibid.*
3. Gulbadan, *Humayun Nama*, tr. by A.S. Beveridge, 1902, pp. 58, 239.
4. *Ibid.*, pp. 59, 239.
5. Farishta, *Tarikh-i-Farishta,* tr. J. Briggs, vol. II, p. 211. The wet nurse herself in Turki is called "Anka" but is read as "Ankah" or "Anagah", and her husband and male relations are called "Atka".
6. Pichah Jan Anagah was the wife of Khwaja Muqqud Ali, a servant of Akbar's mother.
7. Jiji Anagah was the wife of Shams-ud-din Muhammad Atgah Khan.
8. *A.N.*, vol. II, p.183 – One petitioner refers to her as '*Walida*', which definitely was not meant for Miriam-Makani (Hamida Bano Begum).
9. Badauni, *Muntakhab-ut-Tawarikh,* tr. Ranking, vol. I, p. 580. Also refer to Nizamuddin, *Tabqat-i- Akbari,* in Elliot & Dowson, *History of India as Told by its Historians* (hereafter cited as ED), vol. V, pp. 240-41 (*Tabqat,* vol. II, p.112).
10. According to some historians the name of his father is unknown. He

was evidently a royal bastard (Abul Fazl, *Ain-i-Akbari*, tr. Blochmann, vol. I, p. 390, Beale mentions that he "appears to have been an illegitimate son of the emperor Humayun." (Beale, p.34).

11. Baqi Muhammad Khan took part in the battle against Iskandar Khan and Bahadur Khan (*A'in*, vol. I; p.381). In the battle of Khairabad he fought under Muizul-mulk, in this battle Budagh Khan was captured. Due to the personal grievances of Baqi Khan, Mahdi Kasim Khan and Husain Khan Turk Riyah against Muizul Mulk and Raja Todar Mal, this battle was lost. When his marriage was celebrated by his mother Maham Anaga, Akbar himself came to this auspicious occasion (Shahnawaz Khan, *Maasiru'ul Umara* (hereafter cited as *M.U.*), tr. Beveridge, vol. I, pp.384-85). He rose to the rank of 3,000. He died in September 1584 AD in his fief Garh Katanga—*see Badauni*, vol. II, p.385. Also see *A'in*, vol. I p.381, *M.U.*, vol. I, p.385.
12. Shahabuddin Ahmad, a Sayyid of Nishapur and Tardi Beg's successor in the government of Delhi, *Tabqat*, in ED, vol. V, p. 262.
13. Von Noer, *The Emperor Akbar*, vol. I, 1890, p. 83.
14. *A.N.*, vol. II, p.141, *Tabqat*, vol. II, p. 238.
15. *Tabqat*, in ED, vol. V, p. 263.
16. *Ibid.*, p. 264.
17. *Ibid.*, pp. 267-68.
18. Nizamuddin Ahmad (ED, vol. V, p.268) says, "An Afghan named Mubarak Khan Lohani whose father had been killed in an action with the Mughal, "came to wait upon the Khan Khanan with the intention of wreaking vengeance upon him. When they were shaking hands he assassinated him with the dagger."
19. Von Noer, *The Emperor Akbar*, vol. I, Calcutta, 1890, p. 94.
20. V. A. Smith, *Akbar the Great Moghul*, Delhi, 1966, p. 36.
21. Shamsuddin Atka Khan was the son of a simple farmer of Ghazni. He entered the service of Kamran as a common soldier. He saved the life of Humayun when he was defeated in the battle of Kannauj. Humayun appointed his wife as a wet-nurse to Akbar and conferred upon her the title of 'Jiji Anaga'. He defeated Bairam Khan near Jalandhar and received the title of Azam Khan by Akbar. He became the prime minister in 1561 AD. He was murdered by Adham Khan on 16 May, 1562 AD, who was jealous to him. (*A'in*, vol. I, p. 321, Badauni, *Muntakhab-ut-Tawarikh*, tr. W. Haig, vol. III, pp. 308-9.
22. *A'in*, vol. I, pp. 333-34, Munim Khan – In 961, he was appointed *Ataliq* of Prince Akbar and when Humayun invaded India, Munim

was left as governor of Kabul in charge of Mirza Muhammad Hakim, Akbar's brother, then about a year old. In Kabul Munim remained till Bairam fell into disgrace. He joined Akbar in 967, at Ludhiyana where Akbar encamped on his expedition against Bairam, Munim was then appointed *Khan Khanan* and *wakil*. In the seventh year of Akbar's reign, when Adham Khan killed Atgah Khan, Munim who had been the instigator fled twice from court but was caught but later restored to his former honours.

23. *A.N.*, vol. II, p. 208.
24. Baz Bahadur's original name was Malik Bayazid. After the death of his father Shujat Khan (a Sur) he ascended the throne and assumed the title of 'Baz Bahadur'. He had shown his capabilities in his early career and after defeating his opponents established himself as an independent ruler. But when he attacked on the neighbouring state of Gondwana, he was defeated by Chandel queen Durgawati. Being repulsed by a woman he felt so much humiliated that he gave himself fully to wine, music and women and ignored the state affairs — *see M.U.*, vol. I, pp. 394-96.
25. *A.N.* , vol. II, p. 213. Faristha, vol. II, pp. 205-10.
26. *Ibid.*, p. 213. Also *see* V.A. Smith, *Akbar, the Great Mughal*, p. 37.
27. *A.N.*, vol. II, p. 221.
28. *Ibid.*; *M.U.*, vol. I, p. 146.
29. *Ibid.*, p. 221.
30. *Ibid.*, p. 218.
31. *Ibid.*, pp. 149-50, Von Noer, vol. I, p. 90.
32. *Ibid.*, p. 151; *M.U.*, vol. II, p. 847.
33. Dr. R.P. Tripathi, 'Maham Anaga and Akbar', *Journal of Indian History* (hereafter cited as *JIH*), vol. I, No.1, p. 343.
34. *A.N.*, vol. II, p. 230.
35. *Ibid.*, p. 231.
36. Tripathi's article, *JIH*, vol. I, No.1, p. 343.
37. *A.N.*, vol. II, p. 235.
38. *Ibid.*, p. 275.
39. *Ibid.*, p. 230.

Chapter – 15

Gender Discrimination

Madhubala Kumari

The empowerment of women is one of the central issues in the process of development of countries all over the world. Empowerment is the multi-faceted, multi-dimensional, and multi-layered concept. Women's rights and issues have been a subject of serious concern for academicians and policy makers. From the pastoral society to the contemporary information and global society, the role of women has changed drastically. The role of a typical housewife who catered to all the requirements of the household in various job roles of daughter, daughter-in-law, mother, mother-in-law, sister, aunt including upbringing of children, has been played by women quite efficiently. With the process of globalization, modernization and industrialization, showing its deep impact on the human society, the role and responsibilities of women has attained new definition and perspective.

Liberal feminists stressed on the democratic values of human dignity, freedom and equality. They outlined the position of women as a dependent being in our society. They tried to explain and understand the common assumption that justify the gender differences and agree for secondary position of women in the family and society. Their thoughts are mainly concerned with ensuring women equality, need for legal amendments, access to equal opportunities, women's rights to participate in social activities and freedom to develop and realize one's potential as a human being.

Despite of all afforts done for the empowerment of women, a major issue of gender discrimination is still a serious problem, creating a great obstacle in women upliftment.

Although, law forbids any kind of discrimination, on the ground of sex, but even in the present global and advanced society, women are discriminated from men in all walk of their life. Women's right, around the world, is an important indicator to century, the majority of the world's nations a few decades ago. Yet, despite many successes in empowering women, numerous issues still exist in all areas of life, ranging from cultural, political and the economic. For example, women often work more than men, yet are paid less; gender discrimination affects girls and women throughout their lifetime; and women and girls are often the ones who suffer the most.

Many may think that women's rights are only an issue to be discussed, but when we read the report about the 'United Nation's Women's Treaty' we can see how an increasing number of countries are lodging reservations, will show otherwise.

When we see deeply, we will see that women are discriminated throughout their life time, right from their birth to their old age. The discrimination, which women face throughout their life, on various stages, can be summarized as follows:—

1. Feticide and Infanticide

Even before birth feticides are discriminated, UNICEF notes that "where there is a clear economic or cultural preference for sons, the misuse of (pregnancy diagnostic tools) can facilitate female feticide." Today India is taking a leap towards becoming a developed nation, but their mentality is still in the 17th and 18th century. Although, there have been improvement in the condition of women, but still it is more or less the same story being repeated.

It is really difficult in the male dominated world to give women their rights. From the birth itself till death, they are discriminated and exploited by thousands of ways and one of the worst examples is female feticide. Female feticide, the killing of infant girl child is a heinous act and on the other hand it is a grim threat to women's existence, and if not controlled within time constrained, it is going to have a serious and lasting consequence, creating a big rift in gender count. We are leading to population imbalance, which would develop violence in society. The 2001 census shows, that the sex ratio for India is 933 female per 1000 males, which is lowest in the world, even after Government has enacted Pre-natal Diagnostic Technique (Regulation and prevention of measure) Act in the year 1994 itself. The decline of sex ratio has been particularly striking in the age group of 0 to 6 years in recent years. This decline has been registered in all states and Union territories except Kerala, Mizoram, Sikkim, Tripura and Lakshadweep. The decline has been particularly sharp in prosperous states like Punjab, Haryana, Maharashtra and Gujarat. In Punjab the gap in the sex ratio has widened to more than 200 per 1000 children. Unfortunately, we have not been successful in arresting the trend by raising female literacy during the decade. This shows a deep seated prejudice against the girl child in the country, which legal awareness has not been able to eradicate.

2. The Middle Years

A principal focus on the middle years of the childhood and adolescence is ensuring access to, and completion of quality, primary and secondary education is seen in favour of boy child. With a few exceptions, it is mostly girls who suffer from educational disadvantage. The following data will clearly show the plight of women even in this decade. The 2001 Census shows that percentage of female literacy in India is 54.16 against male literacy of 75.85 per cent. Although, after Independence, India has seen various reforms and programmes for the upliftment of women of all communities in pursuance of the Constitutional guarantees provided for the development of women, a number of educational, health and economic programmes were undertaken. One of the major changes, which has taken place in Independent India is the importance given to the education of women. The planners have looked upon education as the chief agent of modernization and social change. It was also believed that education was the crucial agent in achieving economic as well as political transformation. For modernizing India, education has been considered a significant determinant of aspiration, towards technology, productivity and mobility. Education, besides being given support as means for women to fulfil their traditional domestic and family roles, was considered a good level for getting employment. Concerted efforts were made, after independence, to advance the education of girls and women, but still expected results are not seen. It is worst mainly in the remote and rural areas and so a lot has to be done to bridge the gap in the sphare of gender literacy rate.

3. Adolescence

"Among the greatest threats to adolescent development are abuse, exploitation and violence and the lack of vital knowledge about sexual and reproductive health, including HIV/AIDS." Specific areas that UNICEF highlighted were female genital mutilation/ cutting.

Women have been marginalized and continues to remain socially challenged, despite contributing towards national economy and social sustenance. In India, women's representation in Parliament and in the State Assemblies has never gone up beyond 8 to 10 per cent respectively. Mere 2.3 per cent women are administrators and managers. There is a huge need for awareness among people towards these statistics which reflect the condition of women to be dismal. Surprisingly, this situation exists despite the various provisions made by the government which has been sensitive enough to include the principle of gender equality in the Preamble of the Constitution of India, as well as in Fundamental Rights, Fundamental Duties and Directive Principles. The Constitution not only grants equality to women but also empowers the State to adopt measures of positive discrimination in favour of women, but still result is not satisfactory at all.

4. Motherhood and Old Age

These are two key periods in many women's lives when the pernicious effects of both poverty and inequality can combine. Shockingly, "It is estimated that each year more than half a million women—roughly one woman every minute—die as a result of pregnancy complications and childbirth." 99 per cent of which occur in developing countries. Yet, "many of these women's lives could be saved if they had access to basic health care services." In addition, elderly women may face double discrimination on the basis of both gender and age. Many older women are plunged into poverty at a time of life when they are very vulnerable. However, "children's rights are advanced when programmed that seek to benefit children and families also include elderly women."

5. Discrimination at Work Place

Usually women work more than men but are paid less. The informal slogan of the decade of women became "women do two-thirds of the world's work' receive 10 per cent of the world's income and own one per cent of the means of production."[1] Women cultivate, plough and harvest more than half of all the food in the world.

According to Inter-Press Service, "On a global scale, women cultivate more than half of all the food that is grown. In Sub-Saharan Africa and the Caribbean, they produce up to 50 per cent of basic foodstuffs. In Asia, they account for around 50 per cent of food production. In Latin America, they are mainly engaged in subsistence farming, horticulture, poultry and raising small livestock."[2] Yet, women often get little recognition for that.

In fact, many go unpaid. It is very difficult for these women to get the financial resources required to buy equipment etc. as many societies still do not accept, or realize, that there is a change in the traditional role.

UNICEF's main summary of equality in employment includes the following points:—

> "For many women, unpaid work in and for the household takes up the majority of their working hours, with much less time spent in remunerative employment. Even when they participate in labour market for paid employment, women still undertake the majority of the house work.
>
> When women work outside the household, they earn on an average, far less than men. They are also more likely to work in more precarious forms of employment with low earning, little financial security and few or no social benefits.
>
> Women not only earn less than men but also tend to own fewer assets. Smaller salaries and less control over household income constrain their ability to accumulate capital. Gender biases in property and inheritance laws and in other channels of acquiring assets also leave women and children at greater risk of poverty. Paid employment for women does not automatically lead to better outcomes for children. Factors such as the amount of time women spend working outside the household, the conditions under which they are employed and who controls the income they generate, determine how the work undertake by women in the labour market affects their own well-being and that of children."[3]

6. Women and Children

It can also be said, 'The Double Dividend of Gender Equality'.[4] The above title comes from UNICEF's 2007 report on the state of the world's children, where they focus on the discrimination and disempowerment women face throughout their life-time and how that impacts children's lives. The key message that comes from the report are as follow:

1. Gender equality and well-being of the children go hand in hand. Gender equality furthers the cause of child survival and development.
2. Gender equality produces a double dividend benefits *both women and* children. Healthy, educated and empowered women have healthy educated and confident daughters and sons.
3. Gender equality will not only empower women to overcome poverty and live full and productive live, but will better the life of children, families and countries as well.

Conclusion

Thus, we can say that women are discriminated on all walks of their life. Male-domination has been a prominent feature of most of the societies in Indian culture. Over time it has led to severe gender inequality and the twin problem of discrimination and atrocity which persists in some form or the other till date.

Now, to combat with the problem, it is necessary to have gender-sensitization among people to bring a change in their attitude from within.

J.S. Mill in his book '*The Subjection of Women*' questioned the traditional understanding of work and family, which according to him, was not only limiting and restricting women to the boundaries of her household but also devoids her to the right to choose. Mill's essay supports women's right, equality and freedom in society. In his own words, "The purpose of the 'Subjection of women' was to maintain the claim of women, whether in marriage or out of it, to perfect equality in all rights with the male sex."[5]

Women's equal rights and influence in the key decisions that shape their lives and those of children must be enhanced in three distinct arenas: the household, the work place and the political sphere.

A change for the better in anyone of these realms influences women's equality in the others, and has a profound and positive impact on child's well-being and development.

Our government has introduced welfare measures from time to time for the purpose of women empowerment. Among them are: Support to training for Employment Programme (1987), Mahila Samridhi Yojana (1993), The Rastriya Mahila Kosh (1992-93), Indira Mahila Yojana-1995), DWACRA Plan (1997), but still it will not be successfully implemented unless and until the change occur at personal level in the mindset of each one of us.

Thus we can say that gender equality is not only socially, morally and economically right, it is pivotal to human progress and sustainable development.

Achieving Millennium Development goal promoting gender equality and empowering women — will also contribute to achieving all the other goals, from reducing poverty and hunger to saving children's lives, improving maternal health, ensuring universal education, combating HIV/AIDS, malaria and other diseases and ensuring environmental sustainability.

So, to conclude with it can be said that gender equality furthers the cause of child survival and development for all of the society and for that very reason gender equality should not be underestimated.

Lastly, we can say that to bring gender equality, not only government but women themselves will have to come forward and should be aware of their rights provided by the government and secondly, women should be educated from grassroots level so that each woman can understand the necessity for gender-responsive governance and opt for it. Community consciousness and external support can definitely help the cause, but women should rise to the occasion and try to become agents of their own empowerment. Once gender justice is established in the society in the true sense of the term, all legal and welfare measures will become meaningless.

REFEFRENCES

1. Richard H. Robbins, '*Global Problems and the Culture of Capitalism*' (Allyn and Bacon, 1999), p. 354.
2. Inter Press Service.
3. UNICEF's 'Summary of equality in employment', chapter 3.
4. UNICEF's Report 2007.
5. Ronald Flectcher, Ed. 1971. John Stuart Mill 'A Logical Critique of Sociology', Nelson: London, p. 404.

Chapter – 16

Indianness in the Poetry of Sarojini Naidu

Nibha Singh

The present paper is aimed at to study some of the important aspects of Sarojini Naidu's poetry in the great tradition of Indian poetry in English. We have in India a galaxy of poets and writers in English language. The works of such poets as Romesh Chunder Dutt, Manmohan Ghose and Rabindranath Tagore along with much of the poetry of Sri Aurobindo came out during the period of the Indian Renaissance. All these poets contributed to shape the living tradition of Indo Anglian poetry. Today this Literature has a long chain of distinguished poets and writers who are read and praised in most of the English speaking countries of the world.

If Indo-Anglian prose is proud of such writers as Mahatma Gandhi, Jawaharlal Nehru, Mulk Raj Anand, Raja Rao, Nirad C. Choudhury and R.K. Narayan who have won genuine appreciation on both sides of the Atlantic, Indo-Anglian poetry has the glory of having a no less distinguished set of brilliant poets. If the prose writings of Mahatma Gandhi and Jawaharlal Nehru have been the envy of English people, the lyrics of Sarojini Naidu and ballads of Toru Dutt have won the admiration of such critics as Edmund Goose and Arthur Symons. Tagore's *Gitanjali* shows the realization of the vast potentialities of Indo-4Anglian poetry. It is this *Gitanjali* which brought him the Nobel Prize and world recognition. Again Sri Aurobindo's *Savitri* bears witness to the fact that Indo Anglian poetry can produce a great epic in the tradition of not only the *Ramayana* and the *Mahabharata,* but also of the *Iliad*, the *Odyssey* and the *Paradise Lost.*

It is easy to say that being in India, our poets create Indianness in their poetry. However, it is not easy to define Indianness clearly. Yet, it may be said to be a composite awareness in the matter of race, milieu, language, religion and culture. What are the distinctive Indian elements in the poetry of Sarojini Naidu and how do her poems reflect her attitude towards man, God, society and nature are some of the basic points that this study will highlight.

Prior to coming over to Sarojini's poetic beauty it would be well within the framework of this chapter to present a brief critical estimate of her poetical works such as to name *The Golden Threshold* (1905), *The Bird of Time* (1912) and *The Broken Wing* (1917). *The Sceptred Flute* appeared in America in 1937. Later on in 1943 a one-volume edition of the three earlier works was published in India under the same title by Messrs Kitabistan, Allahabad. Sarojini's songs and lyrics in her works are of rather overlapping subjects with sections like *Folk Songs*, *Songs of Love and Death*, *Songs of the Springtime* and a sequence of love lyrics entitled *The Temple: A Pilgrimage of Love,* which is the concluding part of *The Broken Wing*.

Folk songs, from time immemorial, have influenced the creativity of writers. Especially in poetry the language of folk songs gets an organization and tightening. Sarojini too enriched her poetic diction by resorting to the poetic beauty and sonority of folk songs. In Vedic Literature, i.e. through the composition of seers, folk songs have their composite position and that is representative of village culture. Vedic Literature dated back more than 3000 years ago is indicative of the antiquity of Indian writing. Indianness we find in almost all of Sarojini's poems, viz. *Palaquin-Bearers, Wandering Singers, Indian Weavers, Coromandel Fishers, Snake Charmers, Suttee,* and so on.

In *Indian Weavers* she presents the inherent pain of birth and death. She gives a symbolical touch to three stages of life pertaining to infancy, youth and death. Indian weavers weave a garment at the break of day and that is meant for a newly born child or emphatically for a new arrival. This brings all natural beauty in human life. Beauty intoxicated with a sort of eternal happiness captivates all. Again he weaves a garment at nightfall for marriage. The sartorial make up displays an entire glow of youth and youth remains unaware of the upcoming old age. The weaving in the whiteness of moon draws down upon the curtain of life—so from beginning to end an Indian sensibility the poet has picturised and that too has a universal appeal. Universality has been viewed by critics a permanent quality of all compositions. It symbolizes the colours of morning, day and nightfall and has synchronized time in the passage of life.

In *Coromandel Fishers* she has depicted Indian faith and surrender to God :

What though we toss at the fall of the sun
where the hands of the sea-god drives?
He who holds the storm by hair, will hide
in his breast our lives.[1]

He, whosoever surrenders, knowingly or unknowingly, to the Almighty, achieves the meaning of life. Indians, by and large, do not believe in spending life, merely eating, drinking and sleeping. Through the meaning of life, they give a concept of life which is of paramount value. This must have the blending of immediate experience of life of which the poet is quite aware. To an extent it appears that Sarojini also embraced symbolism and therein Sarojini's writings also visible world is not a reality or invisible merely a dream.

Poems like *Purdah Nashin* and *Suttee* speak of Sarojini's longing for the emancipation of women:

Her days are guarded and secure
Behind her carven lattices...
Who shall prevent the subtle years,

Or shield a woman's eyes from tears?[2]

The concept of *Suttee* is purely Indian. Prior to *Raja Ram* Mohun Roy's reformative spirit this custom was prevalent in India which was quite inhuman. Raja Ram Mohun Roy tried utmost to have it eradicated. Tradition of *Sati Pratha* also moved the writer in Sarojini Naidu. The state of *sati* is quite emotional. She feels that the lamp of her life has been extinguished for ever. And for this extinction she has to pay heavily by sacrificing herself along with her dead husband :

Life of my life, Death's bitter sword
Hath severed us like a broken word.
Rent us in twain who are but one...
Shall the flesh survive when the soul is gone[3]

This mystery is quite in tune with the Indian mysticism. Body departs but the soul remains. The *Srimadbhagvad Gita* also speaks of this dictum. Soul [the *atman*] takes no pain in making a changeover. The *Gita* says:

Vasansi jirnani yatha vihaaya:
Navāni grihnati naro'aparani
Tatha sharirani wihaaya jirna-
Nyanyani samyati navāni dehi.[4]

This is the Indian sensibility of the concept of body and soul. Being Indian in character it has a universal appeal and it speaks of the whole of creative machinery of the Almighty. Sarojini has very beautifully revealed this sense of mysticism in this poem. Definitely it is the philosophy of metamorphosis.

Sarojini's love-poems are emotional in character and temperament. Her philosophy of love is that two hearts beat as one and a single thought prevails, e.g. *If You Call Me :*

Life's dark tides may roll between

Or death's deep chasms divide –
If you call me I will come
Fearless, what betide.[5]

The mind in love is endowed with the power of heavenly flight. The lover's soul pierces into the heart of the beloved through her eyes, as at the first sight the beloved or the lover sees the beauty through eyes and is entirely in rapture. Tulsidas in the *Ramcharitmanas* also portrays this state of mind of Sita:

Lochan mag Ramahi ur aani
Deenhe palak kapaat sayanee[6]

Meaning thereby, that Sita drinks deep the radiating personality of Sri Ram through her eyes and locks it up in her heart. Like Tulsidas, Sarojini Naidu tones up the Indian spirit in her love poems.

Sarojini Naidu also confesses the importance of pain and sorrow in life. In one of her letters to Arthur Symons she wrote that pain and sorrow were very sacred to her. In the poem *To the God of Pain* Sarojini reveals the secret of sorrow, suffering and sense of drying up of life. She has picked up her imagery from Indian religious tones:

For thy dark altars, balm nor milk nor rice
But mine own soul thou'st ta'en for sacrifice:
× × × × ×
I have no more to give, all that was mine
Is laid, a wrested tribute, at thy shrine.[7]

It is almost apparent that sorrow and suffering dry up the fountain of life. This drying up, snatches the beauty of sensibility and longing for being in life. In this context a point is automatically raised that Sarojini has somewhere intolerable weariness and exhaustion. To end all these bitter experiences of life she tries to sleep in the lap of death. It is also known to all that nobody wants to die but sufferings causing suffocation in life compel an individual to have a nearness to the permanent end.

The Temple: A Pilgrimage of Love is a distinct collection of Sarojini's poems. It contains twenty four poems and all the poems are love poems. It forms the concluding part of *The Broken Wing*. *The Temple: A Pilgrimage of Love* has symbols, first being *The Gate of Delight*, then *The Path of Tears*, and lastly *Sanctuary*. These are three stages of pilgrimage of love. In early stage a freshness and enthusiasm prevails and to some invisible extent a sort of sublimation is experienced. The woman fallen in love readies herself to sacrifice all for the lover. She can sacrifice her beauty even, on the altar of love. The poet has compared beauty to a rare blossom and to her, youth is a pearl. In this way she has invented beautiful imagery of passion and it seems that there is no craving for any kind of return. In *Feast* the lover offers some gifts to the beloved as a mark of deep feeling. But for the beloved even a footprint evident on the dust is also a matter of worship:

The entranced and flowering dust
You have honoured with your tread
For mine eyelids and my head.[8]

This is the typical Indian sensibility and beauty of love and love-making. Indian woman possesses boundless love for her lover and she wants only one priceless boon from him:

All the sorrow of your years
All the secret of your tears[9]

She wants all the sorrows that may befall her lover all through his life, to become hers, so that his life may be one of unbroken happiness, of unmitigated smiles. She wants to be unhappy in order that he may be happy. The poet in Sarojini Naidu is quite imaginative to pick up this subtlety of love-making.

Love is a biological urge too, in Sarojini's poems. The body also has its legitimate function in the scheme of life and a healthy love-life is, therefore, a complement of a healthy spiritual life. Sincerity and sacrifice are the two elements of falling in love. To the mind of the beloved everything of the lover is worth possessing and enjoying. It appears to the mind that the eyes are lovely, the voice is lovely and the heart is lovely. The lover also feels moved by the radiance of beauty of the beloved. The eyes of the beloved are lit by celestial fire. The celestial fire is a radiating image entirely Indian in character but fire lowers down the soothing impression gathered at first sight.

Sometimes Sarojini Naidu appears to be thrilled by physical beauty and its enjoying sentiment such as in *The Sins of Love, Ecstasy, The Desire of Love, The Vision of Love,* and so on. The poet believes that the material beauty is a means to the ultimate realization of divinity. To Sarojini, the sense of the beautiful is always the sense of the sublime.

Sarojini then shifts from joy to sorrow and we get this indication from the poems collected in the name of *The Path of Tears.* Here is a serious kind of estrangement between the lover and the beloved and efforts are made to bring about a sort of reconciliation. *The Sorrow of Love* tells us that the poet wants to persuade the beloved that love, true in spirit knows no change. Neither sorrow nor death have got the efficacy to efface it. There is an assurance of sincerity in love. In *The Silence of Love*, Sarojini portrays the miserable condition of the beloved, her longing and languishing. She has endowed her lover with the whole joy of flesh and the entire treasure of her soul, and yet she does not demand any gift from his reluctant hand:

But tho' you are the breath by which I live
And all my days are a consuming pyre
Of unaccomplished longing and desire
And tho' I die, how shall I claim or seek
From your full rivers one reviving shower,
From your resplendent years one single hour[10]

She thus experiences a great restraint and invites danger for herself by repressing her mightiest feelings in regarding herself,

> *Foredoomed to bear*
> *A load of passionate silence and despair*[11]

Similar emotions and pictures of the path of tears in love has been presented in *The Menace of Love, If You Were Dead, Supplication*, *The Slayer*, and *The Secret,* finally in which Sarojini reveals about the heart of the beloved which the lover does not vitalize with his love. In an environment of material splendour, where maids and men come to her with gifts, singing joys of praise.

> *How can they know I have been dead, Beloved,*
> *These many mournful days*[12]

The irony here being that she has to keep up appearances and accept those things so as not to betray her innocent secret:

> *For none save you may know the tragic secret,*
> *O Love, that I am dead!*[13]

Now we come to the third section of *The Pilgrimage of Love,* i.e. *Sanctuary.* She now purifies love from grosser elements. Pure love does not contain envy, fear, despair and alike. These have no place in Sarojini's opinion, in love. *The Fear of Love* presents love as a gross passion. To Sarojini's mind it is a ravening fire. The beloved becomes jealous of even those who even with good intentions praise the beauty of the lover. She wants to hide him even from time and fate in order to have lasting happiness with him. But she confesses that as a matter of fact, she is not fit to love him because she has not been able to save him from the ravening fire of my own heart's desire.[14]

The Illusion of Love indicates a different set of emotions. Here the poet has spiritualized love with the soul and that too in communion with truth and divinity. In this context we can mention

The Worship of Love, The Love Triumphant, The Love Omnipotent, Invocation, Devotion.

Sarojini Naidu in her love poems has coloured the beauty of intimate relations and deep passions of love. Passions and delights stir the emotions of love and with honest

feeling feed the sacred flame of love. It is a dynamic force with her, the understanding of which is the understanding of the secret of the living universe around her. In Dustoor's opinion, the spirit and inspiration in Sarojini's love poetry are such that it " ... could have been written only by a woman brought up in the Hindu way of life and in the tradition of Hindu love-poetry, religious and secular."[15]

According to Padmini Sengupta, Sarojini's biographer, "The love which reigned in her heart was more for a mystic lover than a human being, until God and the Eternal Spirit was a supreme victory — and in His love she found the real love she sought all her life."[16]

In some of her poems on love there seems to be a preoccupation with pain and suffering. There is an apparent glorification of the lover's suffering, even self-annihilation. There is a fascination for the sweetness of sorrow, the pleasure of pain.

In the Indian poetic tradition suffering has never been viewed in a wholly negative light as the sheer opposite of joy. While reading some of these poems it should be borne in mind that Mahatma Gandhi, whose ideas made a profound impression on Sarojini, attached a great importance to the beauty and cleansing power of suffering.

She was also influenced by the conventions of Urdu and Persian poetry in this matter, conventions which must have seemed natural to one who was brought up in the literary atmosphere of Hyderabad. The metaphor of the flame and the moth, the *shama* and the *parwana*, has been employed by the Urdu and the Persian poets very effectively. The moth rushes into the flame, the lover perishes in the very process of being united with the beloved. In the Sufi tradition this has always been a symbol of the finite's longing to lose itself in the infinite, but such is the paradox of love that the pleasure of parting is greater than the joy of union. Love rests on duality though it seeks unity. However, even when there are no mystical suggestions, even when they sing wholly of human love, the classical Urdu poets make liberal use of the idea that in the experience of love, pain itself can become the source of joy and the lover enjoys being a victim.

Sarojini's poems tell us of her fancies and longings, the moments of ecstasy and moments of loneliness. In her thought provoking poems, she speculates on the transitoriness of life and the caprice of fortune, the purpose of life and the mystery of death which she very beautifully exclaims in her poem *The Soul's Prayer* where the soul in its dawn, in its phase of innocence, desires to know the secrets of life and death from God. The soul asks for joy and sorrow, gift and grief, love and death. God concedes and prophecies that after being drunk with joy, burnt by the fire of love, and cleansed by the flame of grief, the soul will be illumined by truth. The poem ends on a mystical note that life and death are both images of God, where God answering the prayer of the soul says:

Life is a prism of My light,
And Death the shadow of My face[17]

Mythology interests her and she sings of the gods and goddesses of her ancient land—Krishna, Lakshmi, Kali and others. She sees the beauty of life in the humblest professions and writes poems on palanquin bearers, bangle sellers, weavers, singers, dancers, corn grinders, gypsies, snake charmers and fishermen. When she deals with some social customs of India like *sati* and *purdah*, she gives us a penetrating *criticism of life which is artistic, not argumentative*. Her poetical works include fascinating subjects from the history of India as well as Indian festivals—Vasant Panchmi, Nag Panchmi and Mohurram; poems on Indian flowers —the red *gulmohar*, the rich *champak* and the lovely *asoka*. She sings of the seasons of her land—autumn and its sadness, spring and its joy and she recaptures the scenery around her—dawn over fields full of harvest, blossoming woods in summer, sunset in June, twilight over the hills and nightfall in the city of Hyderabad.

Sarojini saw in India two fundamental qualities, continuity in the midst of change and unity underlying diversity. To her, India was something more than a mere geographical entity, a portion of the earth with an area measured in square miles and population counted in millions. Nor was it an intellectual conception, India ageless though in time, and one though infinitely diversified, was something felt in the blood and experienced by the senses, the heart and the head. However, for Sarojini it was neither a search nor a discovery, she was content to experience, enjoy, celebrate and worship it. India was an ever present reality; it was everywhere: in the paddy fields of Bengal and the black cotton soil of the Deccan, in the valleys of the Ganga and the Yamuna, in the orchards of Kashmir and the beaches of Orissa, it was in the thoughts, feelings and skills of the people; it was in the ancient temples and medieval tombs and mosques; it was in mango groves and lotus pools, it was in thatched huts and royal palaces, in classrooms bazaars and jails. Her concept of India was simply a blend of innumerable percepts. Exquisitely, she sang about the beauty of the Indian landscape, about the common man and woman, about the Hindu-Muslim unity and about the subjugation of India. With the publication of her The Golden Threshold itself in 1905, India smiled with broad contentment at her daughter bursting forth into song, which made her 'the Nightingale of India' and 'Bharat Kokila', as Mahatma Gandhi called her.

REFERENCES

1. *Coromandel Fishers*; Naidu Sarojini: *The Sceptred Flute*, Kitabistan, Allahabad, 1943; p. 6.
2. *Pardah-Nashin*; Naidu Sarojini: *The Sceptred Flute*, Kitabistan, Allahabad, p. 53.
3. *Suttee*; Naidu Sarojini: *The Sceptred Flute*, Kitabistan, Allahabad, 1943, p.18.

4. *Srimadbhagavadgita*; Gita Press, Gorakhpur; 162nd Ed, II. 22. p. 40.
5. *If You Call Me*; Naidu Sarojini: *The Sceptred Flute*, Kitabistan, Allahabad, 1943, p.214.
6. Tulsidas: *The Ramcharit Manas*; I. 4. 232.
7. *To the God of Pain*; Naidu Sarojini: *The Sceptred Flute*, Kitabistan, Allahabad,1943, p. 37.
8. *Feast,* Naidu, Sarojini: *The Sceptred Flute*, Kitabistan, Allahabad, 1943, p. 211.
9. *Ibid.*, p. 212.
10. *The Silence of Love*; Naidu Sarojini: *The Sceptred Flute*, Kitabistan, Allahabad, 1943, p.219
11. *Ibid.*
12. *The Secret*; Naidu, Sarojini: *The Sceptred Flute*; Kitabistan, Allahabad, 1943, p.223.
13. *Ibid.*, p. 224.
14. *The Fear of Love*, Naidu, Sarojini: *The Sceptred Flute*, Kitabistan, Allahabad, 1943, p.226.
15. Dustoor, P. E: *Sarojini Naidu;* Rao and Raghavan, Mysore,1962, p.40.
16. Sengupta, Padmini: *Sarojini Naidu – A Biography*; Asia Publishing House, Bombay,1966, p.110.
17. *The Soul's Prayer*, Naidu Sarojini: *The Sceptred Flute*, Kitabistan, Allahabad, 1943, p.124.

Chapter – 17

Tagore's Portrayal of Female Consciousness in the Home and the World

Seema Prasad

"Tagore's work is a constant music of the over passing of the borders, a chant filled realm in which the subtle sounds and lights of truth of the spirit give new meanings to the fine subtleties of life." —Sri Aurobindo[1]

Truly Sri Aurobindo called Tagore a 'wayfarer' of all times. Tagore's reaction to the national resurgence caused by the partition of Bengal came through his many songs, stories and speeches. He imagined a world where every nation would 'keep alight its own lamp of mind as its part of the illumination of the world'. Tagore's vision goes beyond the national and he imagines one universe, one world. And, it is for this that Tagore has won universal acclaim and attention. A recipient of the Noble Prize for Literature, Tagore's contribution to literature has been a source of inspiration to mankind. The anti-nationalist sentiment—that nationalism is a sense of war and courage, death, destruction and divisiveness rather than international solidarity that induces a larger and more expansive vision of the world—remains at the heart of Tagore's imagination in most of his writings: his letters,

> essays, lectures, poems, plays and fiction. Originally written as *Ghaire Baire* (1914), and translated in the year 1916 as *The Home and The World*, the novel has been resurrected at different times for different purposes. It can be read in conjunction with the themes of Nationalism, Traditionalism and the emergence of Feminism in Bengal.

1905 was a very significant year in the history of Bengal; the partition of Bengal was decreed by the then Viceroy, Lord Curzon, on the pretext that Bengal had become too large a province to be managed efficiently. As a reaction to the partition, the Indian nationalist movement took place. The *Swadeshi* Movement was an integral part of this movement. It fostered a new spirit in the country — a spirit that compelled Tagore to react. There was a new national construct not only geographically but also in terms of political ideology. *The Home And The World* is Tagore's anti-revolutionary response to the critics of his time, as well as his bold *portrayal of the emerging woman.* Bimala's story in the novel is one tentative step towards the *study of the evolution of the new* woman who, when empowered with education and freedom, can think and act with a mind of her own. She creates her own identity, political or cultural.

Today India celebrates 150 year's Birth Centenary of Tagore. Remarkable years of struggle and survival have gone into the making of the country. The early years of the twentieth century was a time of change in the socio-cultural and political consciousness of Indian life and in the closed life of the woman. The torch lit by Raja Ram Mohan Roy was blazing. There was a new concern for woman's equality. All human works arise out of historical and sociological conditions.

Rabindranath Tagore's reaction to the turbulence of the age comes through this novel *The Home and the World.* The book can be read as a historical document of Tagore's views on nationalism and modernism. To give expression to his thoughts on the problems and solutions of the age, Tagore created poignant woman characters as well — Binodini, Bimala, Charulata will in all ages to be, be concerns of feminine study. Throughout the vast expanse of his work, Tagore maintained that India's immediate problem was not political but sociological and cultural. Issues of caste, religion, gender and race could be resolved by establishing an order of equality of existence. Root evils had to be got rid of. Education was a tool to overcome this social stagnation. Tagore seeks to empower his heroines with an educated and an aware mind. These characters can hold themselves as models to the rest of the world. It becomes important to look back at these characters, study their relevance then and relate them today.

'Bimala' is the central female protagonist of the novel, *The Home and The World.* My concern is to look back into the character of Bimala and connect her to the new generations of women to follow. Tagore has created multiple levels of understanding through the characterization of Bimala. On the one hand he wishes to project Bimala as an icon of the liberated woman who is granted free excess to the world; on the other hand her failed relationship with the reactionary, Sandip, signals a re-entry into the home. Of particular interest is Tagore's position on the status of women and the manner the italicized 'new woman' becomes a sign and symbol of the cultural destiny of the nation. The 'woman' does not exist in isolation. In an age of great political movement 'a new spirit' in the country prevails. It is in the backdrop of such considerations that we witness the awake of the female consciousness of Bimala.

Tagore would not barter India's history, tradition and culture and bring them under the shadows of the West; neither did all that belonged to the West had to be boycotted. The story of Bimala is that of a traditional Bengali girl who gains education in her husband's house through 'the exercise books' given to her by him, and an English woman whom he engages tutor to her. At this time, in the western world, education to women was a means to achieve economic independence; in the east, however, it was meant to be a source to create awareness. Bimala empowered with education and encouragement tentatively enters the roads of nationalism only to realize that universal truth and peace are more important than the petty concerns of nationalism.

> "The Nation with all its paraphernalia of power and prosperity, its flags and pious hymns. Its blasphemous prayers in the churches and the literary mock thunders of patriotic bragging, cannot hide the fact that the Nation is the greatest evil for the Nation, that all its precautions are against it, and any new birth of its fellow in the world is always followed in its mind by the dread of a new peril."[2]

Tagore wrote *The Home and the World* as an autobiographical novel through which Tagore explains his concern for social reform, women's liberation and also appreciates the traditionalism of Indian society. He uses three voices: Nikhil's, Bimala's and Sandip's. Through Nikhil, Tagore insinuates harmony, wisdom and awareness; through Bimala Tagore desires education and empowerment to women achieved by a free spirit; through Sandip Tagore launches a fierce attack on the corrupt political ideology set by Nationalists.

The story is told through the internal monologue of the three characters—Bimla, Nikhil and Sandip; for Bimla, this is the most suitable. Tagore's choice of the autobiographical mode is apt. After all, the 'outer world identity' had not been manifested to women. Tagore names his heroine Bimala which actually means 'pristine'. Bimala gives a very clear and honest account of her evolution. The doors to a traditional feudal Bengali household are opened. Bimala is a happy, Bengali bride, married to Nikhil or Nikhilesh, the 'Lord of the Universe'. Nikhil is the kind, caring husband and an enlightened and benevolent *zamindar*. Nikhil's ideology of nationalism is contrary to the spirit of the age. His is the true voice of Tagore. Nikhil claims that he is "willing to serve his country; but (his) worship he reserves for Right which is far greater than (his) country." His concerns are humanitarian. As a *zamindar*, the spirit of the Swadeshi Movement and the volatile atmosphere created by it are not acceptable to Nikhil. He wants Bimla to live a life of equal existence. As a husband, he has given Bimala unprecedented freedom: freedom of movement, the freedom to take English lessons, the freedom to meet other men. Later on in the novel, when he realizes that Bimala is attracted to Sandip, Nikhil allows Bimala the freedom to choose between him and Sandip, for, Bimala's early marriage to Nikhil had not granted her the freedom to choose what she wanted from life.

We need to remember that women during this period lived a life of segregation; women had their own separate rooms with the span of literacy and culture trapped within the walls of these rooms. Early marriage was common. In an age where a woman's world was governed by restrictions, Bimala's is unrestricted. Nikhil's voice carries the political philosophy and ideology of Tagore. Tagore wrote: "I have been chosen by destiny to ply my boat there where the current is against me". "Politics is wholly against my nature; and yet, belonging to an unfortunate country, born to an abnormal situation, we find it so difficult to avoid their outbursts."[3]

In Nikhil we find, similar thoughts and a humanitarian reformer of all times. Of her relationship with Nikhil, Bimla writes:

> " I distinctly remember after my marriage, when early in the morning I would cautiously and silently get up and take the dust of my husband's feet without waking him, how at such moments I could feel the vermillion mark upon my forehead shining out like the morning star."

And she continues :

"I can never forget the shame of being detected... It was my woman's heart which must worship in order to love."[4]

Nikhil represents the humanitarian side of existence. Nikhil is Tagore's alter ego in the novel. Like Tagore, Nikhil understands human minds and relationships and does not place the nation above truth and conscience. Bimala is encouraged by him to interact with the outside world and Sandip enters her life like a shaft of light. Whereas Nikhil is concerned with the inner, Sandip's concern is with the outer.

Bimla is introduced to Nikhil's childhood friend, Sandip. The Swadeshi Movement, which was a part of the Indian nationalist movement, had fostered a new spirit in India. Sandip is a national leader—charismatic and valuable, and carries with him this spirit. Bimala is attracted to the nationalistic ideals of Sandip but is initially hesitant to let go of conventions and fails to recognize the humanitarian ideology of Nikhil. She emotionally trips and vacillates between Nikhil and Sandip. She tries to fulfil her duties in the house towards Nikhil—*ghaire* (home) and Sandip—*baire* (the world). The focus of her life changes from the fair and gentle Nikhil to the forceful and aggressive Sandip. Of Sandip, Bimla says:

> "I do not know how it happened, but I found I had patiently pushed away the screen from before me and had fixed my gaze upon him. Yet there was none in the crowd who paid any heed to my doings. Only once, I noticed, his eyes, like stars in *fateful* Orion, flashed full on my face."
>
> "I was utterly unconscious of myself. I was no longer the lady of the Rajah's house, but the soul representative of Bengal's womanhood."... "I returned home that evening radiant with a new pride and joy."[5]

Though, it is Nikhil who has empowered Bimala with freedom and education, it is through Sandip, and not Nikhil that Bimala feels emancipated and empowered. Sandip makes her aware of her strength and associates it with the divine—*shakti*. She starts working with Sandip in the nationalist movement. In order to please Sandip, Bimala steals money from Nikhil's treasury under the justification that Nikhil's money belongs to the country and not to an individual. She begins to question her marriage with Nikhil. Self-realization comes to Bimala when she is asked by Sandip to steal from her own house in the name of *Swadeshi*. For Sandip "self-interest is the end, brute force the means, conscience is taboo". Bimala becomes aware of Sandip's Machiavellian intentions. Ultimately, it is Bimala's recognition of ultimate truth which triumphs. She realizes that for Sandip, end justifies means:

> "I could not think of my house as separate from my country: I had robbed my house, I had robbed my country. For this sin, my house had ceased to be mine; my country also was estranged from me."[6]

It is here that she understands that people like Sandip corrupt the nation and rob it of its wealth. Earlier Bimala could not understand Nikhil's unwillingness to participate in patriotic endeavours. Tagore explains his spurning of nationalism through Nikhil: "A cruel epidemic of evil,... sweeping over the human world, of the present age and eating into its moral fibre." Earlier Bimala had no "patience with his patience". But now she experiences a new love and respect for her husband. With the death of the young Amulya in the rally and Nikhil wounded, Bimala returns to her house—finally, educated and with a mind of her own.

> "I now fear nothing—neither myself, nor anybody else. I have passed through fire. What was inflammable was burnt to ashes; what is left is deathless. I have dedicated myself to the feet of him, who has received all my sins into the death of his own pain."[7]

An insight into the character of Bimala reveals Tagore's desire for liberated woman—a woman with a mind of her own and a spirit to carry on. Critics have argued that the new liberation of women in Tagore's time was contradictory to the spirit of the age. Tagore was plying his boat against the tide of time but through Bimala's tentative steps we see him making a change take place in the consciousness of the Indian women. The important fact is that through the characters like Bimala, Tagore opened the doors of Indian feminism to the world.

REFERENCES

1. Sri Aurobindo, *The Future Poetry*, Sri Aurobindo Ashram, Pondicherry.
2. Rabindranath Tagore, *Omnibus III, Nationalism, Nationalism In The West*, Rupa & Co., New Delhi, 2005.
3. Available online at *http://mukto-mona.net/Articles/rabindra_probondho/Quayum_on_tagore.htm*
4. Ajanta Dutt (ed.), *Home And The World*, Doaba Publication, 2002, p. 4.
5. *Ibid.*, p. 15.
6. *Ibid.*, p. 111.
7. *Ibid.*, p. 157.

SUGGESTED READINGS

1. Sandip Kumar Datta, *Rabindranath Tagore's "The Home and the World": A Critical Companion*, Delhi: Anthem Press, 2005.
2. Rabindranath Tagore, *Nationalism*, New Delhi: Rupa Publications, 2002.
3. Rabindranath Tagore, *The Literature Network*. Available online at www.onlineliterature.com.
4. *Imagining One World: Rabindranath Tagore's Critiques of Nationalism*. Available online at mukto-mona.net.
5. Mohammad Quayum, "Ghare Baire", *The Literary Encyclopedia*. 22 April, 2005.

Chapter – 18

Status of Women in Buddhism

Praveen Kumar

Indian Society is a patriarchal in nature, wherein status of women was never good right from the Vedic time. The social attitude towards women in Pre-Buddhist days can be traced from the early Vedic literature, such as the *Rig Veda*. There is evidence indicating the honour and respect which women received in their homes. However in the realm of religion, too, they had access to the highest knowledge of the absolute or *brahma*. However, such a liberal attitude towards women changed with the due course of time, under the influence and dominance of the priestly caste with their priestly crafts, animal sacrifices and other ritualistic practices. Thereafter, although, new interpretations were given to the scriptures, yet women came to be considered as greatly inferior to men both physically and mentally.

A woman was looked down upon as a mere possession or a thing. Her place was at the home, under the complete whims and fancies of her husband. She not only had to perform all the domestic chores, but also had to bring up a large family. Some of the priestly caste, Brahmins, married and lived with their wives, yet regarded food cooked by women as impure and unfit to eat. A myth was built up that all women are regarded as sinful and the only way to keep them out of mischief was to keep them endlessly occupied with the task of motherhood and domestic duties. If a married woman had no child or failed to produce any male offspring, she might be superseded by a second or third wife or even expelled out of the house. There was the strong belief that there must be a male child for the continuance of the family line and the performance of the rites of the ancestors. The traditional belief was that only a son could carry out such rituals, which were thought to be very necessary for bringing peace and security to father and grandfather after their death. Otherwise, they might return as ghosts to harass the family. Uncertain were the lives of married women. No less uncertainty awaited the unmarried ones. As marriage was considered a holy sacrament, a young girl who did not marry was badly criticized and despised by society.

In the field of religious practices, the position once enjoyed by women was denied to them. A woman was believed unable to go to heaven through her own merits. She could not worship by herself and she was believed that she could only reach heaven through unquestioning obedience to her husband, even if he happened to be a wicked person. The food left over by her husband was expected to be eaten up by them.

In such adverse environment in the society, Buddhism appeared in 6th century B.C. It was movement both having the characteristier of reform and revolution. Buddha was the first religious teacher who gave women equal and unfettered opportunities in the field of spiritual development. The Buddha opened the gates for the full participation of women in the field of religion by making them eligible for admission to what was known as the *Bhikkuni Sangha*—the order of Nuns—that truly opened to women new avenues of culture and social services and ample opportunities for public life. This brought recognition to women of their importance to society and greatly enhanced their social status. As Susan Marcutt comments.[1] "The nuns *Samgha* was a radical experiment for its time. Earlier, Buddha was also reluctant to permit women to join his monastic community. But after the request of Ananda, and several visits of Mahaprajapati Gotami, he permitted women to join his monastic community and fully participate in it although there were certain provisions of *garudhammas*[2] :

(1) A nun who has been ordained even for a hundred years must greet respectfully, rise from her seat, salute with joined palms, do proper homage to a monk ordained.

(2) A num must not spend the rains in a residence where there are no monks.

(3) Every half month a nun should desire two things from the order of monks, the asking as to date of the observance (*uposatta*) day, and coming for the exhortation.

(4) After the rains, a nun must not invite (*Pavarna*) before both orders in respect of three matters , namely what was seen, what was heard, and what was suspended?

(5) A nun offending against an important rule must undergo *manatta* discipline for half a month before both orders.

(6) When, as a probationer, she had trained in six rules for two years, she should seek higher ordination from both orders.

(7) A monk must not be abused or reviled in anyway by a nun.

(8) From today, admonition of monks by nun is forbidden.

It appears from the *Atthagurudhamma*, that right from very beginning status of nuns was subordinate to their male counterparts.

However, some western scholars like I.B. Horner claim that *Atthagarudhamma* is a latter interpolation and not the Buddha's words. Some are of the opinion that Buddha wanted to protect the *Bhikkunis* through the *Atthagarudhamma*. Whatever the reason behind *Atthagarudhamma,* one thing is certain that establishment of the *Bhikkhuni Samgha* was the revolutionary event in India, with regard to the status of women. Large number of women from different classes of the society took advantage of that, left the home and gave their important contributions in development of Buddhism.

Therigatha and its commentary *Parmathadipani*[3] informs us about important nuns like Mahaprajapati Gotami, Chanda, Patachara, Subha, Dhammadina, Matrika, Dantika, Siha, Sujata, Purnika, Rohini, Citra, Sukla, Anompa, and Amrapali. They left the home due to different reasons, entered into *Samgha* and played a significant role in development of Buddhism. They occupied places within the *Samgha* as teachers and without taking help of anyone, helped other women in getting liberation. They had their own group of discipline, we get a good deal of information about it from *Therigatha.* One *Bhikkuni* Chunda[4] appreciated the quality of *Patachara.* How Patachara helped her in *Pabbaja.*

Patachara had 30 disciples and they all admired the quality of Patachara, Amrapali another nun played important role in development of Buddhism. Mahaprajapati Gotami who was the pioneer of *Bhikkuni Samgha* left the world with 500 *Sakaya* women. She also played a significant role in spreading the message of the Buddha.

Paramathadipini, which is one of the important text of the fifth century[5], informs us about the causes and circumstances under which different women left their home, renounce the world and entered into Buddhist Samgha. Mutta and Purna got *pabaja* due to their enlightenment. Mutta, Gupta and Subha left the home due to the family burden, Dhamnania, Matrika, Dantika, Sita, Sujata, Purnika, Rohini, Subham, Chitra, Sukla, Amrapali, Anopama, some left the world due to their respect for Buddha, whereas Shyama, Ubberi, Kisagotami, Vasatti, Sunidrinanda, Chanda, Patachara, Mahaprajapati Gotami, Vadrakundalakesa, Risidasi left the world due to the bad character of her husbands. All these nuns entered into the Buddhist Samgha from different class and communities. It appears from above description that the woman were not happy in their previous life and their circumstances compelled them to join the Buddhist Samgha, were they got opportunity to improve their status.

All these women in Buddhist *Samgha* did not come from one class and community, but they were from different classes and communities. For example, Khema, Sumana, Shella came from royal family of Magadha.

Mahaprajapati Gotami, Tissa, Abhirupa, Nanda, Sundari, Jenti, Sita, Dhira, Mitra came from feudal family of Licchavi. Matrika, Chala, Upachala, Rohini, Subha came from Brahmin family. Purna, Chitra, Shyama, Sukla, Uttara, Bhadra-kundalakesa came from business class family. Athakasi, Abhayamata, Vimala, Amrapali were from harlot *(ganika)* class. Thus, we find from different caste, class and occupation women left the world and entered into Buddhist Samgha. These women in the form of nuns played a significant role in the development of Buddhism. They had an extraordinary talent and skill to understand the teachings of the Buddha and this way, they played a significant role to spread the message of the Buddha among ordinary masses.

Once, they proved their abilities, Buddha also appreciated them although he did gave some negative remarks also about women.

When Ananda asks, "master, how shall we behave before women?" The Buddha says "you should shun their gaze and if you happen to see her, you should not speak to her and if you should speak to her, you must watch over yourself.[6]

In answer to a question, put by Ananda, the Buddha once said "women are soon angered, Ananda, women are full of passion, Ananda women are envious, Ananda, women are stupid".[7] Once Buddha says to Ananda, if Ananda women had not received permission to go out from the household life and enter the homeless state under the doctrine and discipline proclaimed by the Tathagata, then would the pure religion, Ananda have lasted long, thousand years. But since, Ananda, women have now received that permission, the pure religion Ananda will not stand last so long; the good law will now stand fast for only five hundred years.[8]

There are other passages in the *Samyutta Nikaya* and *Anguttara*

Nikaya[9] where the evils of women as a race are brought out at length. "Women folk are uncontrolled, Ananda, women folk are envious, greedy, weak in wisdom, based on these passages one can think of the misogynistic attitudes of Buddha towards women. But there is passage in the *Tipitaka*, which indicates the positive attitudes of the Buddha also. When a messenger told King Pasendi that queen Malika had given birth to a daughter, he became very sad[10]. The Buddha's outlook, which is evident from what he said to King Pasendi on the occasion, is quite different from the general public opinion, which prevailed at that time. His appreciations of the qualities of women are couched in excellent language.

A woman child,' or lord or man, may prove even a better offspring than a male.[11] Buddha did not have prejudice against women and unlike others very frankly admits that the door of salvation is not closed for women as they are unfit by their nature to attain *nirvana*.

In the *Anguttara Nikaya*[12] also he says that both mother and son can overcome the three terrors by following the eight fold path.

From all this, it is clear that the Buddha did not say anywhere that women cannot get *nirvana*. He never presumed that the nature of women stands in the way of realizing *nirvana*. Now the question arises, that despite the extraordinary contributions played or made played by women, and Buddha's positive attitude towards women why *Bhikkhunis* were treated as marginalized and why by the 3rd century A.D., when the Chinese traveller visited India, *Bhikkhuni Samgha* had lost their identity.

In post-*Mahaparinibbana* period, the Buddhist Samgha became an institution dominated by an overwhelmingly endocentric power structure. The canon was edited and revised to go with this kind of mentality. With the passage of time, ascetical misogyny of *Brahmanism* was adopted by the Buddhist Samgha which associated women almost invariably with adjectives like imperfect, wicked, base, deceitful, destructive, treacherous, ungrateful, untrustworthy, vice, degraded, lustful, envious, greedy, unbridled, foolish and profligate. Such an attitude asserted that women must be suppressed, controlled and concerned by men. This type of logic obviously rooted out the existence of the *Bhikkhuni Samgha* and reduced women in general to a state of marginal existence[13].

By the third century A.D., the *Bhikkhuni Samgha* in India appears to have virtually disappeared from the official order. We know, from the report of the Chinese pilgrim in India, for example, the female monasteries continued to exist well into the 7th century A.D. and beyond, yet there is no record of what these women achieved in their practice or what they contributed to the larger community.

Anywhere in the Pali *Tripitaka*, if we get the misogynistic attitudes towards women just like example. In the Agana Sutta, women are held responsible for the downfall of the human race. However, Buddhist interpretation is generally showed, in general, woman are causing the downfall.

In the Mahayana schools, Buddhahood is the universal goal for Mahayana practitioners. The Mahayana sutras maintain that woman can become enlightened only not in the female form. For example, the *Bodhisattvabhumi* dated to the 4th century states that a woman about to attain enlightenment will be remaining in the male form.

The region for all these anti-woman statement, it may be pointed out that major portion of the Pali *Tipitaka* were written by male dominated society, lisides it may be pointed out that major person of Pali *Tripitaka* appears to have been completed at the third Buddhist council. In this and the earlier two councils, called to decide the *Buddhavacana*, the domicile and androcentric patricidal monks were able to carry through their own points of view.

It appears from the above discussions, that women had played significant role in development of Buddhism. Due to androcentric patricidal nature of the society their achievements and contributions for Buddhism could not be highlighted much. The advent of *Bhikkhuni Samgha* was certainly a revolutionary event in the history of ancient India. It gave the new opportunity to suffering women to improve their social status. What Christianity gave freedom to women in year 1990 Buddhism did it 2500 years ago. Today in the 21st century of globalizing world we are fighting for women liberation and empowerment which Buddha did two thousand five hundred years ago in an ancient time. Certainly *Bhikkhuni Samgha* was landmark contribution to society.

REFERENCES

1. Murcott Susan (1991) – The first Buddhist women translation and commentary on the Therigatha parallax Press, p. 4.
2. Avinash Kumar Srivastava, *Living Buddhism*, Impression Publication, Patna, 2011, p.154; *Cullavaggapali* (Nalanda edition), p. 573.
3. *Thergatha-Therigathapali,* edited by D. Shastri, Buddha Bharati, Varanasi.
4. *Ibid.*
5. *Ibid.*
6. *Aspect of Buddhadhamma* edited by A. Choudhury.
7. *Ibid.*
8. Sace, Ananda, nalabissamathagamotathagatapaveditedhammavina-yeagarasmaanagariyampabajjacirathitikam, anandabrahmachari-yamabhavissavassasahasam, saddhammotithiyyayatochachoaanda, matugamo – pabajjitonadanibrahmanchariyamcirathittikamananda-bhavissatipanchevadaniannadavassavatanisaddhamothassati. *Culla Vagga* (Nalanda edition), p. 377.
9. Kodhano, ananda, matugamo, issuki, ananda, matugamo, macchari, ananda, matugamo, dupannoannadamatugamoayamkhoanandahetu-ayampachayoyenamatugamonevasabhaytamnisidetikamman-tampayosetinakammojamgachhati (*Anguttara Nikaya* 287 (Nalanda edition).
10. Living Buddhism, Impression Publication, Patna, 2011, p.157; *Samyutta Nikaya* Pali (Nalanda edition) .
11. *Ibid., Samyutta Nikaya*, p. 85 (Itthipihiekacciya, seyyaposajanadhip-amedhavanisilavatisassudevapatibbata-tassayojayatipososurohotidi-sampati/tadisasubhagiya putto rajjampianusyati.
12. Ayamkho, bhikkave, maggoayam, patipadaimesam ca tinnamsam-ataputtikanambhayanamimessamcatinnamamataputtikanambhay-anampatanayamsamatikkamayasamvatti (*Anguttara Nikaya* 167 (Nalanda edition).
13. Sarao, K.T.S.– *Origin and Nature of Ancient Indian Buddhism.*

Index